Africa-China Partnerships and Relations

Africa-China Partnerships and Relations:

African Perspectives

Edited by
Kwesi Djapong Lwazi Sarkodee Prah
&
Vusi Gumede

AFRICA WORLD PRESS
TRENTON | LONDON | CAPE TOWN | NAIROBI | ADDIS ABABA | ASMARA | IBADAN | NEW DELHI

AFRICA WORLD PRESS
541 West Ingham Avenue | Suite B
Trenton, New Jersey 08638

Book design: Lemlem Taddese
Cover design: Ashraful Haque
Cover art: © Derejeb | Dreamstime.com (used here with permission)

Library of Congress Cataloging-in-Publication Data

Names: Prah, Kwesi Djapong Lwazi Sarkodee, 1980-
    editor, author. | Gumede, Vusi, editor.
Title: Africa-China partnerships and relations : African
    perspectives / edited by Kwesi Djapong Lwazi
    Sarkodee Prah & Vusi Gumede.
Description: Trenton : Africa World Press, 2017. |
    Includes bibliographical   references and index.
Identifiers: LCCN 2017039842| ISBN 9781569025772 (hb)
    | ISBN 9781569025789 (pb)
Subjects: LCSH: Africa--Relations--China. | China--
    Relations--Africa. | Africa--Foreign economic relations.
Classification: LCC DT38.9.C6 A37 2017 | DDC
    337.6051--dc23
LC record available at https://lccn.loc.gov/2017039842

TABLE OF CONTENTS

=================❖=================

ACKNOWLEDGEMENTS

The Thabo Mbeki African Leadership Institute (TMALI) Africa-China research project proudly presents this book, which makes important contributions to on-going research on relations between Africa and China.

Dr Kwesi Djapong Lwazi Sarkodee Prah thanks Prof Vusi Gumede, the Director of TMALI, his former Post-Doctoral Supervisor and the co-editor of this book, for granting him the opportunity to research, teach and build on his expertise at TMALI. It has proven to be an invaluable experience for which Dr Prah is grateful.

He would also like to thank all the staff at TMALI who supported and encouraged him. Special thanks to Kulani Mashele and Hlengiwe Khuzwayo for their tireless and unwavering support at times when there seemed to be none. Sonja Geyer, Kennoton Mkansi, Tshepo Neito, Phoebe Mushwana, Stevens Mohapi, Victoria Qhobosheane and Serges Kamga also deserve mention and thanks for their assistance in organizing what proved to be a very successful Symposium in 2015; the Symposium from which the material for this book was presented and collated.

We are sincerely grateful to all the authors for all the research and effort put into the various papers presented in this book. It is through their insights that this book gains its value as an important contribution to our progress as Africans. We can only hope they are satisfied and proud of their contributions in this regard.

Dr Prah would like to extend a special thanks to Grace Naidoo, and all the staff at the Center for Advanced Studies of African Society (CASAS) for their assistance regarding the initial type-setting of the manuscript. He would also like to thank Barbara Harthorn for the mammoth task of initial proof-reading, and editorial work on the manuscript. Dr. Kassahun Checole and his staff at Africa World Press also deserve special thanks for their editorial work, reviewing, typesetting, and publication of this manuscript.

Lastly, Dr Prah wishes to extend his gratitude to the Department of History at the East China Normal University, Shanghai, for their support and assistance in finalizing and completing the editing of the book. He has also used the material of this book to further his research on Contemporary Afro-Chinese Relations (under the Chinese National Project; 16ZDA142).

We are proud of Dr Prah for having started the Africa-China research project at TMALI. TMALI acknowledges support from the Thabo Mbeki Foundation and the University of South Africa, without which projects that result into books like this one would not exist.

Victoria Qhobosheane
Research Coordinator: TMALI

FOREWORD

================= ❖ =================

It is a welcome addition to have another book on the relations between Africa and China. This important contribution is a collection of chapters that examine relations between Africa and China through a variety of perspectives including culture, politics, ideology, populism, soft power, nationhood, myths, media perceptions, economy, and policy formulations strategies. The book will help in further improving our understanding of the complex interface between Africa and China. It addresses diverse levels of relations, from questions such as how Africans and Chinese people perceive one another, to challenging the world monetary system and suggesting that the latter should be replaced by 'exchange systems that encourage restorative based-creativity and production'. This is not merely a book on "Afro-Chinese" relations, but one which questions the very essence of world economic domination and global distribution of wealth.

The book is a Pan-Africanist appeal to constructive partnerships and cooperation amongst Africans. It calls for an African strategy and better policy formulation that will enable Africa to benefit from Afro-Chinese relations. It also calls on all African nations to converge and devise a strategy that will help the continent benefit from the presence of China on the continent. The book offers an understanding of standard perspectives on Chinese economic policy-approaches in Africa.

In the context of a rapidly changing political and economic landscape some chapters suggest that Africa should rework the notion of soft power to suit its realities. The general slant of some of the chapters suggests that an African "power of attraction" derived from its possession of natural resources should serve as a foundation for African global appeal. Africa should not attempt to emulate industrialized countries who simply rely on their cultures and standards of living as a way to persuade other nations to look at them favourably. Instead, Africa should construct a 'power of attraction' based on its possession of natural resources prior to these materials entering world markets.

The book from the onset establishes symbolic premises for studying the relations between China and Africa by moving away from the traditional wording of "Africa-China" relations to that of Afro-Chinese partnerships. In doing so it addresses two premises that have been taken for granted so far. First, it addresses the performative impact of always placing China before Africa when referring to the relations between the two parties. Secondly, it ideally qualifies the relationship between the two parties by referring to it as partnership, in a manner of speaking, challenging the dominant rhetoric of donor-recipient undertones.

The book revisits not only the beginnings of Afro-Chinese partnerships but also delineates a periodical sequence as a background to current relations between Africa and China. Claiming that ancient contacts between the two parties did not result in the colonization of one by the other offsets the Fear Factor rhetoric that China's sole intention is to recolonize Africa.

This book provides a broader platform for studying relations between African States and China by moving away from the Panda Huggers and the Fear Factor dichotomy. It attempts to tease out the good that is manifest in these relations and to establish possibilities on how to correct perceived asymmetries between Africa and China.

The book is not limited to discussions on Africa-China relations. It goes a step further by analyzing the role of partnerships with Euro-American States in the face of a developing China. Such an exercise allows the reader to draw parallels between old and new economic powers, and the impact these powers have on the development of African economies.

Africa-China partnerships and Relations is a timely book anchoring possible strategies for Africa to take the center-stage using spaces provided by the immense presence of China on the continent. The book becomes ever relevant in an Africa currently spiralling out of control in a search of solutions for social, economic and industrial development. The multidisciplinary nature of this book makes it relevant to a wider readership as it approaches the subject of Afro-Chinese relations from a variety of accessible perspectives.

INTRODUCTION

========================❖==============

Since the "opening up" of China in the latter half of the twentieth Century, there is no doubt that definitions of development in relation to Chinese and African realities, in terms of economic, political and social change, have taken on new meanings. Urban and rural pressures to sustain the growing human population, political stabilities and social cohesion, economic stability and sustainability, and environmental protection, serve as the main themes that contextualize definitions of progress in these narratives.[1] Whether one disagrees or agrees on a set of definitions, or areas of focus regarding these areas of development, the Communist Party of China has developed a reputation for possessing an uncanny ability to dictate its own terms and conditions with regard to how a state catalyzes and facilitates rapid societal change.[2] Contemporary historical records that make up this book reflect experiences such as the Great Leap Forward, the Cultural Revolution, and the "Opening Up and Four Modernizations of

---

1. Prof Chung-ying Cheng offered a broad, but succinct "Chinese" observation on these narratives – He stated that "...China's revival and development have three connotations: National self-improvement, national development and cultural renaissance. These three relate to each other in body and function." See: Institute of China Studies, *China's Road*, 60; 77–84. In a Southern African articulation of these narratives and their contexts, see Professor Sifiso Mxolisi Ndlovu's chapter in: Busani Ngcaweni, ed. *The Future We Chose*, 77–78.

2. Recently, China's official notice of its domestic developmental challenges and intentions have been outlined, organized and analyzed within themes such as accelerated development of impoverished areas, better and fairer education, improved housing security and supply, and peoples' lives first. See Xi Jingping, *Governance*, 209–225; Feng Cheng et al., *Success Communist Party China*, 55–69.

China." Furthermore, both Africans and Chinese have survived and built on political economic challenges and legacies differently, and these experiences have clearly defined their global presence in recent times.[3] It is no coincidence that colonialism; the politics of non-alignment in international relations; the challenges of "structural adjustment" within the international financial system; and the notion of South-South economic partnerships all became the defining paradigms and living experiences of the twentieth and twenty-first century for the Chinese and the African world, and they continue to serve as examples of converging interests and their legacies.[4]

The book wrested with questions such as: what principles behind Chinese policies in Africa correspond to the diverse policy interests of African states? What avenues are currently sought in building partnerships that complement strategic African interests? Have the outcomes of these partnerships had any measure of success? What possible alternatives are there regarding the building of further partnerships?

It is within these contexts, and through these questions, that foundations are laid for further discussion on strategic partnerships between Africa and China, and their implications. Through relating some of the discussion by a dynamic group of African scholars, this edited collection of papers sheds light on the meaning of strategic and converging interests for the purposes of understanding frameworks for future partnerships. Therefore, the main thrust of this edited book is to highlight strategies that are fundamental to an African development agenda.

Afro-Chinese Partnerships: An Appraisal

Between the emergence of sovereign China in 1949 and the decade of African independence (1960 – 1970), "Afro-Chinese" relations were relatively thin and mainly confined to theoretical views and

---

3. See Dani Wadada Nabudere, *The Crash of International Finance-Capital and its Implications for the Third World.* These challenges are exacerbated by the fact that certain media conglomerates perpetuate a conversation of dependency and backwardness apparently endemic to African realities. In an example of this type of journalism on Afro-Chinese relations, see "One among many" *The Economist Online.*

4. Li Anshan provides a more holistic perspective on the dynamism of Afro-Chinese partnerships in recent history. See Axel Harneit-Sievers et al., 2–24.

explanations about the Chinese "modern" experience; and the emerging neo-colonial, African political economy. This was in as far as lessons could be learnt on both sides about the emergent possibilities for fruitful cooperation between China and Africa. Within three decades, the quantity of exchanges between China and African states has increased significantly.

One author understood the reasons behind a dynamic and growing Afro-Chinese partnership in the following manner:

> the recent Chinese engagement in Africa needs to take into consideration four developments in the 1990s: (a) after being isolated again by OECD [Organization for Economic Cooperation and Development] countries after 1989, the Chinese government decided to resume its efforts to expand its relations with those 'old friends who gave China the necessary sympathy and support'... - that is, the recent engagement in Africa was initiated for political and diplomatic reasons; (b) as the country became a net oil importer in 1993, a couple of large SOEs [state-owned enterprises] pioneered China's outward push into global oil equity markets, especially in countries and regions which international oil companies had either abandoned, such as Sudan, or perceived as too risky to invest...; (c) following the Asian financial crisis of 1997–98, many affected countries, China included, started building their foreign reserves and by the first half of the 2000s, the government was urged by experts to transfer foreign exchange reserves to large SOEs to seek overseas assets...; and (d) with the reforms in the late 1990s, SOEs were stripped of government, regulatory and public responsibilities and exposed to domestic and international competition while formal ownership remained in the hands of the state...[5]

Data documenting the changes in policy and related impacts is revealing. In a typical example highlighting vast increases in trade cooperation, one study revealed that "while in 1992 Sino-South African trade totalled US$ 14 million, it had grown to US$ 26.6 billion in 2010, making China South Africa's biggest trading partner. South Africa is one of the top ten recipients of China's Official Finance to Africa and from 2000 to 2011 received an estimate of US$ 2.3 billion."[6]

---

5. Xing and Farah, *Africa-China Relations*, 88–89.
6. Anthony Ross et al., *South Africa's Relations*. For more recent data, covering the period 2005-2017, see the websites: https://saiscari.word-

Furthermore, through the Forum on Africa-China Cooperation (FOCAC), "…Africa and China formalized their historic relations into a result-driven mechanism based on long-observed tenets of equality and mutual benefit that has characterized the two sides' relations. Therefore, the two sides and above all China believe that FOCAC represents a new strategic partnership that emphasizes political equality and mutual trust, economic win-win cooperation and cultural understanding."[7]

Therefore, it is not difficult to understand the nature and influence of China, and its key interests in Africa. Luo Jianbo and Zhang Xiaomin summarize a now-standard perspective on Chinese economic policy-approaches in Africa:

China's economic development benefits from Africa-China economic and trade cooperation. According to statistics, the bilateral trade rocketed from $10.6 billion in 2000 to $198.4 billion in 2012. Since 2009, China has been the largest trade partner of Africa, surpassing the United States and Europe. China's outward foreign direct investment (FDI) stock in Africa increased fast from $400.9 million in 2003 to $21.2 billion in 2012. China began to import crude oil from Africa in 1992. The amount increased from 500 000 tons in 1992 to 64.69 million tons in 2010. In recent years, crude oil from Africa accounted for 23.9 percent of the total of China's imported oil. China's economic interest in Africa lies in many fields, while the most important and urgent is to realize the diversification of its import of resources and energy. Like any other big power which has its own definite overseas energy interest and energy strategy, China doesn't need to skirt around its energy demand from Africa. When facing Western criticism of Africa-China energy cooperation, China should not feel stampeded or panic.[8]

This is also in conjunction with a rapid increase in Chinese investments throughout the continent in sectors such as mining, fishing, precious woods and telecoms, but also in less profitable sectors neglected or abandoned by the West (transport and related services).[9]

---

press.com/Africa-China-trade-data/ or https://tradingeconomics.com/china/exports-to-south-africa

7. Bankie andZimunya, *Sustaining New Wave*, 210–211.
8. Jianbo and Xiaomin, "China in Africa."
9. Kwesi Kwaa Prah, *Afro-Chinese Relations* 1–2.

4

Nevertheless, these public and private exchanges have yielded mixed results. China can thus be seen to be pursuing its own national interests, as would any other country. Trade often tends to create deficits that continue to be detrimental to African partners. Significantly, not all parties view this rapid, lopsided growth to be as mutually beneficial. Debt-generation continues to hinder the development plans of many state-economies in Africa, including China's biggest trading partner in Africa; South Africa. Furthermore, not only do cheap Chinese consumer products fulfill predictions which indicate how they destroy local industries but, across Africa, the supply of many Chinese imports are owned and directed entirely by Chinese enterprises. Cheap Chinese textile and clothing products have flooded many African markets, seriously jeopardizing the survival of indigenous African manufacturers. Some critics have also voiced concerns over how Chinese-owned firms are treating African workers. Popular protests in Zambia, pay disputes in Namibia and Zimbabwe, and illegal mines in Ghana, all begin highlighting growing problems related to gross lack in corporate social responsibility, limited cultural assimilation, criminality and environmental degradation in Africa. In all respects, African and Chinese interests are at the core of these interactions, and must always be, given the contentious nature of the political and economic environment worldwide.

Despite the Pan-Africanist appeal for constructive partnerships and cooperation amongst and from Africans, many "Africa-China" watchers continue to adopt non-applicable models of social and political development, as a basis for economy and sustainability in Africa. Land, energy, food security, human labour and natural resources are the battle grounds for debates on bilateral and multilateral relations. These battlegrounds have caused some watchers to reconfigure the classic Western, political narrative on "superpower" rivalries, and use terms such as "South-South" and "North-South" essentially to distort inter-related causes of political and economic inequality (through populist methods), and entrench the validity of the international trading system, its global legal and banking appendages, and corresponding political backing. Financing and settling of sovereign debts, financing infrastructure developments, balancing rural-urban divisions of labour and related demands; and at the same time ensuring market growth, profiting off consumer trends, investing in high technology that secures these varying interests are the typical factors fuelling "Africa-China" theories on development. Christopher M. Dent noted, "The inherent problems of China's dualistic development (e.g. divergent incomes, employment, welfare and skills levels between core urban-industrial zones and peripheral rural-interior areas) also confront many African countries."[10] However, what Dent and most of his colleagues have failed to understand or fully interrogate in their arguments are the continuing and growing systemic dependencies that most, if not all, African states have on political and economic prescriptions, as well as colonial legal and institutional inheritances. Instead of acutely taking into account the challenges being presented by current popular protest and action (with varying degrees of radicalism) against economic exploitation and political oppression, most African countries are classified as underdeveloped or developing, due to standards inconspicuously set by Western economic policy makers and analysts, which Chinese journalism and scholarship far too willingly oblige at times.[11] Thus concerns about value and competitive strength continually evade Africans and their efforts to address these issues in any concrete, coherent and cooperative manner.

The collection of these differing approaches to understanding the impact China has had in Africa all indicate that strategy is key to securing interests. Theories on national development (championed by various political parties and constituents) in Africa need to be scrutinized and moulded to suit a rapidly changing political and economic landscape. K. F. Hirji suggests that alternative approaches to utilizing political ideology, and moulding economic transactions to suit and sustain indigenous diversity, need to be grounded in the following principles: intellectual independence, stellar scholarship, integrated conceptualization, understanding history, and intellectual integrity.[12] Furthermore, one "... must actively start to create new and more 'people to people' institutions across our borders, institutions which serve the emergent needs of Africans as a whole. Institutions, which focus on particular economic, social, cultural and political objectives, which strengthen the democratic basis of everyday life,

10. Christopher M. Dent, *China and Africa*, 5.
11. See Yao and Wheatley, "Insight: Changing China." See also Xing and Farah, *Africa-China Relations*, 29–43.
12. Karim F Hirji, *Cheche*, 186–189.

enhance the emancipation process and serve the material needs of life."[13]

Perspectives

The symposium, between March 30th and April 1st in 2015, focused on revisiting partnerships between African states and China in African perspective. The papers addressed the following questions:

- What are the current outcomes and realities stemming from Afro-Chinese relations between 1975 and 2005?
- What factors could be found to influence countries' economic development strategies, and how have these factors influenced past and present economic relations between Africa and China?
- What diplomatic activities, and people-to-people connections have highlighted a specific focus on inter-cultural development (between China and Africa), and how have these activities strengthened, or weakened the development of relations between Africa and China?

Analyses of these relations, in specific contexts and case studies, across Africa, fell under specific thematic guidelines:

- The role of culture as a platform in the development of State Public Policy
- Nationalism and propaganda
- Energy, environment and public participation
- Examining the impact of state-owned enterprises (SOEs) and/ or small and medium-sized enterprises (SMEs), community-based and/ or grassroots initiatives in Afro-Chinese partnerships

To address these wide-ranging contexts and their specificities, this book is divided into two parts. The first part outlines the general themes, perspectives and discourses that have come to characterize Afro-Chinese Relations. The second part focuses more on case studies, and specific issues related to Afro-Chinese realities.

---

13. Tunde Babawale et al., *Pan-Africanism*, 21

Part one begins with Siphamandla Zondi's discussion on Afro-Chinese partnerships, in which he suggests key questions that Afro-Chinese relations pose with regard to global coloniality and imperialism, as well as outlining possible answers that arise if studies employed a decolonial, Afrocentric epistemic lens regarding developments underpinning Afro-Chinese relations. By contextualizing the nature of the modern world system and the complicated location of China and Africa in it, the chapter describes the challenges that this poses regarding the interpretation of international relations and Africa's international diplomacy in particular. On this basis, he proposes and justifies a decolonial, Afrocentric angle of analysis. Zondi then uses this theoretical platform to interpret what has become of Afro-Chinese diplomatic relations in the past decade, with special reference to the Group of 77 and China (G77+China), and the Brazil, Russia, India, China, & South Africa (BRICS) political grouping. Zondi concludes by suggesting key questions and issues that arise from this with respect to Africa's international diplomacy.

In chapter two, Lloyd G. Adu Amoah specifies the critique on Afro-Chinese partnerships by highlighting and explaining the debate in which China is represented as an exploitative partner. He demonstrates that China's deliberate, organized, self-conscious and self-interested strategic manoeuvers are responsible not just for the advantages they have extracted, and are extracting from Africa, but are also responsible for its global ascendancy. Furthermore, Amoah argues that Africa's incapacity to take advantage of her burgeoning relationship with China, despite the wealth of opportunity, is a manifestation of African states' lack of strategic vision and resources. He explains that this incapacity is located in current approaches to policy formation in Africa that inordinately privilege a focus on responding to short-term policy problems, and almost ignore anticipating and preparing for long-range ones. He concludes the chapter by suggesting a strategic framework that outlines practical approaches for African states, regarding their long-term strategic thinking as a key part of public policy formation.

Paul Z. Tembe builds on Amoah's critique and the need for strategic vision in chapter three. He argues that scholars have raised concerns that prevailing political rhetoric, which tries to explain the nature of Afro-Chinese relations, tends to replicate China's domestic ideals within African strategic analyses and spaces. This is witnessed

8

by the coupling of a so-called "China Dream" and "Africa Dream" in general descriptions of relations between the African world and China. He argues that the slogan, "Africa Dream", is mistakenly framed within the historical trajectory of the "China Dream", and that this inadvertently articulates China's reform-policy implementation goals for the twenty-first century. Therefore, this chapter distances itself from the usual discussion of how China benefits Africa and vice-versa. Instead, it poignantly reminds readers that the "China Dream", and its replication within an "Africa Dream", constitutes a strategic narrative that is meant to shape the development of international relations within Chinese contexts. Tembe concludes by suggesting that the African world must explore the possibility of establishing a "power of attraction" model that is able to shape Africa's strategic role at an international level, and within Afro-Chinese contexts and partnerships.

Similarly, in chapter four, Heather Chingono argues that Africa should have a specific set of policy plans related to Afro-Chinese partnerships. She indicates that this African deficit in policy regarding a coordinated, relevant, and informed development action plan more often than not advances China's policy interests in Africa. This makes many of China's engagements with African states lopsided. She then emphasizes that it is important to understand this position, and explains how it relates to the need for uniform action amongst African peoples.

Antoine R. Lakongo, in chapter five, suggests that if the African world wants to locate and solidify its own development path by promoting science and technology, it has to rely on its own diverse traditions and cultures to define and situate international scientific developments within African contexts. He bases this assertion on the argument that in many African philosophies, there are little or no divisions between the natural and the supernatural, between the physical and metaphysical, and between the spiritual and the material world; and therefore, there are no divisions between science and culture. Thus, according to Lakongo, Africa's abundance in natural and cultural resources, as well as its young population, allows it to pursue its own development path. He concludes by suggesting that strategic Afro-Chinese analyses must regard African cultures as key elements in the scientific and technological innovation of the African world – by using African languages to develop science; by giving priority to rural development and grassroots development community mobilization; by

9

locating African women as key drivers in the economic emancipation of the African world; and many other constructive suggestions.

Ogundiran Soumonni then expounds on these issues of technology transfer and scientific development in chapter six. He "interrogates the apparent lack of a strategy on the part of African countries for acquiring technological capabilities (including both technical and managerial know-how) from foreign direct investment (FDI) and other economic relations with other nations." He argues that "while many African governments have praised the preferential trade and loan agreements they have with China, there has also been some measure of displeasure within segments of civil society about the disadvantages of these investments with respect to the lack of job creation, poor quality goods, or the crowding out of locally manufactured products from the domestic market. Some of these commentators even lament the lack of 'technology transfer' from China in its dealings with Africa." His analyses grapple with the intricacies of how these "transfers" must play strategic roles in the overall development of a given African political economy. In his words, when dealing with "… the context of this book's focus on the Afro-Chinese partnership, the question of what understanding or framing of 'Africa' is most germane for bringing about a mutually beneficial and reciprocal relationship between the two peoples cannot be circumvented."

The book then begins part two with Samuel O. Oloruntoba's chapter (i.e. chapter seven), which steers the discussion towards the economic dimensions of these relations. He argues that the relationship between Africa and China provides opportunity for Africa, particularly with regard to the issue of diversification within trade partnerships. However, Oloruntoba explains that these relationships present challenges too. Focusing on Nigeria as a case study, he examines the extent to which Nigeria and China can leverage their bi-lateral relationship, so that the relationship facilitates the realization of their interests. This is examined within the context of rising economies. He argues that Nigeria has economic and political leverage as the most populous country in Africa, and he points out that it has the largest growing economy on the African continent. This relationship would be a good way to strategically augment and counter-balance Western interests in the region, as well as to inform China's engagement with Africans.

In chapter eight, Ng'wanza Kamata interrogates the issue further by examining the impact of relations between Tanzania and China over a fifty-year period, and questions whether China has created new possibilities for Tanzania in this regard. Drawing from lessons learnt in recent history concerning Tanzania's political economy, he highlights how structural adjustment programmes debilitated its economy. Furthermore, these structural adjustment programmes inadvertently created a new scramble for Africa's natural resources. He argues that the renewed scramble over Africa's resources are occurring at a time when Africa has not resolved or recovered from the political and economic fragmentation caused by European colonialism. According to Kamata, the need to understand strategic dimensions, and the facts with regard to how Afro-Chinese partnerships have altered Tanzania's political economy, is very important, as this would offer useful precedents and reference points for future Afro-Chinese partnerships at bi-lateral or multi-lateral levels.

A cultural dimension to perspectives on Afro-Chinese partnerships is explored further in chapter nine. Maitseo M. M. Bolaane widens and expounds on this angle of perspective by arguing that there has been a rise in academic and journalistic literature emerging in recent years that has spoken to growing interest in the globalization of Chinese soft power; specifically, regarding the development of the Confucius Institute (CI) as an innovative tool in championing China's cultural diplomacy. She argues that it is important to look into realities regarding cultural diplomacy, and to look closely at CIs because of the proliferation of these institutions on the African continent. She chooses the University of Botswana as a case study to investigate the "nature" of these institutions as a form of cultural diplomacy, or "nation-branding." Furthermore, Bolaane argues that the discourse on higher education and economic development shifted toward promoting investment in technology and natural scientific studies, while the social sciences and humanities suffered. This trend had to change, if strategic interventions within Afro-Chinese relations were to succeed.

Chapter ten also extends the cultural perspective and discussion. Part T. Mgadla and Oarabile Makgabana-Dintwa elaborate on this case study in Botswana. Their chapter identifies some of the common myths, stereotypes and misconceptions that exist among the Chinese and Africans living in Botswana. The result of the investigation aims to promote an understanding between African and Chinese peoples in general, and that of the Batswana and the Chinese in particular. The chapter also highlights the purpose of culture, through language and systems of governance from the two societies, to explain various contradictory and complimentary factors. They argue that understanding negative attitudes and beliefs held by either of the two societies will be instrumental in any constructive approach aiming to dispel these myths and stereotypes, in order to foster better working relationships and mutual understanding between the two societies.

In chapter eleven, Muhidin J. Shangwe explains that primarily through Western media houses, the "Dark Continent narrative" has spread and shaped perceptions of people in other parts of the world, and that China was not immune to this. However, contrary to conventional understanding, Chinese society harboured deep- rooted pessimism about Africa, which was mostly attributed to the influence of colonial scholarship on Africa. He stated that in China, like in so many other parts of the world, Africa was always reported on within the contexts of poverty, war, famine and disease. The general understanding of Africa beyond these tragedies, was, as a result, limited. The same could be said about Africa in the context of Afro-Chinese cooperation, where the lack of resources and too much dependency on Western media as the main "source" of information meant that news about China was always presented to Africans through a Western lens. The result was the same –Africans were fed with information that had been filtered by Western media for Western audiences and interests. Moreover, at a time when China is investing heavily in soft power, media reporting about Africa in both China and Africa is increasingly in favour of China, at least through the eyes of state-owned media. Shangwe concludes his arguments by stating that it was important the media provided reliable information that was crucial in the promotion of knowledge and understanding between the two regions and peoples.

Kwesi D.L.S Prah rounds off the discussion on the cultural dynamic of Afro-Chinese relations in chapter twelve. He focuses on populism and the state in China and Africa; and unpacks how China and certain African states use populism as a vehicle for furthering the interests of the state, and also as a means of expressing and responding to trends in social organization and governance, laws and customs amongst the citizenry. These appeals to common interests shared between the State and the citizenry, he argues, focused attention on the need for a technical and scientific modernization along scientific socialist principles. This influenced populist ideas of economic self-sufficiency, social harmony, and common scientific purpose in China and in the majority of African states. Prah concludes by offering recommendations on how to understand and utilize populist Africanist notions of self-sufficiency and constructive economic, political, and social development within Afro-Chinese contexts.

Concluding remarks

In essence, chapters in this book cover important themes and discussions related to the strategic development of studies on Afro-Chinese partnerships. As the African world grapples with continuing and recurring phenomena of "under-development" and related impacts, the need for focused and serious studies on the strategic benefits and negatives of particular international partnerships become even more critical. The concluding chapter outlines the recommendations from the analyses contained in the chapters that make up this book, and offers a clearer picture of the way forward.

Bibliography

Axel Harneit-Sievers, Stephen Marks, Sanusha Naidoo, eds. *Chinese and African Perspectives on China in Africa*. Cape Town: Pambazuka Press, 2010

Bankie F. Bankie, and Viola C. Zimunya, eds. *Sustaining the New Wave of Pan-Africanism*. Windhoek: NYCN / Nigerian High Commission, 2011.

Dent, Christopher M., ed. *China and Africa Development Relations*. New York: Routledge, 2010.

Fengcheng, Yang, Su Haizhou, Geng Huamin, Yan Maoxu, Zhao Shumei, Wu Wen Long, Zhang Siyang, eds. *The Success of the Communist Party of China*, China: Remin University Press, 2012.

Hirji, Karim F., ed. *Cheche; Reminiscences of a Radical Magazine*. Dar es Salaam: Mkukina Nyota, 2010.

Institute of China Studies, Shanghai Academy of Social Sciences, ed. *China's Road and Prospect; Record of the 5th World Forum on China Studies*. Beijing: China Intercontinental Press, 2013.

Jinping, Xi. *The Governance of China*. Beijing: Foreign Languages Press, 2014.

Luo Jianbo and Zhang Xiaomin. China in Africa: Devil or Angel?, *Pambazuka News*, February 19, 2014. http://pambazuka.org/en/category/features/90638.

Nabudere, Dani Wadada. *The Crash of International Finance-Capital and its Implications for the Third World.* Cape Town: Pambazuka Press, Cape Town, 2009.

Ngcaweni, Busani, ed. *The Future We Chose: Emerging Perspectives on the Centenary of the ANC.* Pretoria: Africa Institute of South Africa, 2013.

"One among many: China has become big in Africa. Now for the backlash", *The Economist Online:* January 17, 2015, accessed August 20, 2015. http://www.economist.com/news/middle-east-and-africa/21639554-china-has-become-big-africa-now-backlash-one-among-many.

Prah, Kwesi Kwaa, ed. *Afro-Chinese Relations; Past, Present and Future.* Cape Town: Center for Advanced Studies of African Society, 2007.

Ross Anthony, Sven Grimm, and Yejoo Kim, eds. *South Africa's Relations with China and Taiwan.* Stellenbosch, South Africa: Policy Briefing, Center for Chinese Studies, November 2013.

Tunde Babawale, Akin Alao, Tony Onwumah, eds. *Pan-Africanism, and the Integration of Continental Africa and Diaspora Africa (Volume 2).* Lagos: Center for Black and African Arts and Civilization (CBAAC), 2011.

Li Xing and Abdulkadir Osman Farah, eds. *Africa-China Relations in an Era of Great Transformations.* UK: Ashgate, Farnham, 2013.

Yao, Kevin, and Alan Wheatley, "Insight: Changing China set to shake world economy, again," *Reuters Online*; September 10, 2013, accessed October 9, 2013. http://www.reuters.com/article/2013/09/10/us-china-economy-transformation-insight-idUSBRE9891HN20130910.

PART I

Chapter One. The Rise of China, the Rise of Africa: A Convergence of Emergence and Implications for Africa's International Diplomacy

====================❖==================

Siphamandla Zondi

Introduction

The rise of China in its role as an economic superpower is seen as a "peaceful emergence" by the Chinese and by some in the global South; but it is a concerning if not threatening appearance for the dominant global North. Furthermore, the prospects for sharing a central zone in the dynamics of global power, and the impact of this, an independent, different and powerful non-Western country, threaten the continuities of a Eurocentric world system in more ways than is generally accepted. The end of the Cold War opened up space for elements in the global periphery to emerge from the margins of a world the West had made on the basis of economic development, self-awareness and a sense of agency, rather than through the enabling guidance of the West in a process akin to how Japan became a global power. In this process, not only is China threatening the very idea of superiority of the West and its claim to control over the centre of world power, but other developing regions and countries are also threatening the structure of global power that generally took the form of the West being the apex of the hierarchy, or the centre of concentric circles of power. During this period, Africa is transforming in ways that are elevating its significance in the world, from an epitome of decline to a narrative of a rising region. The continent has become the focus of both the global northern and southern countries seeking to expand their global economic power, thus giving it an opportunity to play a critical role in the transformation of the world towards the birth of a truly pluriversal world system.

This chapter reflects on the implications of the rise of China, in this context, on African diplomacy as a tool for expressing, advancing, projecting and defending Africa's interests and values in world affairs. Both Africa's diplomacy generally and Afro-Chinese diplomatic relations are important in this regard. There seems to be a convergence in diplomatic postures, ambitions and concerns about Africa and China around the search for significance in the world, in response to the post-Cold War international environment and the exploitation of South-South cooperation to drive economic development and human well-being. There are divergences around questions of a state model, political and economic power, and ramifications of commercial interpenetration. This chapter seeks to unpack the implications of this growth in "diplomatic capital" generated by African states and China, and explores the possibility for greater convergence in the diplomatic capital of Africa and China with a view to recommend ways in which the two could transform international diplomacy, and make it work to their advantage.

The Rise of China and its Diplomacy

China is perhaps the biggest beneficiary of the changes that have taken place in the world since the Cold War. In a short space of time, it has become the second biggest economy in the world and thus presents a threat to the hegemony of the West and its civilization in the world through inspiring calls by others for a post-Western world order.[1] No part of the world, including China's arch-enemies in Asia and the West, can avoid seeking stronger and more beneficial relations with China. For China to sustain this, which it calls a "peaceful rise" in world affairs, it cannot avoid growing its relations with Africa – its major source of natural resources, the major consumer of its goods and services and a major voting bloc in global diplomacy. It is no wonder that as these changes happen, so have diplomatic, economic, and political relations between China and Africa grown dramatically.

---

1. Amitav Acharya, *The End of American World Order* (Cambridge: Polity Press, 2014).

A major part of Africa's growing agency in international diplomacy has to do with its adoption of common negotiating positions in international negotiations, thus enabling otherwise diplomatically small and weak countries to pool their strengths in order to punch above their weight.[2] While this has enabled Africa to increase its significance with countries like China and regions like Europe, which have established strategic partnerships with the continent, it is debatable whether the continent has harnessed this to gain optimal advantage in terms of trade, investment and cooperation opportunities. There is room for Africa to use its new-found diplomatic capital to enhance further the global stature needed for the winning of concessions in international negotiations; and also, to rebalance its relations with key partners like China. China's willingness to explore an equal partnership based on mutual benefit is a huge opportunity for Africa, so also is its willingness to support Africa's agenda in various international forums.

Few countries have experienced the kind of economic and human development expansion such as that experienced by China since the 1980s. Between 1979, when economic reforms were introduced to open the Chinese economy up to foreign trade and investment opportunities, and 1994, the economy grew at an annual average rate of 9.8 percent, well above the world average estimated at about 5 percent in the same period.[3] At some points, the annual growth rate exceeded 10 percent, as occurred between 1983 and 1985; 1992 and 1995; and 2005 and 2007. In 1984, 1992, and 2007, the annual economic growth rate exceeded 14 percent.[4] What made this expansion even more remarkable was the rate at which the primary industry and manufacturing sector grew during the period, expanding at an average of 5.2 percent. The secondary industry rose by an average rate of 11.4 percent and the tertiary industry grew by 9.8 percent. During this period, China registered a remarkable 17 percent increase in the volume of exports and 15.9 percent in imports, making it a new

2. Siphamandla Zondi, "Common Positions as African Agency in International Negotiations," in William Brown and Sophie Harman, eds, *African Agency in International Politics*. Routledge Studies in African Politics and International Relations. (London: Routledge, 2011).

3. Li Jingwen, *The Chinese Economy into the 21st Century: Forecasts and Policies* (Beijing: Foreign Languages Press, 2000), 1–7.

4. Wayne M. Morrison, *China's Economic Rise: History, Trends, Challenges, and Implications for the United States*, (Washington: Congressional Research Service) 3–5.

centre of international trade.[5] Domestic and corporate savings grew remarkably, enabling Chinese households to invest in human development like education, health and social security, as a result of which they increased their potential to prosper. Hundreds of millions of poor Chinese were taken out of poverty in the process. China moved from being ranked number eleven in economic size in 1979 to becoming number two, twenty-three years later in 2002. By 2011, its gross domestic product (GDP)was 31 percent of that of the United States (US), measured by market prices and about 60 percent in terms of purchasing power parity. It is expected to become the biggest economy in the world by 2020 when it is anticipated that it will overtake the US economy.[6]

China also became the largest manufacturer of goods in the world with its gross value-added manufacturing accounting for about 32 percent of the GDP in contrast to Japan's 18 percent and the US's 12 percent. This means manufacturing is much more important for China's own economic development than it is for other major economies.[7] According to the China Statistical Yearbook for 2011, China had registered 445,244 foreign-invested enterprises (FIEs), which employed some 55-million employees, making FIEs key players in China's industrial production. FIEs account for a significant share of China's industrial output. They also dominate China's high-technology exports.[8]

The introduction of price and ownership incentives for farmers enabled China to benefit from decades of growing produce and from small-scale agriculture as part of building collectives. There were 1.5 million rural enterprises in 1978 and by 1995, they numbered 22 million; this represented a monetary value of 22,9 billion yuan in 1978 to 1,2 trillion yuan by 1995.[9] Four special economic spheres were established along the coast to attract foreign investment, to boost foreign trade, and to dramatically increase China's access to new

5. Li Jingwen, *The Chinese Economy*, 1–7.
6. Lu Ding, "China's Path to the World's Largest Economy: Limits of Extrapolations," accessed September 13, 2013, http://www.eai.nus.edu.sg/Vol2No4_LuDing.pdf.
7. Deloitte, "Press Release," January 22, 2013, accessed September 13, 2013, www.deloitte.com/view/en_CN/cn/Pressroom/pr/105280463d16c310VgnVCM2000003356f70aRCRD.htm.
8. China Statistical Yearbook for 2011.
9. Li Jingwen, *The Chinese Economy*, 108–25.

technology. To this end, tariffs and non-tariff barriers to foreign trade were removed. This strengthened the use of public enterprises, positioning them to drive industrial and broader economic development. Citizens were encouraged to own enterprises and use free market principles to achieve their own prosperity.

The Chinese approach to economic reforms during the age of globalization was gradual, endogenous and staggered in the sense that China remained in control of its economic reforms and was able to choose policies that produced positive economic and developmental outcomes for itself in special economic zones, so that they could ascertain what worked in which parts of the country. This is what the Chinese leader, Deng Xiaoping, called "crossing the river by touching the stones". It involved investment in research and development, partly to understand the impact of policy choices being made by the Chinese and by others in order to develop further strategies for supporting the growth of their country.

The social outcomes of this economic rise have been equally remarkable. Some 620-million ordinary Chinese people came out of absolute poverty and improved their standard of living significantly, mainly because employment grew substantially with 51 percent of the population having become employed by 1994. On this basis, China alone accounts for the bulk of the dramatic decline in world poverty. Countries like Brazil have also added to this positive development. Per-capita household income rose by 15 percent between 1979 and 1995 with rural households registering slightly higher income increases than urban ones. This was also linked to improved productivity of rural households, especially in respect of small-scale agriculture.[10] China registered substantially positive educational outcomes right through all levels of education. The average years of schooling for adult segments of the population up to sixty-four years increased from five to nine years, while the numbers of those with secondary education increased two-fold. The country also witnessed massive decline in infant, child and maternal mortality. Immunization of children against tuberculosis and measles reached 98 percent. Life expectancy rose to a respectable seventy-one years by 2000. The health standards of the Chinese

---

10. Ibid., 196–201.

population and country generally quickly matched those of the highly-industrialized economies with a long history of stable health systems.[11]

Although the global economic crisis that began in 2008 affected the Chinese economy negatively, China retained its position as one of the best performers on all fronts. Economic decline in the US – China's largest export destination – and in the European Union, its main source of imports, negatively impacted China's economic performance with the result that some 20-million Chinese workers lost their jobs in the export sector between 2008 and 2010. In 2007, the Chinese Premier, Wen Jiabao, referred to "structural problems in China's economy, which cause unsteady, unbalanced, uncoordinated and unsustainable development."[12] He identified excessive credit, trade surpluses, current-account surpluses, overheating of investments and urban-rural disparities as among the key problems with which China was dealing. The Chinese government was quick to put in place a stimulus plan in 2009, which boosted domestic demand and increased health and social security spending, thus contributing to employment recovery in low- and high-end skills sectors. At the same time, the state increased the amount of capital available for Chinese enterprises plying for opportunities in the global environment through its large development finance and credit assurance institutions.[13]

Emergence and Implications for the Global Power Structure

The rise of China, even if it is seen as peaceful and is intended to be so in Beijing, threatens the very structure of global power as we have known it since the fifteenth century: Ramon Grosfoguel describes this as an entanglement of multiple and heterogenous global hierarchies with race as the organizing principle. It manifests as hierarchies of

---

11. World Health Organization and China State Council Development Research Centre, "China: Health, Poverty and Economic Development," (2005), accessed November 12, 2014, http://www.who.int/macrohealth/action/CMH_China.pdf.
12. "Officials have no power except for the people," (March 19, 2007), accessed October 13, 2013, http://english.people.com.cn/200703/19/eng20070319_358925.html.
13. Linda Yeuh, "China's Strategy towards the Financial Crisis and Economic Reform," accessed January 12, 2015, http://www.lse.ac.uk/IDEAS/publications/reports/pdf/SR012/yueh.pdf.

power along political, economic, spiritual, linguistic, cultural, sexual/gender, epistemic and racial lines with North America-Western Europe as the apex of heterarchies.[14] On this basis, he proposes that non-European nations live under a regime of global coloniality driven by the US and previously managed primarily by West European colonial empires of Britain, France, Germany, Portugal and Spain. In this sense, the collapse of colonial rule throughout the world especially after the so-called Second World War turned out to be a transition from global colonialism to global coloniality.

According to Wallerstein,[15] this structure of power takes the form of a system with boundaries, structures, member groups, rules of legitimation, and coherence, whose underlying logic is a strong centre made up of Western powers and peripheral areas occupied by others through processes of domination and exploitation. For Walter Rodney, this structure of global power is premised on the realities that peoples of the world outside the centre experienced. He described it as imperialism, "which for many years embraced the whole world – one part being the exploiters and the other the exploited, one part being dominated and the other acting as overlords, one part making policy and the other being dependent."[16]

China's remarkable economic surge has also brought an immense international influence and political significance in world affairs. The country's steady growth in military power, which has been financed through the windfalls from its global trade, has enabled China to become more than a regional or middle power in world affairs. The country has all but become a major global power that is taken very seriously, albeit with some paranoia on the part of dominant Western powers as they seek to preserve and defend their global power and diplomacy. This reality has caused a mushrooming of academic and policy documents explaining how the US might influence China to

14. Ramón Grosfoguel, "A Decolonial Approach to Political-Economy: Transmodernity, Border Thinking and Global Coloniality," *Kult 6 – Special Issue*, Fall: 10–38, 18.
15. Immanuel Wallerstein, *The Modern World-System: Capitalist Agriculture and the Origins of the European World-Economy in the Sixteenth Century*, (New York: Academic Press, 1976).
16. Walter Rodney, *How Europe Underdeveloped Africa* (Nairobi: East African Educational Publishers Ltd, 1972), 14.

"adopt international norms",[17] a euphemism for Western models of arranging power, and to adopt policies that are compatible with US interests in the world; meaning to subordinate China into another of the many US proxies in the world. It is in this context that China-West relations have become more tense over the past two decades.

What lies at the heart of this tension is not the shift from a subdued Chinese foreign policy to an assertive one, as some have posited, but rather the fact that the Western-centric world has not been ready for the implications of such a rise. In fact, there is sufficient evidence to show that the West has not been ready to share global significance and even hegemony with anyone that is not produced by itself. Besides Japan, no non-Western or non-white state actually occupies the centre of global power under Western control today. Japan did not rise on its own; it did not assert itself to a point that it forced the West to accept it is as a partner in shaping world affairs. But Japan rose in a manner that assured the West that its global power and privilege would be secure: it did not align itself with the idea of reforming world affairs in order to democratize them in the manner China has. It did not behave like a state willing to take an independent line on matters concerning the structure of global decision-making, the composition of leadership in institutions of global governance, global economic and financial governance, matters of underdevelopment in the developing world, questions of sovereign equality of states, and neocolonialism and global imperial designs that have continued to this day. Instead, Japan accepted its subservient position in relation to the US-led West and used this to its economic advantage, thus also avoiding tensions. Countries like South Korea and Singapore have also chosen subservience as a non-confrontational position in the face of Western hegemonic tendencies even in their neighbourhood.

Therefore, the growing tensions between Western powers and China do not arise because China is a rising Asian power, but because China is rising in a manner that does not assure the West that its hegemony is intact. This is evident in US commentary, public discussions and scholarship on China, with the underlying logic that China should not be different from the US or the West in its ideological outlook, its domestic power arrangement, its economic model, and its normative framework. There is a subtle demand that

---

17. Robert G. Sutter, "China in World Affairs – US Policy Choices", *Congressional Research Service*, 95, 295, (January 1995): unpaginated.

any rising power in the global South must accept tutelage from the US and the West about its domestic affairs and international role; it must have its place in world affairs carved up in the West. At the core of tensions that have flared up from time to time since the late 1980s, is – in terms of US thinking (both scholarly and public) – the question of human rights. The US had long decided that China must become an "open" society,[18] a term used to mean adopted political liberalism in the Western sense, including liberal democracy within competitive elections and guaranteed individual human rights. Any other model for protecting human rights, including an emphasis on group rights and socio-economic rights, is considered to be non-action until individual civic rights are guaranteed. In effect, this is a demand for countries to completely Westernize their political system. As a residue of the Cold War ideological prism, the US objects to a communist option in political and economic affairs, no matter what empirical research on living standards there is, and no matter what the attitude of citizens might be. It has long chosen that its preference must be a preference of others – what we will call internationalization of particularities in order to make them universal.

It is near impossible to understand this without appreciating the logic of the global structure of power and how it leads to this posture on the part of the US. The works of decolonial thinkers are useful in describing this briefly.[19] Although diverse in their ideas, they privilege

---

18. US government officials, from Ronald Reagan to Obama Administrations, have insistently used the idea of "open society" as their basic demand on Chinese leaders. George Bush's senior minister, Robert Zoelick, explained this most succinctly, making obvious the real intent, in Robert Zoelick, "Whither China: from Membership to Responsibility," *NRB Analysis*, 16,4, (2005): 6–7.

19. The brief outline is based on the following works of scholars from the global South: A. Quijano, 2000. "Coloniality of Power, Eurocentrism and Latin America", *Neplanta: Views from the South*, 1,3 (2000): 533–80; L. Alcoff, and E. Mendieta, *Thinking from the Underside of History: Enrique Dussel's Philosophy of Liberation*(Lanham: Rowman and Littlefield, 2000); E. Dussel, *The Underside of Modernity*(New Jersey: Humanities Press, 1996); S. Amin, *Eurocentrism*(New York: Monthly Review Press, 1989); N. Maldonado-Torres, *Against War*(Durham: Duke University Press, 2008); W. Mignolo, *The Darker Side of Modernity: Literacy, Territoriality and Colonization*(Ann Arbor: University of Michigan Press, 1995); Grosfol Ramón Grosfoguel, "A Decolonial Approach to Political-Economy: Transmodernity, Border Thinking and Global Coloniality," *Kult 6–Special*

a historical perspective that shows continuities in the evolution of the modern world since the European arrival in the Americas and Africa in the 1490s. They use the term modernity to describe what the so-called "modern" world sought to bring, mostly on the basis of what key actors in this process themselves proclaimed. The constitution of this world happened through conquest and violence; the construction of a new structure for control of labour and resources; the invention of race to make a distinction between the conquerors and the conquered or to normalize the relations of domination; the "eurocentrification" of the world economy and political power through the construction of Euro-North America as a centre while condemning others to the periphery; and the accompanying ethnocentrism that enables the West to export its culture and knowledge to the world to displace other cultures and knowledge. In this sense, although modernity was presented as a force of good for all – as was evident in the increased human and economic contact, expansion of technology, new and advanced rational science (expanded knowledge), salvation of lost souls, liberty, human rights, democracy, and development – behind this veil of salvation lay a treacherous penchant for conquest, domination and universalism.

So, modernity has in its salvation narrative the civilizing mission, a hidden underside called coloniality as a model of power, as an approach to knowledge, and as a worldview. Western Europe and North America globalizes by colonizing and overcoming others, thus building the world on the basis of the hegemony of the West at the expense of original heterogeneity and diversity of peoples and civilizations. Through successive world orders, from the conquest and the naming of the Americas by Europeans through to modern slavery, global colonialism, neocolonial arrangements after 1945, and to globalization, the West has succeeded in imposing its civilizing mission on others through a combination of open and subtle violence. This has produced a world in which the West occupies the centre, a position of power and privilege both because of its hard power currency built over years of domination, and because of its cultural hegemony most evident in the imposition of one form of knowledge as the only way of knowing throughout the world.

Issue, Fall, (2009): 10–38; Ngugi wa Thiong'o, *Globalectics: Theory and Politics of Knowing*(New York: Columbia Press, 2012) and F. Fanon, *The Wretched of the Earth*(New York: Glover Press, 1963).

This model of power with its logic of hierarchies (white, male, capitalist, Christian, eurocentric and so forth) and its homogenizing tendencies (globalizing or universalizing North American/European ways so that they become internationalized) has continued in spite of the end of colonial rule. It is evident in the inception period between the fifteenth and sixteenth centuries. It is evident in the period following the eighty-years-war in Europe that ended with the construction from 1648 of a new Western world order premised on the idea of one nation, one state, which became known as nation states, as the foundational logic of international relations. It is evident in the inception of the ensuing order with Britain, France and Germany in the driving seat, the age of the extension of colonial power in the seventeenth to the nineteenth century, including the Berlin Conference that invented modern Africa as a group of largely unviable nation states. It is evident in the UN-based world order following the shift in the balance of power in the West from western Europe to the US, an order in which western Europe now shares its central role with the US. Ramon Grosfoguel explains this as follows:

> One of the most powerful myths of the twentieth century was the notion that the elimination of colonial administrations amounted to the decolonization of the world. This led to the myth of a 'postcolonial' world. The heterogeneous and multiple global structures put in place over a period of 450 years did not evaporate with the juridical-political decolonization of the periphery over the past 50 years. We continue to live under the same 'colonial power matrix.' With juridical-political decolonization we moved from a period of 'global colonialism' to the current period of 'global coloniality.'[20]

The US has, since the middle of the Cold War, acquired even greater confidence and the collapse of the Communist Bloc in 1989 has left the US without any illusion that it is the lone superpower with greater responsibility for the defence and advance of Western civilization in the face of rising non-Western polities.[21] US hegemonism found expression also in concepts of "an indispensable nation", an "exceptional superpower" that US government officials

---

20. Ramón Grosfoguel, "A Decolonial Approach,"219.
21. See Samuel Huntington, "Lonely Superpower," *Foreign Affairs*, 78,2 (1999): no pagination.

and politicians used frequently in the 1990s and early 2000s.[22] The US assumed that it had the licence to build a unipolar world by ensuring that its superpower status is unrivalled, reacting negatively to an emergence of global powers that did not belong to its coalition of states. In the process, it has committed to building global unilateralism in which it shares the privilege and power over world affairs with western European states and its clientele states elsewhere. In this, the US has been driven by assumed "American uniqueness, American virtue, and American power". The uniqueness illusion arises from its interpretation of Western civilization as triumphant in the manner both Samuel Huntington[23] and Francis Fukuyama[24] imply. American virtue is best expressed in the demand that US norms – liberal values of human rights, democracy and governance – can be imposed on others as universalized norms. It is in this context that one can appreciate the US and Western response to the rise of China without falling into the trap of either accepting the modernist narrative in which the Western core interests are wrapped, or of projecting that China is merely a victim.

Some in US-based scholarship and political thinking about China's role in world affairs worry about maintaining the US leverage over China in defence of a number of principles and values that actually represent Western civilization. In this, the encirclement or isolation of China in Asia and in Africa is justified in sophisticated ways.[25] The emphasis is on warning China not to be confrontational with the US without advising the US not be offensive towards China, thus suggesting that US hegemonic tendencies are natural and resistance to them is somewhat ill-advised. Prominent US thinkers constantly warn China to choose cooperation with the US at the time when the US is working to isolate Beijing from its neighbours by escalating military presence in Asia. It does not occur to them that by lecturing China very publicly on how to run its domestic affairs, giving it only one

22. Ibid.
23. Samuel Huntington, "Clash of Civilizations," *Foreign Affairs*, 72,3(1993): 22–49.
24. Francis Fukuyama, "End of History?" *National Interest*, Summer edition (1989):1–8.
25. John Lee, "Lonely Power, Staying Power: the Rise of China and the Resilience of US pre-eminence", *Strategic Snapshot*, 10 (September 2011):1–3. See also Katrin Bennhold, "As China Rises, Conflict with West Rises too," *New York Times*, January 17, 2010.

option – Westernize through Western-style democracy or perish – is in fact a way of starting a confrontation. Somehow, the imperialist tendency is again naturalized as normal, its language is seen as the norm and its conduct is perceived as somewhat exemplary (as implied by Nye's concept of soft power[26]), while an attempt by China to peacefully defend its choices, to disagree with US and Western advice, and to demand that they respect its different choices in domestic and foreign policy, is projected as unnatural and even unwise. This is an outcome of an embedded paradigm of international relations as premised on Western civilization, Western ways, Western ideas of political arrangement and Western choices as "international" in and of themselves. It is the paradigm ingrained in the very idea of the world that the West is building through imperialism, colonialism, neocolonialism and globalization; it is a world where others must follow its dictates. It is a world in which its particularities are extended over the whole world to internationalize them: the particular values, ethics, norms, interests, models and so forth.

Now, what has been the logic of the foreign policy as pursued by the Chinese during the period of emergence? In the period immediately after the Cold War, China's foreign policy was undergirded by the idea of *taoguang yanghui* (韬光养晦), which means keeping its international relations role subdued while building its national strength or domestic strength, and buying time before asserting itself globally. It kept a low profile on major global issues and worked hard to avoid confrontation with Western powers already worried about the implications of its rise. It was in this context that the Chinese government described its attitude to the US as "learning to live with the hegemon", a logic of power that is the direct opposite of the logic of power as dominance or competition prevalent in Western thinking about international relations, which encourages domination or confrontation as witnessed in their kneejerk response to Chinese government's suppression of the Tiananmen Square protests in 1989.[27] It focused a lot more on more on good neighbourliness, the idea of co-existence rather than dominance, achieved by strengthening

---

26. See, for instance, Joseph Nye, *Bound to Lead: The Changing Nature of American Power* (New York: Basic Books, 1991); and Joseph Nye, *Soft Power: The Means to Success in World Politics* (New York: Basic Books, 2004).
27. Baohui Zhang, "Chinese Foreign Policy in Transition: Trends and Implications," *Journal of Current Chinese Affairs*, 39, 2(2010): 30–68.

relations in Asia to improve conditions for its economic development. Buoyed by its massive economic development, enabling it to overtake Japan as the second biggest economy in the world, after rising past a few G7 economies in a matter of a decade, China's foreign policy posture shifted gear a bit as it became more assertive especially in respect of its national interests. Tensions with Western powers became a lot more apparent in the UN Security Council as well as in relation to the issue of territorial disputes in the South China Sea and the Taiwan issue. For instance, it warned the US about the repercussions of its very public reception to the Tibetan leader, the Dalai Lama, and its intended arms' sale to Taiwan; it suspended economic ties with Denmark after it had received the Dalai Lama; and even cancelled the China-European Union (EU) Summit over the French reception to the Dalai Lama. During the period, China continued accelerating the modernization of its military capability, investing heavily in cutting-edge technology for land, water, air and space activities.

China's military role expanded from securing national sovereignty to securing the sea lanes and shipping lines especially in South China Sea, partly in response to the policy of encirclement pursued by the Bush and Obama administrations in the US in tandem with Japan, Australia and other powers. This has heightened tensions in the region, especially with Vietnam, the Philippines and Japan at a time when the US was working to isolate China by strengthening its military relations with these and other countries in the Asia-Pacific area. In the same period though, China has worked to build cordial relations across the Taiwan straits, allowing economic cooperation to grow exponentially, thus creating a situation where the political relations are lukewarm. However, Taiwan's economy is virtually integrating with that of the mainland economy in China. It has also massively expanded its relations with the US neighbourhood, almost completely taking over as key trade partner in South America and the Caribbean. In addition, it has displaced Western powers as the leading trade and investment partner to Africa, parts of eastern Europe, western Asia, and the Pacific. With this economic pre-eminence, the need has arisen for China to defend its global interests, hence its willingness to confront other global hegemons when these are threatened. It is thus teaching Western powers to learn to co-exist with an independently minded, ideologically distinct and assertive non-Western power in place of their tendency to dominate and lead others in the direction towards subservience.

The dominant analysis on China's foreign policy is premised on assumptions that the country's new stature and role is bad for democracy; it is bad for human rights and for the world itself because its values, conduct and actions are not compatible with those of Western powers. So, compatibility with the current centre of global power, the North America-western Europe axis, is turned into a standard for measuring significance and value in international relations. There is worry about whether China will use its new-found global economic power to assert its national interests at the global level, an expectation born of the assumption that all states are like modern Western powers; given a chance, they would dominate and colonize the world. Many in the West fear China's motives and calculations; this stems from the knowledge of the dark underside of Western modernity over the past 500 years. In this sense, it matters little whether indeed China is moving in this direction or not. The Western writings on China's role in Africa see the rise of a colonial empire intent on plundering Africa's resources for its own national interests and placing Africa under its global wing as it plans, many in the West presume, to challenge Western power globally.

This is why African and other subaltern thinkers, who are writing about Africa-China relations, face the real danger of replicating the Eurocentric paranoia about China and other emerging powers. There is every danger that we could repeat to the world the exaggerated threat that the dominant West see in China's global presence. African, and South thinkers and people, have huge concerns of their own about China as one might be concerned about any country with massive power, but the fear is not that China would dislocate the West, but how its power impacts on the African dream and aspirations of the periphery generally. This includes the fact that like other emerging powers, China can be seen on the periphery as increasingly becoming a pillar of the western world rather than an alternative one. The tendency of these countries, which in Wallerstein's analysis could be classified as semi-periphery, is to act like the Westernized *bourgeoisie* by being willing to reach some consensus with global power or to strike pragmatic deals. This creates concerns among the subalterns that emerging powers like China gravitate towards sub-imperialism to the benefit of the Western imperial order continuing longer.[28] These large

---

28. Patrick Bond, "Sub-imperialism as Lubricant of Neoliberalism: South African 'deputy sheriff' duty within BRICS," *Third World Quarterly*,

states of the South are criticized for playing a role in re-legitimizing failed Western liberalism, from a Western model of democracy in the case of Brazil, India and Turkey, for example, to neoliberal economics in the case of China and others. Africans and other subaltern critics also have concerns about the conduct of Chinese business enterprises in relation to importing labour or their massive purchase of land alongside a number of others emerging powers and so forth. There is also interest in the danger of uncritically copying the Chinese models and the challenges relating to weak strategy regarding what Africa needs from China.[29] There are debates about translating Chinese investments in commodities and infrastructure to drive effective development.[30] There are also critical discussions on the implications of relations with China on African cultures and languages, both positive and negative ramifications.[31] Yet, the danger of replicating the Western narrative that projects the Chinese presence as colonial in order to have the Chinese share the huge historical burden that the West have over Africa's underdevelopment, carries the danger of replicating messaging that is part of normal propaganda in the battle for global power.

The geopolitics and biopolitics of knowledge under modernity have been such that the Western knowledge has attained the status of being the universal and hegemonic way of knowing; its theories, philosophies, paradigms, tools of analysis and methodologies have become hegemonic. The coloniality of knowledge was achieved alongside the coloniality of being (the creating of inferior and superior subjects), and the coloniality of power that we have outlined above; and it manifested in universalization of eurocentrism. This is what the Nigerian thinker, Professor Claude Ake,[32] concluded from his studies

34,2(2013):251–70. See also Ruy M. Marini, Subdesarrollo y Revolucio☐n (Mexico City: Siglo XXI Editores, 1974): 1–25, accessed February 12, 2015, translated on http://mrzine.monthlyreview.org/2010/bt 280210p.html#_edn13.

29. Garth Le Pere, *China: Mercantilist Predator or Partner in Development* (Midrand: Institute for Global Dialogue, 2007).

30. Garth Le Pere and Garth Shelton, *China and South Africa: South-South Cooperation in a Global Era* (Midrand: Institute for Global Dialogue, 2007).

31. Kwesi Kwaa Prah, *Afro-Chinese Relations: Past, Present and Future* (Cape Town: CASAS, 2007).

32. Claude Ake, *Social Science as Imperialism: The Theory of Political Development* (Ibadan: Ibadan University Press, 1982).

that social science as we know it is imperialism par excellence. To know is to acquire the Western lenses of knowing; to educate is to introduce others to Western knowledge. This was achieved through process of epistemicide, the deliberate murder of other ways of knowing and knowledges deemed by the Western scholar as irrational; the erasure of others in the realm of knowledge production so that the archive, which should shape what the world knows and thinks, should be Western; and the silencing of voices about the very nature of modernity and its dark underside. Under these conditions, the Western subject is centered in all ways of knowing and others are de-centered, prevented from understanding phenomena authentically through their own loci of enunciation. The difficulty is that modernity functions on the basis of illusions that hide the darker side of its motives; so, it presents itself as an objective, universal and disinterested discourse when in fact it conceals the violence of its epistemic imperialism. We on the African continent experience this to this day as Western discourses continue to shape what we think and say about ourselves, Africa, the South, and the world. This reduces our inputs to mimicry. For this reason, the first task for a subaltern thinker is to unmask the silences, distortions and illusions of the dominant discourse.

Implications for Rising Africa's Diplomacy

Africa has also been on the rise in the period after 1990, but it is a rise that is somewhat different from that of China and other emerging powers. This difference forms part of the distinction that must be made between the emergence of major powers in the global South and the rise of the rest of the South. In the first two decades after independence, Africa's GDP grew at an average of 4.5 percent, its export growth rate at 2.8 percent, agriculture grew at 1.6 percent and manufacturing at 6 percent, making it one of the growing regions of the world. But according to Abdulla Bujra, "the strong optimism of the 60s concerning economic development, slowly gave way, first to hesitation, then to pessimism and by the end of the 70s, to a consensus of gloom."[33] This marked a surge of pessimism after a period punctuated by the euphoria of independence and the disappointment at the collapse of first independent governments under the weight of military take-overs and political assassinations that we now know

---

33. Abdalla Bujra, ed., "Editorial," *Africa Development. A Quarterly Journal of CODESRIA*, 7(1,2) (1982): i–vi.

involved imperial forces keen to clampdown on anti-imperialist tendencies in the newly independent African states. Africa reached an economic crossroads with three options before it, according to the UN Economic Commission of Africa (ECA) at the time: self-reliance and self-sustenance that would require a strong vision and leadership; surrender of economic sovereignty and reliance on foreign aid and tutelage; or adopting a wait-and-see approach while using conventional measures to avoid antagonism and hoping for a positive turn in the economic situation.[34] Working with the ECA, the Organization of African Unity (OAU) convened dialogues with the continent to fashion a vision for an African economic renaissance in a period of global economic meltdown. These discussions culminated in the famous Monrovia Declaration, through which African countries announced their commitment to a vision for chance within the timeline 1979–2020, underlining self-reliance, self-sufficiency, democratic national development, equitable economic development and solidarity in world affairs.[35]

The Monrovia Declaration inspired the development of a concrete plan for economic rejuvenation through regional integration based on industrialization, expanded trade and stability, the Lagos Plan of Action of 1980. Through this, the OAU hoped to succeed in stimulating economic cooperation and integration on the basis of regional institutions for integration, the so-called regional economic communities. Six principles were agreed on as the basis for this, namely: self-reliance as the basis of development; equity in the distribution of wealth; expansion of the state/public sector as an essential element of development; direction of external capital aligning them with domestic imperatives; inter-African economic cooperation and integration; and a commitment to a New International Economic Order as part of the broader Third World campaign. The Plan set the vision for an African Common Market by 2000. But the incidence of conflict worsened, economic challenges deepened, and despair grew in the 1980s, giving the Plan no chance of ever taking root. The dream was thus deferred as governments fell and juntas emerged, as authoritarianism grew bolder in the context of the Cold War stalemate and big power support for dictatorships. During this period, economic

---

34. Abdalla Bujra, "Editorial."
35. Organization of African Unity, "What Kind of Africa in the Year 2002?" (Addis Ababa: OAU, 1979).

imperialism and the neoliberal onslaught on African economic sovereignty helped entrench economic stagnation and support economic dependency, and the underdevelopment of Africa for the development benefit of Western economic powers grew.

The end of the Cold War opened up opportunities for African economies to expand and grow, and for its politics and diplomacy to emerge as crucial for major decisions in the global environment. Africa is a complex geopolitical map made up of fifty-five countries designed in an arbitrary process of imperial expansion from Berlin, Germany, in western Europe. The story of economic development in Africa is also complex. Six countries are said to have dramatically transformed their per capita economic growth with positive effects on social and human development between 1970 and 1995, but two of these – Cote d'Ivoire and Zimbabwe – stagnated and even regressed in the 2000s. This is part of the story of African economic growth that is marked by ebbs and flows, inconsistencies relating in most cases to incidences of political instability and conflict, as well as instability of commodity prices in the world markets. To keep the dream alive, the OAU and ECA came up with an accelerated special programme to respond to the specific challenges of the 1980s, the African Priority Programme for Economic Recovery, 1986–1990, with a strong focus on the rehabilitation of agriculture, alleviating external debt and strengthening regional economic communities. In 1989, they also produced an African Alternative to Economic Structural Adjustment Programme to respond to the Western neoliberal onslaught on African economic independence through the International Monetary Fund (IMF) and the World Bank. Both initiatives did not enjoy the support of the powerful in the world, including the IMF and World Bank, and they had power to marginalize, undermine and suffocate these initiatives. Conditions of failure of governance – with the spread of dictatorship, economic decline and collapse of social development as structural adjustment programmes – simply deepened and did not allow these programmes to have the desired effect.

In 1991, Africa took advantage of the improving political situation and adopted the Abuja Treaty towards Establishing an African Economic Community that consolidated the various measures agreed on in the past and placed a strong emphasis on making regional economic integration work in order to produce an African economic community by 2025. This helped re-energize regional bodies and their focus on economic consensus. But the post-Cold War dynamics and their positive impact of reform of political arrangements towards democratic forms of statehood, collapse of military governments, decline of conflict and violence, and improved social situation, meant that this consensus needed to be strengthened to respond to new opportunities that Africa needed. It is in this context that Africa took the decision to transition from the OAU to a new organization with a stronger focus on the economic question, the African Union (AU) and the adoption of a new all-embracing development plan for Africa, the New Partnership for Africa's Development (NEPAD) in 2002.

In the period after the Cold War, Africa's economies also began to register steady growth: in many cases, there was a dramatic rise in growth rates, especially in resource-based economies. Between 1995 and 2010, Africa's average growth rate was 5 percent and per capita income also started to rise, registering a 2.6 percent rise year on year, after a decade of stagnation and regression. By 2010, Africa's per capita income had grown by 46 percent. Africa continued to experience an economic upswing in spite of the debilitating global economic crisis from 2008, so that in the period 2008–2014, when global economic giants were registering extremely low growth rates, Africa continued to report an impressive average 2.6 percent growth rate.[36] Big African economies like South Africa, Egypt and Nigeria grew, diversified further and this enabled them to play significant roles in the world. Resource-based economies like Angola, Equatorial Guinea, Gabon, the Democratic Republic of Congo (DRC), and others, have generally registered very high economic growth rates.

In the same period, Africa has also increased its political clout on account of the emergence of new African leaders and governments willing to assert the interests of the continent at the centre of global power more forcefully than before. African multilateral diplomacy has been on the rise ever since, as evidenced by the large number of common negotiating positions on a range of major global issues and in relation to matters of global decision-making. This includes common positions on the external debt, global multilateral trade, global climate change, intellectual property regimes, the reform of international finance institutions, the UN Reform, global development agenda, international security and terrorism and so forth. These

---

36. African Development Bank, ECA, and UNDP, *African Economic Outlook 2013: Structural Transformation and Natural Resources* (Addis Ababa, 2014).

positions demonstrate two crucial facts about growing the African agenda in world affairs: the first is the intention on the part of Africa to contribute in South-led efforts to transform the world system towards the birth of a new one, where all are equal and the agenda is really shared. The second is the realization that Africa has the advantage of numbers that is crucial in multilateral negotiations both in terms of shared agenda and during voting; therefore, Africa has decided to use its leverage with regard to the number of its states in international negotiations to advance its shared interests.

African countries individually too have raised their stature and significance in international affairs with a number being invited into global decision-making platforms such as Egypt and South Africa that are members of the Group of Twenty global economies (G20) responsible for global economic governance; Nigeria is now a member of the Mexico, Indonesia, Nigeria, and Turkey (MINT) diplomatic club, Egypt is also member of Colombia, Indonesia, Vietnam, Egypt and South Africa group (CIVETS) and so forth. Countries are playing more active role in structures and alliances of the South such as the G77+China and Non-Aligned Movement (NAM). Africa has become a centre of new mega-strategic partnerships, having signed partnerships with China, Japan, Turkey, the US, South Korea, South America, Asia, the EU, and the Caribbean.

Implications for Africa-China Relations

Both Africa and China confront the challenges and opportunities that come with the convergence of their emergence from the periphery of a Western-centric world. Their rise, as we have argued, inevitably opens up spaces for rising powers and regions to exercise their agency in a world designed to marginalize them in order to enhance their significance, pursue their interests and contribute to the change that they think is needed. Their rise enhances their strategic significance in world affairs in the sense that no major discussion, no global consensus and no key international decision can be taken in their absence without legitimacy questions arising.

In the case of China, of course, this rise is a bit more consequential for the world itself and the structure of global power as we have argued. For this reason, China has acquired much leverage in the form of economic clout for use in influencing decisions and shaping the evolution of global economic governance. In the case of Africa, the leverage is potentially substantial depending on whether Africa succeeds in pooling its capacities together through shared positions and collective action on a number of fronts, including negotiation reforms in international systems of governance.

Both have become major sources of economic growth globally. To regain growth, the world economies need access to Africa's vast commodities. In order to increase trade and investment, they need relations with China as a large growing economy with huge reserves in a period of financial crisis in Western economies. Africa has been the focus of the scramble for natural resources involving both emerging powers like China and Western powers. The continent has seen a rise in exports and export earnings in foreign currency due to this growing demand for natural resources like minerals, oil and gas, marine and forestry resources. China has been able to acquire stakes in major stock exchanges across the world and its investments are driving growth in regions like Latin America, the Caribbean, the Pacific, West Asia and Africa. Of course, China's story is much more positive being about sustainable economic activities that are in its favour, but Africa's opportunity remains vulnerable because of the tendency to focus on, and not go beyond, the export of primary commodities with little or no beneficiation.

Therefore, Africa has a lot to learn from the Chinese success over several decades in order to turn the potential economic benefits into reality. China's economic success has been driven by its ability to excel in manufacturing and other parts of the primary industry. Africa's hope to increase beneficiation of natural resources and to export manufactured goods on a greater scale will be strengthened by strong relations with China. Africa also stands to gain from applying lessons China learned and contextualizing these to African conditions. Africa needs industrialization, integration and equitable sharing of wealth, and China has the experience into which Africa needs to tap for this purpose.

The Africa-China diplomacy can be of real value for both sides if nested properly in the growing agency and significance of the global South. The relations have a potential for contributing concretely to the growing volume and value of South-South cooperation, especially in the areas of trade and investment, technical cooperation, cultural exchange, science and technology transfers, and cooperation in the knowledge sector. Increase in Africa-China trade and investment, for instance, contributes to the volume and value of South-South cooperation when figures are developed. The sheer size of the entities involved means that they could account for at least half of South-South cooperation.

Both are key components of the global South with Africa epitomizing the rank and file of the South and China representing the big and advantaged members of the South. On this basis, both could play a critical role in bridging the divide between big players, the emerging powers, and the rest of the South, which has been apparent in recent years such as during climate change negotiations in Copenhagen in 2009, where emerging powers brokered a compromise with Western powers to the chagrin of smaller South countries that hoped to see their demands accepted for greater action by the developed countries. They have an opportunity to understand together and separately the dynamics facing either side so that the rift within the global South is resolved before it worsens. In this process, the two could facilitate linkages between big South multilateral platforms like the G77+China and the NAM with the smaller diplomatic clubs that emerging powers have established recently, including partnerships between Brazil, Russia, India, China and South Africa (BRICS); and India, Brazil and South Africa (IBSA); and CIVETS for the purposes of promoting a stronger South alliance on major international affairs where the interests of the poor are at stake.

But this will require that both parties also work through a host of challenges. The role of China in Africa is increasingly subject to criticism for being too dominant and therefore posing a danger of entrenching power asymmetry between the two. There are concerns about the conduct of China in Africa, especially as is seen in the conduct of big and small enterprises in African countries, which shows the abuse of workers, poor working conditions and the import of poor Chinese as labour. The motives of China in Africa are coming under strong criticism as critics decide to go beyond nice-sounding declarations and pleasantries and expose the realities of resource hunger, commercial competition and civilizational clashes at times. Africa's relatively weak leadership at the moment means that the continent may not come up with an overarching strategy for dealing with China. There is the process of deciding on "the Africa we want" through extensive consultations conducted by the AU Commission, but whether this will lead to clarity of vision practically is a subject for debate.

Conclusion

The prospects of sound diplomatic coordination between Africa and China is not about relations between the two alone, but how all this is nested in international diplomacy generally and how it also contributes to global South agency. Africa and China find themselves is a strategic position in world affairs on account of their economic growth over the past three decades, enabling them to increase their economic and political clout. They have gained stature and significance. This convergence of emergence offers both opportunities and challenges for Africa and China in international diplomacy. Key among challenges is that there are major differences between the two. Among the opportunities is that the two countries could scaffold their international diplomacy on alignment between small and big South multilateral institutions for greater harmony in the pursuit of the common agenda.

Bibliography

African Development Bank, ECA, and UNDP, 2014. African Economic Outlook 2013: Structural Transformation and Natural Resources, Addis Ababa.

Ake, C., 1982, Social Science as Imperialism: The Theory of Political Development, Ibadan: Ibadan University Press.

Alcoff, L. and Mendieta, E. 2000. Thinking from the Underside of History: Enrique Dussel's Philosophy of Liberation, Lanham: Rowman and Littlefield

Amin, S. 1989. Eurocentrism. New York: Monthly Review Press.

Bennhold, K, 'As China Rises, Conflict with West Rises too', New York Times, 17 January 2010.

Bond, P., 2013. 'Sub-imperialism as Lubricant of Neoliberalism: South African "deputy sheriff" duty within BRICS', Third World Quarterly, 34 (2), pp. 251-70.

Bujra, A. (ed.), 1982. "Editorial', Africa Development. A Quarterly Journal of CODESRIA, 7(1,2), pp.i-vi.

China Statistical Yearbook for 2011.

Deloitte, 'Press Release', 22 January 2013. Available at *www.deloitte.com/view/en_CN/cn/Pressroom/pr/105280463d16c310V gnVCM2000003356f70aRCRD.htm* (accessed on 13 September 2013).

Ding, L. China's Path to the World's Largest Economy: Limits of Extrapolations.   Available   at *http://www.eai.nus.edu.sg/Vol2No4_LuDing.pdf* (accessed on 13 September 2013).

Dussel, E. 1996. The Underside of Modernity, New Jersey: Humanities Press

Fanon, F. 1963. The Wretched of the Earth, New York: Glover Press.

Fukuyama, F., 1989. 'End of History?' National Interest, Summer edition, pp. 1-8.

Grosfoguel, R. 2009. 'A Decolonial Approach to Political-Economy: Transmodernity, Border Thinking and Global Coloniality', Kult 6- Special Issue, Fall: 10- 38.

Huntington, S. 1993. 'Clash of Civilizations', Foreign Affairs, 72 (3), pp. 22-49.

Huntington, S., 1999. 'Lonely Superpower', Foreign Affairs, 78 (2), no pagination.

Jingwen, L. 2000. The Chinese Economy into the 21st Century: Forecasts and Policies, Beijing: Foreign Languages Press, pp. 1-7.

Lee, J., 2011. 'Lonely Power, Staying Power: the Rise of China and the Resilience of US pre-eminence', Strategic Snapshot, 10, September, 1-3.

Le Pere, G., 2007. China: Mercantilist Predator or Partner in Development, Midrand: Institute for Global Dialogue.

Le Pere, G. and Shelton, G., 2007. China and South Africa: South-South Cooperation in a Global Era, Midrand: Institute for Global Dialogue.

Maldonado-Torres, N. 2008. Against War, Durham: Duke University Press

Marini, RM. 1974. Subdesarrollo y Revolución, Mexico City: Siglo XXI Editores, pp 1–25, translated at *http://mrzine.monthlyreview.org/2010/bt280210p.html#_edn13* (accessed on 12 February 2015).

Mignolo, W. 1995. The Darker Side of Modernity: Literacy, Territoriality and Colonization, Ann Arbor: University of Michigan Press

Morrison, W.M. 2012. China's Economic Rise: History, Trends, Challenges, and Implications for the U.S., Congressional Research Service, Washington: CRS, pp.3-5.

Nye, J., 1991. Bound to Lead: The Changing Nature of American Power, New York: Basic Books; and Nye, J. 2004. Soft Power: The Means to Success in World Politics, New York: Basic Books.

OAU 1979. 'What Kind of Africa in the Year 2002?', Addis Ababa: OAU.

'Officials have no power except for the people'. 19 March 2007. Available at *http://english.people.com.cn/200703/19/eng20070319_358925.html* (accessed on 13 October 2013).

Quijano, A. 2000. 'Coloniality of Power, Eurocentrism and Latin America', Neplanta: Views from the South, 1 (3), pp. 533-80

Prah, K.K., 2007. Afro-Chinese Relations: Past, Present and Future, Cape Town: CASAS.

Rodney, W., 1972. How Europe Underdeveloped Africa, Nairobi: East African Educational Publishers Ltd.

Sutter, R.G. 1995. 'China in World Affairs - US Policy Choices', Congressional Research Service, 95 (295), January, unpaginated.

Wallerstein, I., 1976. The Modern World-System: Capitalist Agriculture and the Origins of the European World-Economy in the Sixteenth Century. New York: Academic Press.

Wa Thiong'o, N. 2012. Globalectics: Theory and Politics of Knowing, New York: Columbia Press.

WHO and China State Council Development Research Centre, 2005. 'China: Health, Poverty and Economic Development'. Available *http://www.who.int/macrohealth/action/CMH_China.pdf* (accessed on 12 November 2014).

Yeuh, L. 'China's Strategy towards the Financial Crisis and Economic Reform'. Available at *http://www.lse.ac.uk/IDEAS/publications/reports/pdf/SR012/yueh.pdf* (accessed on 12 January 2015).

Zhang, B., 2010. 'Chinese Foreign Policy in Transition: Trends and Implications', Journal of Current Chinese Affairs, 39(2), pp. 30-68.

Zoelick, R. 2005. 'Whither China: from Membership to Responsibility', NRB Analysis, 16 (4), pp. 6-7.

Chapter Two. Africa-China Relations and Africa's Strategic Deficits

══════════════❖══════════════

Lloyd G. Adu Amoah

On the whole, Chinese policy in Africa has resulted from the diplomatic initiative of the People's Republic of China, rather than of the African States themselves.

–Alaba Ogunsanwo

Introduction

In the popular imagination and even in informed and enlightened circles in Africa today, it would seem that Africa-China relations are a very recent phenomenon. The evidence, however, in ancient Chinese records and those unearthed by sinologists point to a quite long provenance going as far back as early Han Dynasty times (when the Chinese might have reached Africa overland) through to the Song, Tang and down to the Ming Dynasties.[1] It is instructive to note that by medieval times, trade between the two peoples was to prove the most compelling evidence of early contacts in the form of coins and porcelain[2] exchanged for Africa's exotica (precious objects and rare animals). For China, greater sophistication in its maritime technology

---

1. Teobaldo Filesi, *China and Africa in the Middle Ages* (London, England: CASS, 1972).
2. Most of the Chinese coins found on the East African coast are linked to the Tang and Song Dynasties. By the Ming Dynasty era, the use of coins (replaced by porcelain) for trade had been banned by stringent regulations accompanied by stiff punishment in case of any violations.

made possible this interaction. Teobaldo Filesi[3] informs us that by the seventh century, the Chinese had become "the boldest seamen of the Orient", culminating in the great expeditions to Africa in the Ming era. It is worth quoting Filesi in full here:[4]

China's peaceful ventures into the exotic world of Africa – a remarkable episode in the history of civilization – were the product of national propensities, of commercial interests, of technical ability and of the nautical knowledge acquired by the Chinese. If even today this nautical knowledge evokes profound admiration, it must have seemed even more prodigious to peoples of long ago, of whatever race or continent.

Though the basis for closer and deeper ties had thus been laid via the mediation of the Indian Ocean, the peoples of Africa and China had to wait for the twentieth century to realize this more concretely and actively.

Africa-China Relations: The Central Place of Bandung and Involutionary Impulses

Diplomatically, politically and economically isolated[5] from the richer Western nations after China's Communists defeated the Kuomintang in 1949 on the battlefield (and with that Chiang Kai-shek whom the US had supported with more than £3billion),[6] China had to reappraise her geo-political strategy. The urgency for this reconfiguration was further exacerbated by internal political questions. Key among them was responding to the activities of the remnants of the Kuomintang on the mainland in the vital effort of consolidating its power and engendering political stability. The isolation had to be broken in part for the sorely needed economic benefits this would bring and how this would redound on the internal political calculus (stability) as well. The Asia-Africa Conference of Heads of State and Governments (the Bandung Conference) of 1955 was to offer the institutional, albeit

3. Filesi, *China and Africa.*
4. Ibid., 13.
5. The Sino-Soviet Treaty signed between Mao Zedong and Joseph Stalin soon after the establishment of the People's Republic of China served to guarantee China's economic and military aid from the Soviet Union and firmly ensconced the Asian nation into the Communist bloc.
6. Ogunsanwo, *China Policy in Africa,* 5, quoting *The China White Paper* (US Department of State, August 1949), re-issued (Stanford University Press, 1967), 969.

transient, opportunity for this. China utilized this opening to the hilt. Ismael[7] underlines this: "We may say that from their assumption of power in 1949 until the Bandung Conference in 1955 the Chinese People's Republic showed little interest in Afro-Asian affairs, and no interest in Africa."

The Korean War had demonstrated to the Chinese, given the country's isolation, the critical "interlocking of her African policy with her international strategic interests and thus the relative incomprehensibility of the former without the latter."[8]It must be noted that China's participation in the Korean War led to a total embargo (initiated by the Truman Presidency)[9] on unlicensed financial and commercial transactions between United States (US) nationals and China (and North Korea as well) under what came to be known as the Foreign Assets Control Regulations (FACR) of December 17, 1950. China's geo-strategic policy after Bandung came to be marked unambiguously by developing ties of friendship with African countries as it cast itself it as a champion of Afro-Asian solidarity and interests.[10] To be sure, Zhou En Lai had gone to Bandung with the diplomatic masterstroke encapsulated in the PanchSheel Treaty (also known Five Principles of Peaceful Co-Existence) signed with India over Tibet in Beijing a year earlier on April 29, 1954. The Five Principles were to find expression, albeit in a modified form, in the enunciation of ten principles ensconced in the final communiqué issued at the end of the Bandung Conference on April 24, 1955. In Bandung,[11] China's vision of how it wished to engage with both Africa and Asia in particular gained critical diplomatic purchase. China took full advantage of this in blistering diplomatic, economic and cultural overtures directed at the African continent just a year after Bandung.[12]

---

7. Ismael, *"The People's Republic of China and Africa"*, 512

8. AlabaOgunsanwo, *China Policy*, 3.

9. The Americans subsequently pressured Britain to follow suit. See David Clayton, *Imperialism Revisited.*

10. Alaba Ogunsanwo, *China Policy,* and Ismael *The People's Republic of China and Africa*

11. Noted African-American writer Richard Wright, in his work *The Colour Curtain*, felt that Nehru, one of the key figures at Bandung, was being used by a wily Zhou Enlai who presented a friendly, reasonable and accommodating China to the world.

12. Alaba Ogunsanwo, *China Policy*, 9.

In 1956, Chinese cultural missions visited Egypt, the Sudan, Morocco, Tunisia and Ethiopia. China also made commercial inroads into Africa with large cotton purchases from Egypt, followed by her first commercial contracts with other African countries – beginning with the Sudan and Morocco. On the diplomatic front, she succeeded in obtaining diplomatic recognition from Egypt in May 1956. The first Chinese embassy in Africa was established in Cairo, with the wider function of contacting as many African groups as possible and making a concrete analysis of the general African situation. Ambassador Ch'en Chia-k'ang was sent to Cairo, where he remained until December 1965.

It must be stated that just four years after this flurry of Chinese activities on the African continent, concentrated around the Northern extremity, Ghana established diplomatic relations with China on July 1, 1960: the first and longest running (albeit with a break after the coup d'état in 1966) to date involving countries south of the Sahara. Arguably Africa-China relations from the 50s to the 70s which were characterized by the strains and stresses of Cold War politics and China's own external and internal concerns and limitations (regional questions and economic challenges), achieved by the mid-1980s[13] to the turn of the twentieth century a certain stability and solidity even though there were still residual tensions.

Amoah questions[14] the simplifying, rigidifying and simplistic dualization of Africa-China relations along the axes of gain and loss[15] evident in very recent writings on the subject and proffers a new interpretation (see Figure 1.0) which is sensitive to the notions of loss and gain (but is not held captive by it) yet draws attention to the involutionary nature (and therefore the value of temporality) of the relationship which is framed in recent times by power, resources and developmentalism.

---

13. China had become more economically buoyant (see table 1.0) by the late 1980s after China under Deng Xiaoping adopted the raft of policies under the Reform and Opening up Period (*gaige kaifang*) (1979–1994).

14. Lloyd G. Adu Amoah, "China in Africa." This section and others following it draw textually and ideationally on the author's previous works to provide the necessary background for readers unfamiliar with them.

15. Chris Alden, *China;* Johan Norberg, "China Paranoia"; Ian Taylor, "Beijing's Arms"; Taylor 2006b, "Sino-African Relations."

Table 1.0[16] – China's Economic Transformation Indices

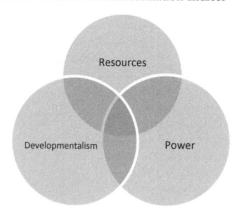

Figure 1.0. Re-interpreting Africa-China Relations (Cognitive Map)

Indices	year	year	year	year
	1978	2006	1986–1996	1996–2006
Per Capita Gross Domestic Product (GDP)	381yuan	16084yuan		
GDP (percentage growth)		10.7	10.1	9.0

Africa, China and Strategy

Africa-China relations have been marked by contradictions. These are empirical facts that cannot be wished away and require addressing if Africa in particular is to benefit far more than it has in its relations with China. Such contradictions include China's purported land grabs in Africa; deleterious labour practices (using Chinese labour in Africa for projects and reported ill treatment of African workers)[17], dumping of fake and low-quality goods on Africa; and a suspicious interest in Africa's natural resources (in Ghana for example this has led to alarming environmental degradation) including oil among others.

---

16. Source:http://www.stats.gov.cn/tjsj/ndsj/2007/indexeh.htm.
17. See Sautman and Yan, "East Mountain Tiger."

These have been rationalized as being the corollary and evidence of China's exploitative and imperialist[18] designs on Africa via an explanatory framework that refuses to differentiate between contradictions that arise, and will continue to do so, as the two parties interact far more intimately than before historically (C_1); and those reflecting deliberate policy formation in pursuit of strategic advantages (C_2). This paper focuses on C_2 (which have a dual quality in being advantages/gains if one considers them from the vantage point of China; and disadvantages from the African view point) and seeks to explain how these have emerged. These are the substantive questions on which Africa must focus as it engages China, given that C_2 are a sufficient condition for C_1 and therefore logically the attempt to resolve the former has a direct bearing on minimizing the emergence of the latter.

It is our contention that C_2 have emerged in Africa-China relations because China, unlike Africa, has a robust, strategically alert, nimble and constantly adaptive and evolving policy-formation[19] infrastructure in place. Strategy employed in this work ties in with the massive literature on this idea across a wide range of disciplines that fundamentally connects it with the search for power.[20] Amoah[21] identifies and therefore delimits its use within the context of the policy sphere of circumstanced developing countries which desire (and act as well) to rapidly transform. In this sense, Amoah[22] defined strategy in policy formation terms at the national level (the centre) as a pattern of decisions and actions (which change in response to changing international and national conditions), undergirded by a clearly articulated world view aimed at meeting specific goals within a given time frame to ultimately gain a position of relative competitive advantage and / or benefit. The Mandarin rendering of strategy, *zhanlue*

---

18. Hilary Clinton's 2012 veiled swipe at China in a speech at the University of Dakar is a classic reflection of the "Fear Factor" camp's view that China is simply in Africa to exploit. http://www.theguardian.com/world/2012/aug/01/hillary-clinton-africa-china.
19. Refers to policy making from the formulation, implementation, monitoring stages right through to policy change and termination phases.
20. Lawrence Freedman, *Strategy: A History,* an excellent encyclopedic treatment of the subject matter.
21. Amoah, "The Strategy approach"; Amoah, "Public policy formation"; Amoah, "The Rise of Telcos".
22. Ibid.

(战略), in the field of politics and economics is apt: "a plan, policy or tactic with overarching, comprehensive, and decisive implications."[23] Strategy therefore for the circumstanced developing nation, desirous of rapid independent national transformation is directed at a peculiar kind of power that allows it to meet its development goals on its terms, as it navigates a competitive and even combative geo-economic and geo-political terrain.

It is hardly mentioned in recent discourse on Chinese policy formation (nor are the necessary vital linkages drawn) that those who took up the mantle of steering the Chinese state immediately after 1949 were essentially former guerrillas who had come to power after winning decisive battles against armies that were much more well-armed and equipped. Guerrilla fighters essentially start a war from a position of weakness[24] (just like a circumstanced developing country in her attempt to transform) and must actually depend on the weapons of their enemies[25] and the masterful and judicious use of the benevolence of the surrounding physical and natural terrain to pursue the objectives of their campaign. Constant strategic decisions will be required in such a context and the Chinese Communist Party leaders who finally took up residence in *Zhongnanhai* (中南海), Beijing in 1949 (among them Mao Zedong, Zhu De, Lin Biao, Deng Xiaoping, Chen Yi, Zhou Enlai, among others) definitely honed their strategic thinking through all the epic military campaigns (against the Kuomintang and the Japanese) they had gone through. Mao Zedong[26] points to this experience as he and his comrades consolidated their power in Beijing in 1955: "We had twenty years experience in the base areas, and were trained in three revolutionary wars; our experience [on coming to power] was *exceedingly rich...*" (italics mine).

Our argument is that such strategic thinking was brought to bear on the myriad of tough policy questions that China faced and has

---

23. Xia and Chen, *Cihai [Seas of Word]* (Shanghai: Shanghai Cishu Publisher), 6th edition, 2009.

24. See Guevara, *Guerilla Warfare*.

25. David Chambers, "A lantern in the dark night", shows in a fascinating account how China's Signal Intelligence (SIGINT) service, the 3rd Department of the People's Liberation Army General Staff (3PLA), was in its institutional formative years wrought from purloined equipment from the battlefield.

26. Schram, *The Thoughts*, 113.

faced, including the African question. Such thinking has a very long provenance in Chinese international relations, marked as it has been by "an underlying strategic acumen and longevity,"[27] going back to the days when dynastic China, surrounded by mounted, more mobile nations on its frontiers, had to find the ways and means to ward them off. In the event, African nations (as opposed to the continent which is a civilization in her own right) have faced, and continue to do so, a distinct disadvantage interacting with a China which Lucian Pye[28] has described aptly as "a civilization pretending to be a nation- state"; a reality further exacerbated by the long, virtually unbroken, record and history of China's geo-economics and geo-politics. In dealing with Africa therefore, especially in recent times, the Chinese strategists at the centre framed the continent as a vital strategic matter and deployed the necessary resources (ideational, material and organizational) in search of benefits as theorized by the Strategy Approach.[29] In spite of all the public discourse from both the African and Chinese sides, it is naïve to assume that the interests of the two parties will be homogenous, let alone that they will coincide, and that either party realizing an advantage will not exploit it. As Chinese scholars Feng and Huang[30] have shown, China is engaging with the world, including Africa, on the basis of two logics – defensive and assertive – by which she safeguards her core national interests and pursues others of a material and moral nature. The Chinese are brutally clear on their interests.[31] "Our demand for energy and resources will grow. We must take part in the global reallocation of resources in a more active manner."

From the Forum on Africa-China Cooperation(FOCAC) to Xi Jinping's 4631 Idea

China's 2006 Africa Policy Document is a potent literary statement of China's strategic acuity in its engagements with Africa. What the document essentially does is to synthesize the critical policy insights

---

27. Kissinger, *On China,* 19.
28. Pye, "Social Science Theories", 1162.
29. For economy of space kindly see Amoah (2009, 2011b, 2014) for a detailed explication of the Strategy Approach.
30. Feng and Huang (2014)
31. Zhang Xiaoqiang, vice-chairperson, China's National Development and Reform Commission.

and experiences China had gathered as she interacted with Africa (going back as far as the mid-twentieth century) especially through the Forum on Africa-China Cooperation (FOCAC) process. The FOCAC process does institutionally for China what the 2006 document achieves textually: it provides China with a strategic advantage to define and dictate its interactions with African nations in the pursuit of her long-term national interests which spawns the C_2.

Forum on Africa-China Co-operation(FOCAC)

Type of Conference	Year	Host	Key Textual Outcomes
Inaugural Ministerial Conference	October 10–12, 2000	Beijing, China	Programme for Africa-China Cooperation in Economic and Social Development
2nd Ministerial Conference	December 15–16,2003	Addis Ababa, Ethiopia	Addis Ababa Action Plan (2004-2006).
3rd Ministerial Conference and Summit	November 4–6, 2006	Beijing, China	Beijing Action Plan (2007-2009)
4th Ministerial Conference	November 8–9,2009	Sharm el Sheikh, Egypt	Sharm el-Sheikh Action Plan (2010-2012)
5th Ministerial Conference	July 19–20, 2012	Beijing, China	Beijing Action Plan (2013-2015)
6th Ministerial Conference	2015	Johannesburg, South Africa	Johannesburg Action Plan (2016-2018)

Table 2.0: Africa-China Formal Meetings

To be sure, the Chinese have invested the necessary ideational, financial, organizational, personnel and diplomatic resources to pull this off with the consent of their African counterparts. This is the blinding array of administrative resources (one can imagine the other entailments) that the Chinese have packed behind the FOCAC process:

> In November 2000, the Chinese Follow-up Committee of FOCAC was established, currently composed of twenty-seven member departments or agencies, which are: the Ministry of Foreign Affairs, Ministry of Commerce, Ministry of Finance, Ministry of Culture,

International Department of the Communist Party of China (CPC)Central Committee, National Development and Reform Commission, Ministry of Education, Ministry of Science and Technology, Ministry of Industry and Information Technology, Ministry of Land and Resources, Ministry of Environmental Protection, Ministry of Transport (Civil Aviation Administration of China), Ministry of Agriculture, National Health and Family Planning Commission, People's Bank of China, General Administration of Customs, General Administration of Quality Supervision, Inspection and Quarantine, State Administration of Press, Publication, Radio, Film and Television, National Tourism Administration, Information Office of the State Council, Chinese Communist Youth League, China Council for Promotion of International Trade, China Development Bank, Export-Import Bank of China, Bank of China and People's Government of Beijing Municipality, with the Minister of Foreign Affairs and Minister of Commerce as the honorary chairmen and vice-ministers responsible for the related areas of the two ministries as chairmen. The Committee has a secretariat (comprised of director general-level officials from the Ministry of Foreign Affairs, Ministry of Commerce, Ministry of Finance and Ministry of Culture with the director-general of the Department of African Affairs of the Ministry of Foreign Affairs as the secretary-general) set up at the Department of African Affairs of the Ministry of Foreign Affairs.[32] (parenthesis mine).

The institutions and personnel involved are nested in the highest rungs of the Chinese hierarchy of governmental and administrative power at the centre. At FOCAC ministerial meetings, China has consistently been the benevolent one as African nations completely shorn of strategic initiative and pride are content to extend their begging palms, oblivious of the centrality of self-dignity and self-reliance[33] in Confucian cultures and the signals this sends. After the first FOCAC ministerial meeting, which was essentially foundational in character, China in the second FOCAC "announced that it would further increase assistance for Africa, pledging to train 10,000 professionals in various fields, and give zero-tariff treatment to

---

32. See http://www.focac.org/eng/ltda/ltjj/t933522.htm.
33. Bottelier (2006:15) informs us that China in its engagement with the World Bank serviced their loans "on time".

products exported to China from some of the least developed countries in Africa." For the third FOCAC,

> President Hu Jintao, on behalf of the Chinese government, announced eight measures to strengthen practical cooperation between China and Africa to support national development in Africa, including increased assistance, provision of preferential loans and preferential export buyer's credit, establishment of the Africa-China Development Fund, offering assistance in building the AU conference center, debt and customs exemption, establishment of economic cooperation and trade zones, enhancement of human resources development and cooperation in education, health care and other areas for Africa.

The pattern continued right up to the fifth FOCAC at which President Hu Jintao, on behalf of the Chinese government, unfurled a series of new measures to be implemented in the following three years to support Africa's peaceful development and strengthen Africa-China cooperation in five major areas of investment, finance, assistance, African integration, non-governmental exchanges and peace and security. This included China:

> providing 20 billion dollars of credit-line to African countries to assist their development of infrastructure, agriculture, manufacturing and small and medium-sized enterprises; continuing to increase assistance to Africa and building more agricultural technology demonstration centers as necessary; helping Africa train 30000 personnel in various sectors; offering 18000 government scholarships, and building cultural and vocational skills training facilities in African countries; deepening medical and health care cooperation by sending 1500 medical personnel to Africa and continuing to perform the Brightness Operation offering free treatment to cataract patients in Africa; continuing to carry out well-drilling and water supply projects in Africa to provide safe drinking water for the African people; establishing transnational and trans-regional infrastructural development partnership by supporting the related project planning and feasibility studies and encouraging established Chinese companies and financial institutions to take part in the transnational and trans-regional infrastructural development in Africa. China also proposed to carry out the Africa-China People-to-People Friendship Action; set up the Africa-China Press Exchange Center in China; continue to implement the Africa-China Joint Research and Exchange Program to sponsor 100 projects of

research, exchange and cooperation involving academic institutions and scholars from the two sides; launch the Initiative on Africa-China Cooperative Partnership for Peace and Security to deepen cooperation with the African Union(AU) and African countries in African peace and security by providing financial support for the AU peace-keeping missions and development of the African Standby Force, and train more AU peace and security officials and peace-keepers.

In not one instance of the record of events noted above does one African nation or even a collection of them attempt to offer anything to the Chinese. Ogunsanwo's view that China has always led diplomatic initiatives between her and African nations sounds true today. This is reflected, as argued above, in the overall objectives and key outcomes of FOCAC and vitally in the evolution of Africa-China relations. Having assumed power, President Xi Jinping is tapping into the strategic momentum China has regarding Africa-China relations. Using a "change in continuity" logic, he has recalibrated the relations around the 4613 pivot. The number four represents the foundations of sincerity, real results, affinity and good faith upon which the relations between the two partners is built (derived from China's framing of the issues). The number six captures the major projects in the areas of industry, finance, poverty reduction, ecological and environmental protection, cultural and people-to-people exchanges as well as peace and security that China seeks to pursue in Africa. The number one points to the central place of the FOCAC process, while the number three expresses China's interest in supporting Africa's high-speed railway, highway and regional aviation networks.

Xi Jinping is already making good the Strategic Partnership focus agreed upon at the fourth FOCAC. Egypt's relationship with China under President Xi has been elevated to a "comprehensive strategic partnership", which the Accra based think-pad Strategy3 argues should "see deeper and closer political, economic, military, cultural and technological co-operation between the two sides."[34] The other two African countries, which have a comprehensive strategic partnership with China, are South Africa and Algeria. Nigeria and Angola have strategic partnerships.[35]

---

34. http://www.strategy3online.com/news/index.php?fn_mode=fullnews &fn_id=81
35. We build on the list of Feng and Huang (2014).

The African Response to China

If Africa's response to China's increasingly influential role in the world (and its willingness to actively co-operate with Africa) is one that will benefit her peoples and resolve what seems to be contradictions (our C_2), then it must of necessity be strategic (and therefore take into account medium- and long-term policy questions) and focused. Amoah[36] draws attention to what he calls 3G Public Policy Formation in Africa which refers essentially to policy-making approaches (of the 1980s and 1990s through to the present) shot through by neoliberal ideas. Once planning (centralized or not) was given a bad name and hanged in the mortal ideological battles of the Cold War, the term has become so anathematized that any long-term strategic policy thinking in Africa is subsumed under it and scorched. The upshot has been policy formation focused on the short term to the detriment of the long term, which entails strategic thinking. Mulgan[37] is perceptive in stating that "all successful governments have created spaces for thought, learning and reflection to resist the tyranny of the immediate". And we must add especially that some governments in the Global South have actively done what Mulgan draws our attention to. Too many African governments, it will seem, have been held captive by the "tyranny of the immediate" under 3G Public Policy Formation.

The Strategy Approach provides prescriptions on how to make strategy central to the policy process in developing polities who care deeply about their transformation. Briefly, the Strategy Approach (derived from the policy experience of Singapore and modern China) theorizes that at the core of the rapid transformation mode developing polity's policy formation, will lie questions of strategy encompassing the complex of ideas, processes and actions by which efforts are made to transform the entire life of the citizens through the utilization of its resources (both physical and human) and opportunities. Policy actors in the rapid transformation mode developing polity are engaged primarily with matters of strategy in industrial, economic, external relations, defense, environmental, and educational, etc. spheres.

Any African country serious about engaging China needs to retool its policy formation infrastructure and place strategy at its core as a first vital step. It is this weakness which has prevented virtually all African countries from putting together their own China Policy

---

36. Amoah, "Public Policy formation".
37. Mulgan, *The Art of Public Strategy*, 3.

Documents (one of the key challenges of their relations with China). At the time of writing, no African country had such a policy document in place. This needs to be addressed quickly as a matter of strategic necessity. Amoah[38] has raised this concerning Ghana. Amoah's argument (and this applies reasonably to other African countries) was that without such a document providing vital guidelines and clear deliverables, Ghana's engagement with China "was marked by an uncoordinated set of gestures and activities (of which visits by top state officials to China and vice versa form a key part) which are largely symbolic and often yield marginal benefits." Amoah[39] added further:

> Ghana's policy towards China must be coherent and forward-looking. At present, it is difficult to decipher what interests specifically Ghana seeks to pursue beyond traditional concerns such as the one China policy, fraternal goodwill, south-south co-operation and piecemeal economic, technical and educational benefits that are undermined in the long run because they are not driven by a strategic focus anchored in the national interest.

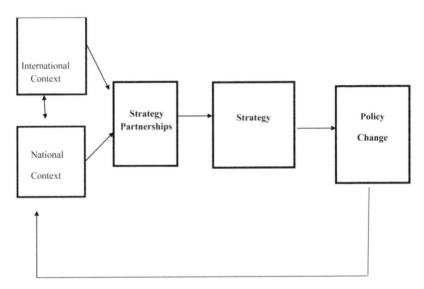

Figure 2.0: The strategy approach in schematic

---

38. Amoah, "Ghana-China Relations."
39. Ibid.

China Policy Documents will provide the sorely needed ideational rudder (to guide policy action) for African countries as they engage with China and will restore Africa's agency more actively and consciously than pertains currently. To be sure, ideas do not mean much until they are translated or translatable into the tangible and empirical. This requires clearly dedicated personnel (well-trained)[40] and resources (pecuniary, power, logistical and institutional); what we will describe as the well-oiled institutional infrastructure. Africa can learn from the Chinese model here, given the blinding range of ideas, personnel and resources she has sunk into engaging Africa. South Africa seems to be showing some signs of building such an infrastructure in the South Africa-China Joint Inter-Ministerial Joint Working Group on Co-operation which held its first meeting on September3-4, 2014, in Beijing (why not Pretoria?). Presidents Zuma and Xi signed the agreement for the terms of reference for the South Africa-China Joint Inter-Ministerial Working Group on Co-operation in Pretoria in 2013. The terms of reference[41]are instructive:

> The *objectives* of the Joint Working Group on Cooperation are to *monitor the implementation of cooperative projects, manage and solve challenges* which may arise during the implementation of such projects as well as elevate bilateral economic relations through the deepening of practical cooperation. (italics mine)

To reiterate our claim: any strategic response by African countries to China must entail initially a policy document and the infrastructure to implement the ideas therein. It is clear we have been focusing more on individual African countries than a regional/continental approach. We do not suggest here an "either-or" approach but postulate rather a pincer movement involving both levels, yet marked by greater thrust on the part of the nation-state because it can be far more nimble, flexible and better organized (it worth noting that China has entered into a strategic partnership with the AU and not a Comprehensive Strategic Partnership; the latter is more encompassing in terms of the

---

40. The author has met several high-ranking officials (including foreign ministers) across Africa in charge of their countries' relations with China who have but a passing knowledge of Chinese culture, history, economy and society, let alone Mandarin.
41. http://www.sanews.gov.za/south-africa/sa-china-joint-working-group-meet.

depth and range of sectors of co-operation; the former is a basis for elevation to the latter.).

Conclusion

This chapter has argued that Africa's burgeoning relationship with China has been marked by C_1 and C_2 contradictions (in the main inimical to Africa's interests as the weaker partner) because at a deeper fundamental level, Africa's public policy formation infrastructure in contemporary times has not prioritized – or ignored entirely – strategic thinking and action. The Strategy Approach is presented as a toolbox for making strategy the core of public policy formation in Africa going forward in order to respond more robustly to emerging policy complexities, among them the emergence of China as a global power. This African response to China, it has been suggested, should focus initially on crafting China Policy Documents and building the necessary infrastructure and formulating the ideas to pursue the key objectives spelt out in these documents. That China has an unquestionable strategic lead over Africa as the two partners interact is not in question. On the basis of China's public declarations and actions stretching back into the twentieth century, it is arguable that the Asian country genuinely wants to partner Africa for the mutual benefit of both sides. Africa must seize this opportunity and exploit it by overcoming the gaping strategic deficits and must do so quickly.

Bibliography

Alden, Chris. *China in Africa*. London and New York: Zed Books, 2007.

Amoah, Lloyd G. Adu. "Ghana-China Relations: From Ambivalence and Fear to Vision and Action." Paper presented at a Roundtable organized by the Development Policy Institute in Accra, November 2007.

Amoah, Lloyd G. Adu. "The strategy approach: Towards a public policy theory alternative for developing polities." Unpublished Doctoral Thesis, Wuhan University, 2009.

Amoah, Lloyd G. Adu. "Africa-China: Planning for the long term." *African Agenda* (March, 5–8, 2010).

Amoah, Lloyd G. Adu. "Public policy formation in Africa in the wake of the global financial meltdown: Building blocks for a new mind in a multipolarworld." In *African engagements: Africa negotiating an emerging multipolar world,* edited by T. Dietz, K. Havnevik, M. Kaag& T. Oestigaard, 327–345. Lieden and Boston: Brill, 2011a.

Amoah, Lloyd G. Adu. "The Strategy Approach: A Response to the Challenge of Ghana's Rapid Transformation by 2037." Paper presented at the European Conference on African Studies. Uppsala, Sweden, June 16, 2011b.

Amoah, Lloyd G. Adu. "Africa in China: Affirming African agency in Africa-China relations at the people to people level." In *Africa-China Partnership: The quest for a win-win relationship,* edited by JamesShikwati, 104–115. Nairobi: IREN, 2012a.

Amoah, Lloyd G. Adu. "Constructing a new public administration in Africa: reflections on philosophical clarity and the process-orientation turn." *Administrative Theory and Praxis* 34, 3 (2012b): 385–406.

Amoah, Lloyd G. Adu. "Accra and Chinese Traders – Transcontinental Dreams, Spaces and Protests." Technical Research Report presented to the African Centre for Integration, Trade and Development, Dakar, Senegal, 2013. http://www.endacacid.org/french/index.php.

Amoah, Lloyd G. Adu. "The Rise of Telcos and Africa's Knowledge Society: What Have Telchambs Got to Do with It?" In *Impacts of the Knowledge Society on Economic and Social Growth in Africa,* edited by Lloyd G. Adu Amoah, 112-133. Hershey, PA: IGI Global, 2014. doi:10.4018/978-1-46.

Amoah, Lloyd G. Adu. "China, architecture and Ghana's spaces: Concrete signs of a soft Chinese imperium?" *Journal of Asian and African Studies,* Vol. 51(2) (2016): 238 –255.

Ampiah, K. and Sanusha Naidu. *Crouching Tiger, Hidden Dragon: Africa and China.* Kwazulu-Natal: Kwazulu-Natal University Press, 2008.

Appadurai, Arjun. "Disjuncture and Difference in global cultural economy." *Theory, Culture and Society*7 (1990):295–310.

Bottelier, P. "China and the World Bank: How a Partnership was built." Vol. 16 (51) (2007): 239-258.

Brautigam, Deborah. *The Dragon's gift: The real story of China in Africa.* Oxford. New York: Oxford University Press, 2011.

Chambers, David Ian. "A 'lantern in the dark night': the Origins and early Development of China's SIGINT Service." *Journal of Intelligence History,* 13(2) (2014):204–222, doi:10.1080/16161262.2014.906147.

Chinweizu, C. "Pan-Africanism and a Black Superpower: The 21st century agenda." Paper presented at the CBAAC Conference on Pan-Africanism, Abuja, Nigeria, 2010.

Clayton, David. *Imperialism Revisited: Political and Economic Relations Between Britain and China, 1950-54.* New York, New York: St Martin's Press, 1997.

Edoho, Felix M. "Globalization and Marginalization of Africa: contextualization of Africa-China relations." *Africa Today* 58(1) (2011): 102 – 124.

Feng, Z and Huang, J. *China's Strategic Partnership Diplomacy: Engaging with a changing world.* Madrid, Spain: FRIDE, 2014.

Filesi, Teobaldo. *China and Africa in the Middle Ages.* London, England: CASS, 1972.

Freedman, Lawrence. *Strategy: A History.* New York, New York: Oxford University Press, 2013.

Hall, R. and H. Peyman. *The Great Uhuru Railway: China's Showpiece in Africa.* New York, NY: Gollancz, 1976.

Guevara, Che. *Guerrilla Warfare.* Lincoln, Nebraska: University of Nebraska Press, 1998.

Hsu, Immanuel C. *The Rise of Modern China.* Oxford, UK: Oxford University Press, 1983.

Ismael, Tareq. Y. "The People's Republic of China and Africa." *Journal of Modern African Studies* 9(4) (1971):507–529.

Kissinger, Henry. *On China.* Penguin, 2012.

Lee, Kuan Yew. *One Man's view of the World.* Singapore, Singapore: Straits Times Press, 2013.

Monson, Jamie. *Africa's Freedom Railway: How a Chinese Development Project Changed Lives and Livelihoods in Tanzania.* Bloomington, IN: Indiana University Press, 2009.

Mulgan, Geoff. *The Art of Public Strategy: Mobilizing Power and Strategy for the Common Good.* New York, New York: Oxford University Press, 2009.

Norberg, Johan. "China Paranoia Derails Free Trade." *Far Eastern Review* 169, 1 (2006): 46–49.

Ogunsanwo, Alaba. *China Policy in Africa, 1958–1971.* Cambridge, UK: Cambridge University Press, 1974.

Pye, Lucian "Social Science Theories in Search of Chinese Realities." *China Quarterly,* 132 (1992): 1161–1170.

Sautman, Barry and Hairong Yan. "East mountain tiger, West mountain tiger: China, the West and 'Colonialism' in Africa." *Maryland Series in Contemporary Asian Studies* 3 (2006): 186.

Sautman, Barry and Hairong Yan. "The Beginning of a World Empire? Contesting the Discourse of Chinese Copper Mining in Zambia." *Modern China*, 39(2) (2013): 131–164.

Schram, Stuart. *The Thoughts of Mao Zedong.* Cambridge, England: Cambridge University Press, 1989.

Snow, Philip. *The Star Raft: China's Encounter with Africa.* New York: Weidenfeld and Nicolson, 1988.

Taylor, Ian. "Beijing's Arms and Oil Interests in Africa." *China Brief* 5, 21 (2005).

Taylor, Ian. Unpacking China's Oil Diplomacy, 2006a. Accessed April 9, 2012. http://www.cebri.com.br/midia/documentos/323.pdf.

Taylor, Ian. "China's Oil Diplomacy in Africa." *International Affairs* 82, 5 (2006b): 937–959.

Taylor, Ian. "Sino-African Relations and the Problem of Human Rights." *African Affairs* 107, 426: (2008): 63–87.

Wright, Richard. *The Colour Curtain.* Jackson. Mississippi: University Press of Mississippi, 1994.

Yu, G.T. "Working on the railroad: China and the Tanzania-Zambia Railway." *Asian Survey*, 11, 11 (1971):1101–1117.

Zheng, Bijian. *China's Peaceful Rise: Selected Speeches of Zheng Bijian (1997–2004).* Washington DC: Brookings Institution, 2005.

Chapter Three. Africa at the Centre of China Shaping the World

Paul Zilungisele Tembe

Introduction

The author suggests a deviation from the tendency of relying solely on events at the expense of theoretical concepts, as is sometimes the case in the analysis of Africa-China relations. If this chapter perceives/regards Africa as a platform for China to shape the rest of the world as the title suggests, it is then befitting that the impact of China's political rhetoric, manifest in Africa-China relations, be examined using conceptual analytical tools from studies of international relations and foreign affairs, with a focus on the use of soft power. Discussions and analysis of soft power usually feature China, India, United States (US) and European Union (EU) relations. If mentioned at all, Africa always features as a recipient of soft power and never the other way round, except in the case of Adams Bodomo.[1] The analysis of soft-power movements reveals a unidirectional pattern. Moreover, the pattern reflects trajectories that are from the developed to less developed nations. The latter assumption may be a cause for concern as it questions the Africa-China relations foundational ethos, expressed using terms such as "mutual interests", "mutual respect", "mutual development" and "win-win situation". Such an observation seems to suggest that the possession of "power of attraction" and soft

---

1. odomo, "Africa-China Relations: Symmetry, Soft Power and South Africa"

power is the prerequisite for successes in economic and military fields, both of which constitute hard power or coercive power. Does such a suggestion ring true to China's emergence and its subsequent ability to use soft power and the "power of attraction" on the international scene? This chapter proposes to align and adapt some features of soft power to suit Africa's specific design of soft power and "power of attraction". It suggests that Africa should construct its own "power of attraction" by prioritizing the extraction industry and the exploration of minerals and natural resources as hard power prior to these elements entering mainstream economies.[2] The reason for such a suggestion is that once Africa's mineral and natural resources enter mainstream economies, their asset value no longer belongs to the continent. Instead, in the mainstream economies, Africa's mineral and natural resources manifest as tools of both hard and soft power used to control the African continent by international market players. In the final analysis, such circumstances leave the African continent with no power, be it as a resource or as an application of a resource.[3]

It is imperative that Africa, and the power it is perceived to possess, undergoes scrutiny when analyzing the dynamics within Africa-China relations. Africa-China relations consist of the two "new kids on the block", one in the form of China and the other Africa, both vying for spaces in the international system. Africa has a history of development by proxy which affects both the ownership and use of its resources and thereby its power for growth and sustainable development.[4]Under such circumstances, the African Union (AU) Agenda 2063 should be regarded as an articulation of solutions meant to dislodge Africa's lack of power.[5] On the other hand, China has been on the back bench of development with a limited role in the international system until the 1978 open-door era of Deng Xiaoping.[6] The interplay between China's1978 reform policies and the AU Agenda 2063 requires a thorough analysis if Africa-China relations are to deliver further benefits to both parties within the ambit of a "win-win situation" and

---

2. See Chen and Chang for the analysis of the interplay between coercion and attraction in the buildup of soft power properties meant to attract the majority of international players.
3. Ibid.
4. Bebbington, *Promoting Development.*
5. Bello, "Towards Agenda 2063."
6. Qiu, *Contemporary Chinese.*

"people-to-people relations." The notion of "people-to-people relations" in this instance ought to be read as a platform meant to safeguard the gains of the Africa-China relations which involve the two newly emerged players in the international system. It is therefore imperative that a platform built on the notion of "people-to-people relations" reflects symmetries at all times.

"China Dream" as an Articulation of China's Political Ideals

The "China Dream", like all previous political slogans in China, is meant to articulate ideals and goals of the Chinese Communist Party (CCP). The maxim "China Dream" has since its inception been disseminated and taught at all levels of society through national, provincial, town and village party organs. Since inception, the People's Republic of China (PRC) has used the tradition of slogans to teach and govern the nation. During the rule of Mao Zedong, "Serving the People" was the flagship of a variety of slogans meant to guide, educate and re-educate the masses through a chain of revolutionary campaigns that took place between 1949 to 1978.

However, the post-Mao era witnessed a dramatic decline with regard to political campaigns and slogans.[7] Instead, each president adopts a maxim which conceptualizes and accompanies their term of office. The slogan "Four Modernizations" (1979–1988) is representative of Deng Xiaoping's term of office, articulating the rationale for the state-led market system. The "Three Represents" (1990–1999) under Jiang Zemin was meant to mitigate the social and cultural changes that emerged with the introduction of the state-led open-market system. The "Eight Virtues and Eight Shames" (2000–2012) is representative of Hu Jintao's term of office and was coupled with the rhetoric of "Harmonious Society" meant to mitigate foreign fears of China's rise. All such slogans, including the current "China Dream" by president Xi Jinping, are maxims which serve to articulate the way forward for China and manifest as vehicles for an all-inclusive policy implementation. Why is it then that the "China Dream", unlike previous political maxims, has found fertile ground beyond China's domestic borders? Is the export of the "China Dream" limited to the African continent as witnessed in the use of the term "Africa Dream" within the framework of Africa-China relations? This chapter attempts

---

7. Ding, *The Decline.*

to answer these questions by tracing the origins and the trajectory of the "China Dream" and what it reveals about China's intentions on the international system.

The Reform and Opening Up of China

Since the inception of the 1978 open-door policies, China has enjoyed immense attention from the entire world.[8] During the first two decades of the open-door policies, the world focused on China's rapid economic growth, political and social events. These new changes shaped China's participation in a variety of international multilateral frameworks.[9] China as a new signatory to a myriad of international multilateral treaties was called to "toe the line" which in most cases meant to mimic the Western political and social traditions.[10]The majority of international players, especially the West, took China's open-door policies to mean that the latter was willing join the political and social systems of the former. However, the continued rapid economic growth led to less attention on China's domestic political and social affairs by the West with the exception of the Tiananmen incident in 1989. Instead, the focus turned to intense head-on competition between China and traditional global economic players who had for the previous five centuries dominated the international system.[11]

The competition among global economic players and the need for natural resources to power economic growth saw China expand its focus and intensify its African relations beginning with the late 1990s.[12] In Africa, China revisited old acquaintances and relations forged during the support of African liberation movements whose members now led legitimate governments and constituted the political elite in the majority of African countries.[13] Such an example is that China, in forging new spaces for its development, did not solely rely on its economic muscle but also strived to do so through non-coercive means.[14] However, China did not move into an "empty" African space.

8. "International attention," *China Daily.*
9. Chachavalpongpun, *Uncharted Waters?*
10. Horsburgh et al., *Chinese Politics.*
11. Obemma, *China and West.*
12. Shinn el al. *China and Africa: A Century of Engagement.*
13. Ibid.
14. Johnston et al. *Engaging China.*

Instead, it moved into a continent pained by its history and relations to former colonial masters. Such a scenario required China to use "power of attraction" that would appeal even to forces critical of its rapid economic growth and expansion into global markets. China did not only focus on convincing the African continent but the trajectory of its reform era reveals attempts at joining forces with nations of developing and emerging economies through a variety of South-South cooperation frameworks. In such strategies, it is discernible that China sought to carve spaces of influence on the international system using non-coercive methods.

The African Turn: African Union Agenda 2063

The rise of China in combination with the subsequent frameworks representative of the South-South cooperation, such as the Forum on Africa-China Cooperation (FOCAC)and the group of countries, Brazil, Russia, India, China and South Africa (BRICS), has altered the representation and role of Africa on the global scene. The South-South cooperation frameworks with China at the helm have provided alternative sources for capital, technology and development of sustainable goals for the continent.[15] Solutions provided by interactions with China have provided Africa with an opportunity to establish home-grown game plans in a variety of fields. However, persisting divisions on the African continent representative of former colonial masters' denominations, such as Anglophone, Francophone and Lusophone, represent a hurdle for synergy among African nations. The above-mentioned divisions are evident in the lack of cooperation among African countries, impacting intra-Southern African Development Community (SADC) trade, which presently is only at 11 percent, while the EU and the Americas enjoy 44 percent and 60 percent intra-continental trade volumes respectively, according to the Organization for Economic Cooperation and Development, (OECD).[16] As a result, the majority of "independent" African countries – despite multiple attempts at establishing feasible and viable political and economic systems – still rely on former colonial masters for day-to-day running of government and the state.[17] Such is evident in that some African states may speak only of "development by proxy",

---

15. Dent, *China and Africa.*
16. OECD, *Policy Priorities,* 2012.
17. Mazrui et al., *Anglo-African Commonwealth.*

despite having resources to catapult their national economies to greater heights.[18]

Since the first wave of independence in Africa, there have been calls for unity of the entire continent.[19] The formation of the Organization of African Union (OAU), established on 25 May 1963, and now referred to as the AU, established on 26 May 2001; and the long and protracted assistance given to a myriad of African liberation movements are some of the results of such aspirations. More than half a century later since the first wave of African independent countries, the AU has grown from strength to strength into a robust framework that rationalizes solutions for problems facing the continent. During the same period, China has become a closer partner to the AU and African countries, a relationship which has become suspect in the eyes of former colonial masters and their allies.[20] However, the closer interactions between China and Africa during the last two decades have provided the latter with opportunities to pave its own agenda in the international system. The articulation of the "AU Agenda 2063 – The Africa we want" document is reflective of the progress made since the initial stages of African independence and attempts at rationalizing local solutions to problems of a cultural, social, political and economic nature in the continent.

The AU Agenda 2063 emphasizes the development of local manufacturing industries and the beneficiation of minerals and natural resources as a foundation for structural, social and economic transformation.[21] The AU Agenda 2063 rationale is that engaging in the above-mentioned strategic areas is the key to sustainable growth and development as enshrined in the Millennium Developmental Goals (MDGs) and Sustainable Developmental Goals (SDG). Both the MDGs and SDGs are sought as a solution to rampant unemployment, poverty eradication and general development in Africa and the world. This chapter argues that the above-mentioned solutions

---

18. Bebbington, *Promoting Development.*
19. Reading from the following maxim by Kwame Nkrumah, it is clear the independence of Ghana marked the genesis of an idea that the unity of the entire African continent was a prerequisite for its development: *"The independence of Ghana is meaningless unless it is linked-up with the total liberation of the African Continent."* (Independence Speech – Kwame Nkrumah March 6, 1957, Accra, Ghana).
20. Brown, *EU-China Relationship* and Goldstein, *Meeting China Halfway.*
21. Bello, "Towards Agenda 2063."

are not feasible without changes in the manner in which Africa presents itself at the international arena. Africa needs to present a proactive, attractive and robust demeanor if it is to achieve the set of goals articulated in the AU Agenda 2063 and the UN Millennium Declaration. The implementation and success of Agenda 2063 rely on Africa's ability to cooperate with other international players from a position of strength. Such ability is possible only if Africa possesses "power of attraction" with which to shape the international system. In accordance with definitions by Joseph Nye,[22] such abilities are only feasible through the use of soft power. Moreover, a current reading of the AU Agenda 2063 reveals that Africa is in possession of rich minerals and natural resources whose conversion to either hard power or soft power has since evaded the African continent. However, the survival and development of Africa relies on the implementation of soft power. This may be garnered from the conversion of hard power whose source consists of African minerals and natural resources.[23]

Minerals and Natural Resources as Africa's Hard Power: Possible Conversion of Africa's Hard Power into Soft Power – "Power of Attraction"

Minerals and natural resources have and continue to constitute a reason for the majority of international players visiting, working and trading on the African continent.[24] Francoise Mitterrand, former president of France, once stated that Europe cannot afford to let go of its interests in Africa because their existence depended upon it.[25] Given the above scenario, why it is that Africa cannot rely on its minerals and natural resources to establish an image as an attractive and powerful player on the global arena? What variables can Africa exploit to turn the attraction of mineral and natural resources into benefits that go beyond limited monetary gains? According to Joseph Nye,[26] monetary gains comprise hard power while culture, political values and foreign policies make up soft power. The suggestion of establishing a type of soft power that may benefit Africa is fraught with

22. Nye, *Bound to Lead*.
23. Such analysis follows the reading of the concept of "soft power" since inception to present.
24. Grant et al., *New Approaches*.
25. Bart-Williams, "Change your Channel."
26. Nye, *Bound to Lead*.

contradictions as the continent consists of a variety of nations with varying cultures, political values and foreign policies. However, heightened Africa-China relations may provide possible solutions for converting Africa's hard power into soft power. The question that arises then is: how can Africa place leverage on the Africa-China relations and other South-South cooperation frameworks to establish its "power of attraction" *à la* soft power that can serve to achieve the goals of the AU Agenda 2063?

China in Africa-Culture and Development of Africa-China Relations

Since the 2006 first Africa-China summit, Africa-China relations have reached heightened levels.[27] The closeness of relations between China and Africa has led to a plethora of publications with varying points of view supporting either the idea that China represents neo-colonial power in Africa, or that this provides opportunities for the continent. China on the other hand has relied on the narrative of long relations with the African continent beginning with the story of the sea-fairing general Zheng He (1371–1435); to the coast of East Africa (1405–1433); to the support for African liberation movements from China (1960–1985); to the Tanzania-Zambia Railway Authority (TAZARA) Railway project (1970–1975) financed by China.[28] However, the world economic crisis of 2008 saw the role of China changing globally in a drastic way.[29] China emerged as a savior to a variety of nations when it provided varied forms of financial relief, in the process mitigating the effects of a global financial meltdown but also enhancing its international image. China used the opportunity provided by its role as a savior during the global financial meltdown to fine-tune its image and strategies by engaging with strategic markets and key players on the international system.

During the same time, Africa-China relations made strides in the process and featured as a primary variable for rationalizing a "new" China approach to the world. Such a statement begs the question: how does Africa feature in the equation of China's acquisition of soft power, specifically aimed at shaping the international system? The answers to this are discernible in the analysis and examination of the

---

27. Tiezzi, "New Relations."
28. Shinn et al., *China and Africa.*
29. Men, "World Financial Crisis."

"China Dream" and its replication into "Africa Dream" within the ambit of Africa-China relations. First, an analysis of 'soft power' and its limitations in the international relations needs to precede any attempts at answering the question.

Definitions and Uses of Soft Power

The concept of soft power is articulated by Joseph Nye:[30] "When one country gets other countries to want what it wants might be called co-optive or soft power in contrast with the hard or command power of ordering others to do what it wants." He goes on to say that soft power found favor with the US government as it sought ways to maintain its super-power status in a post-Cold War world where the appeal of military power was waning. However, China as an emerging economic power-house in the global was thought to have found in soft power a tool to mitigate growing suspicions against its emergence into the center of the international scene.[31]

Definitions of soft power have had two turns as their usefulness was challenged by scholars of international relations and beyond. Soft power is initially defined as the ability to attract and co-opt rather than use coercion (hard power), using force or giving money as a means of persuasion.[32] Nye identifies culture, political values and foreign policy as the three standard features that constitute soft power. Soft power is further defined as an ability to shape the preferences of others through appeal and attraction.[33] The latter definition has become the flagship for soft power implementation at an international level where each nation contends with others in an effort to demonstrate its "power of attraction" with the hope that such will in turn shape the ideals and goals of counterparts. Hard power is said to constitute the two forces of coercion; military and economic power.[34]

Initially, China lacked in all the prerequisites for implementing a successful soft power exercise.[35] China urgently needed a soft power vehicle that would help enhance its international image and appeal. The power of China during the first two-and-a-half decades of its

---

30. Nye, *Bound to Lead*.
31. McClory, "Soft Power Rankings."
32. Nye, *The Future of Power*.
33. Chen and Chang, "The Power Strategy."
34. Copeland, "Hard Power vs Soft Power."
35. Nye, "China's Soft Power Deficit."

open-door policy manifested in its rapid economic growth –this was hard power and not soft power.[36] The fact that the military was identified as one of the areas targeted for "scientific modernization" at the onset of the 1978 open-door policies, did not help the situation.[37] In order to change its international image, China needed to formulate a palatable rhetoric that lacked any signs of real or imagined menace to the world. However, it was hard for China to find such a rhetoric: one that had the ability to appeal to the international community without alienating domestic audiences. China needed a rhetoric abstracted and rationalized within the framework of the inward-looking *nei* (内) Chinese traditional philosophy and history while at the same time appealing to the international community.

Conversion of Hard Power into Soft Power using Traditional Chinese Idioms *chengyu* (成语)

The tradition of using all-encompassing slogans and "power-words" to mobilize, inform and educate the public about current policies is part and parcel of China's political life.[38] The tradition is as ancient as China itself. Michael Schoenhals[39] observes that China has since the beginning of times been preoccupied with the use of proper expressions in the form of formulaic language. Dittmer[40] calls such preoccupation, with the correctness of expressions in Chinese culture, a culture of "politics in command." The inception of the People's Republic of China (PRC) following on the tradition of ancient China was preoccupied with correct formulations, as a way of structuring and disseminating correct ideology.[41] One central aspect of establishing and spreading official terminologies is the process of communal

---

36. Copeland, "Hard Power vs Soft Power."
37. According to the maxim "Four Modernizations" (*sigexiandaihua*) 四个现代化 of 1978, Industrialization, Agriculture, Education and the Military were targeted areas for modernization meant to catapult China into the global international systems.
38. Tembe, *Re-evaluating Political Performatives of the PRC: Maoist Discourse – The Historical Trajectory of the* "Laosanpian".
39. Schoenhals, *Doing Things with Words in Chinese Politics: Five Studies.*
40. Dittmer and Hurst, "Analysis in Limbo: Contemporary Chinese Politics Amid the Maturation of Reform."
41. Hsia, 1961. *Metaphor, Myth, Ritual and the People's Commune.*

exegesis.[42] The process is that of communally studying by heart, if necessary, all government and party maxims at all levels of the country beginning with the capital city and ending with the smallest hamlet in the remote areas of the country. The tradition, which began during ancient China and continued through to the inception of the PRC, is in place to this day and is manifest in all social spheres from education, politics, and recreation and through all party organs throughout the country in the form of moral and patriotic education.[43]

China's foundational problem for spreading the goodwill of its 1978 open-door policies was the lack of tools for addressing an international community, which lacked the traditions of communal exegesis and rote learning. China needed to adopt an amicable approach, palatable to audiences beyond its borders while gradually taking the center stage in the international scene. The first attempt by China to convert hard power into soft power in order to address the international system and in the process mitigate the outward perceived threat may be discerned in the maxim "hide capabilities and keep a low profile" *taoguang yanghui* (韬光养晦), set in place by Deng Xiaoping in the early 1990s.[44]

The maxim "hide capabilities and keep a low profile" (韬光养晦) contained central guidelines for Chinese foreign policy strategy.[45] Although the maxim expressed guidelines for Chinese foreign policy, it still relied heavily on the inward-looking traditional Chinese philosophy. The maxim read more as a directive to domestic entities in China. Scholars, analysts and observers suspected that China used the maxim to evade responsibilities as an upcoming global leader.[46] Some observers were of the idea that China was trying to accumulate strength so that one day it could dominate the region and the world.[47] Despite such suspicions, the maxim did enjoy some success in mitigating perceived China threats towards international community.

---

42. Apter and Saich, *Revolutionary discourse in Mao's republic.*
43. Tembe, *Re-evaluating Political Performatives of the PRC: Maoist Discourse – The Historical Trajectory of the* "Laosanpian".
44. Zhu, *On diplomatic strategy of "Keeping a Low Profile and Taking a Proactive Role When Feasible."* and Wang, "Global Governance."
45. Yang, *My Views about "Tao Guang Yang Hui".*
46. Wang, "Global Governance."
47. Ibid.

However, an analysis into the origins of the maxim reveals that it is a borrowing from two historic proverbs *suyu* (俗语) made popular at different epochs of Chinese history: the (*taoguang*) "to restrain one's light" was first used by Xiao Tong, the crown prince of Liang Dynasty (502–557 A.D.) and the second part (*yang hui*) "to hide from public eye for self-cultivation" first appeared during the Song Dynasty (960–1279 A.D.) in the *History of Jin-Biography Huangpu Yi*.[48] The merging of the two words, *taoguang* and *yanghui*, into a four-character idiom, appeared only during the Qing Dynasty (1644–1912) to mean, "Do what you are capable of, and prevent overarching oneself."[49]

These original meanings and uses of the maxim since ancient times seem to dispel malice on the side of the Chinese politicians. Yang[50] explains that the usage of "hide capabilities and keep a low profile" by China's forefathers reveals that the expression simply describes "keeping a low-key lifestyle." He further states that such a lifestyle implies strategic consideration and not expedient tactics. He concludes that reading from historical and contemporary uses of the idiom nullifies the idea that China uses the *taoguang yanghui* maxim as a strategy to mislead the international community. Remarks by Yang have the support of speeches directed to the international community by Deng Xiaoping during the late 1980s and 1990s.[51] The main themes of the speeches during this period emphasized China's resolve at "keeping a low profile" as an important precondition for "accomplishing something." In most of the speeches Deng Xiaoping "repeatedly emphasized the need for China not to assume the leadership role."[52] In accordance with traditional Chinese philosophy, the maxim translates as "hide one's advantage and improve one's disadvantage." The latter translation befits the position of Deng Xiaoping and that of China during the onset of the open-door policy.[53] The use of the maxim as a guideline for foreign-policy strategy reflects a response by

48. Yang, *My Views about "Tao Guang Yang Hui"*.
49. Wang, "Global Governance."
50. Yang, *My Views about "Tao Guang Yang Hui"*.
51. See details in *Selected Works of Deng Xiaoping Vol. 3 (1982 – 1992)*. Beijing 1990.
52. Spence, *A Search for Modern China*.
53. Yu, *China's Rise: Strength and Fragility*.

Deng Xiaoping when asked to take the leadership of the developing world after the fall of the Soviet Union.[54]

There are several other Chinese traditional idioms that feature in the articulation of China's foreign policy since the inception of the open-door policy. All lead with the message that "it is neither easy nor wise to be at the top". One such maxim of influence in China's foreign-policy strategy says that "when you are on top of the mountain, you are not able to stand up to the cold", (高处不胜寒) *gao chu bu sheng han.*[55] The maxim can be interpreted as "the higher your position, the more problems you face." These two maxims may be categorized as "strategic cultural phrases."[56] Another phrase, which has dominated in the foreign policy of China, reads "you should not have any intention to do harm to others; you should not lack the foresight to safeguard against the harm from others", (害人之心不可有, 防有之心不可无) *hairen zhixin bu ke you, hairen zhixin bu ke wu.* This maxim reflects a "behavioral norm." It reflects China's current power strategy of "attractive defense."[57] Lastly, another prominent maxim used in the Chinese foreign policy circles is "each ordinary man has a duty to ensure the prosperity and security of the motherland", (天下光兴亡匹夫有责) *tian xia guang xing mang, pifu youze.*[58] This last maxim is used to reflect the ideal of the Chinese government and the people who work to maintain regional, and international peace, security, stability and prosperity. It should be observed that all these four maxims do not stray from the "Five Principles of Peaceful Coexistence" of 1954 which to this day serve as a blueprint and a guideline for China's foreign policy strategies.

The question that arises from this summary of China's guidelines for foreign policy strategies is: Does the articulation of the "China Dream" and its export to foreign shores deviate from the Deng Xiaoping's foreign policy ideals? The majority of both national and foreign China scholars and observers have emphasized the need to examine and research traditional Chinese philosophy, history, culture

54. Wang, "Global Governance."
55. Qiu, *Contemporary Chinese.*
56. Yi, *Chinese Foreign Policy in Transition: "Understanding China's Peaceful Development."*
57. Chen and Chang, "The Power Strategy."
58. Qiu, *Contemporary Chinese Relations.*

and their impact on China's foreign policy.[59] The assumption is that it is only with knowledge and understanding of traditional Chinese philosophy and history, that one is able to trace the processes of how China manages to convert its perceived hard power into soft power.

Emergence of the Concept "China Dream"

The phrase "China Dream" was coined in 2013 by president Xi Jinping as a slogan meant for the articulation of China's open-door policy with promises of promoting individual dreams.[60] President Xi has urged young people to dare to dream, to work assiduously to fulfill the dreams and to contribute to the revitalization of the nation.[61] Li,[62] former vice president of the CPC Central Committee's Party School, defines the goal of the "China Dream" as building a moderately prosperous society in an all-round way by 2020, and achieving modernization by 2050.[63] In short, the great national rejuvenation project is meant to achieve modernization. The "China Dream" is also in line with Deng Xiaoping's logic of pioneering the establishment of a *Xiao kang shehui*, a "moderately well-off society."[64] The Central Party School/Central Committee of the CCP defines the "China Dream" as an articulation and a description of the set of ideals in the PRC.[65]

The notion of the "China Dream" may be understood to manifest at four levels. It firstly manifests as a guideline for the implementation of reform policy, as it prescribes and proscribes the roadmap for China's future.[66] Secondly, embedded in the articulation of the "China Dream" is a historical collective memory spanning from a powerful ancient China that regarded itself as the center of the world. It is at this level where the "China Dream" articulates the project of rejuvenation meant for China to rid itself of "national humiliation" caused by the arrival of imperialist Western powers in China at the turn of the

59. Compton, *Mao's China – Party Reform Documents, 1942 – 44.*
60. Wang, *The Chinese Dream: Concept and Context.*
61. Zhang, *Social Media Use Among Youth and Innovations of Moral Education Work With University Students in China.*
62. Li, 2014. *Cited in David Shambaugh's "China's Soft-Power Push.*
63. China Daily, "International Attention."
64. China Daily, "Xi Jinping's explanation of the Chinese people's dream"
65. Creemers, "The Chinese Dream Infuses Socialism with Chinese Characteristics with New Energy"
66. Tembe, "Misconceptions and omissions in the Africa-China discourse."

twentieth century.[67] President Xi Jinping describes the "China Dream" as "national rejuvenation, improvement of people's livelihoods, prosperity, construction of a better society and military strengthening."[68] The third level of the "China Dream" manifests domestically, as a converging point for national unity. Lastly, the "China Dream" is meant to formulate the "power of attraction" meant for helping China's appeal in the international system.

The maxim "China Dream" has, as mentioned before, functioned as the guideline for foreign-policy strategy and as a tool for enhancing China's image and attraction appeal in the international system. The latter part of this statement indicates a change in the manner in which China has decided to use a domestic political idiom in an effort to better its image and in the process, shape the international system. Such a realization gives rise to the following question: How has China gone about designing and implementing the "China Dream" rhetoric so that it is suitable for soft power purposes?

The Design and Power of the "China Dream" Rhetoric

The emergence and implementation of the "China Dream" maxim reveals China's heightened ability in the design of the rhetoric meant to address the international system. There are few signs which reflect that the maxim "China Dream" has managed to curve spaces internationally. Firstly, on more than one occasion president Xi Jinping has used the expression "world dream" in combination with "China Dream" when addressing international audiences. On occasions, the Chinese president has been observed to tailor the expression "China Dream" to target specific audiences, as in the case of "Africa Dream", "Europe Dream" and "India Dream." However, Anny Boc[69] points out that "China Dream" has received the most appeal on the African continent. Such use of "China Dream" should be understood within the premises of recent foreign-policy statements such as "China's development cannot be isolated from the world's development and

---

67. Wang, "Never forget national humiliation." The notion of China's "national humiliation" falls under 'moral education' and 'patriotic education' subjects which form part of school curriculum and people's civic education programmes.

68. Chitty Naren, "The Chinese Dream and international community"

69. Boc, "The Power of Language: Globalizing 'The Chinese Dream'."

vice-versa"[70]or "the Chinese dream cannot be realized without realizing the world dream."[71]

According to theories from rhetorical and performative studies, China has managed to dislodge and own to a given extent the lexical unit "Dream". Derrida and Butler[72] argued that a "break" in the use of a lexical unit from one linguistic/social sphere to another is made possible by changing social dynamics. Such a break, although relevant, is not only bound by the iterability of words.[73] China is not a stranger to changing social dynamics as is discernible in its continuous revolutions of the twentieth century. Changes in China's social dynamics involved finding new formulaic expressions meant to legitimize a new social order or delegitimize old ones. The Yanan revolutionary era (1936–1948), Great Leap Forward (1958–1961), The Great Cultural Revolution (1966 – 1976) and the Open-Door policy (1978– present) all have their distinctive rhetoric and texts that mark China's paradigm shifts throughout the twentieth century. Given the above presentation, how does the maxim "China Dream" differ from the previous rhetoric representative of China's paradigm shifts?

The answer lies in China's domestic speeches and definitions of the "China Dream". The Qiushi, the party's theoretical journal, cites that the "Chinese Dream" is not about individual glory, but about collective Chinese effort.[74] The scope of such a statement is broad, but does not leave the premises of traditional Chinese philosophy and the conceptualization of family as expressed in terms of public/private, (gong/si) 公/私, where the former is superior to the latter. There is a vast body of literature by prominent China analysts and sinologists[75] who affirm the idea that in Chinese culture, the individual is subordinate to the rule of the many, and that it is within this context that morality and general correctness in society is measured.[76]

---

70. Sun, "China's Success Story and Its Relevance to Africa."
71. ibid.
72. Butler, *Excitable speech;* Derrida, "Signature Event."
73. Tembe, *Re-evaluating Political Performatives of the PRC: Maoist Discourse – The Historical Trajectory of the* "Laosanpian".
74. Jin. "The China Dream Vs. The American Dream"
75. Baker, *Chinese Family;* Boden, *Mindmapping China;* Che, *Modern Chinese Family;* Giskin and Walsh, *Introduction to Chinese Culture.*
76. Tembe, *Re-evaluating Political Performatives of the PRC: Maoist Discourse – The Historical Trajectory of the* "Laosanpian".

国是大家，家是小国

"A nation consists of everyone; a family is a small nation."[77]

> The structure of the Chinese family differs from that of other cultures in the way it serves as a foundational field for inculcating and transferring social traditions in that it tends to be manifest within the logic of *gong/si*公/私, where *gong* 公 (public) takes primacy over *si*私 (private), and are strongly reliant on the notions of *rong*荣 (virtue) and *chi*耻 (shame) which serve as a framework that guides and legitimates all practice.[78]

These statements suggest that the "China Dream" does not only not deviate from the foundations of traditional Chinese philosophy and culture but also holds to the idea of political continuities in China's society and foreign policy. The maxim "each ordinary man has a duty to ensure the prosperity and security of the motherland" (天下光兴亡匹夫有责), used during the Deng Xiaoping era, is almost identical to definitions of the "China Dream" with regard to individual obligations towards and relations with the nation. This analysis seems to imply that the "China Dream" has qualities that constitute; i) China's *habitus*, which is responsible for transmitting Chinese culture from one generation to the next;[79] ii) an ability to institute national unity; iii) an ability to co-opt international audiences; and iv) an ability to export traditional Chinese philosophy modes of practice.

Export of People's Republic of China Political Rhetoric into Africa and Beyond

China is not the first nation to use the notion of a "dream" to articulate national ideals. There is an old and well-known maxim, the "American Dream", which describes the national ethos articulated as a set of

---

77. A Chinese folk saying encountered in both the institutionalized and everyday language settings.

78. Tembe, *Re-evaluating Political Performatives of the PRC: Maoist Discourse – The Historical Trajectory of the* "Laosanpian".

79. See Bourdieu (1991) for details on the concept of the *habitus*. cf. Tembe (2013).

ideals: "Democracy, Rights, Liberty, Opportunity, and Equality." Adams[80] states that according to the "American Dream", all should have equal opportunities in life, regardless of background, sex or religion. The "American Dream" is at times referred to as the "American Spirit", describing resilience and perseverance in defense of the ideals featured above. Enshrined in the definitions of the "American Dream" are individual freedoms. The "China Dream" on the other hand focuses on the benefits and defense of a sovereignty.[81] The maxim "China Dream" describes a dream of a collective where the future trajectory of the Chinese nation depends on efforts of individuals. Articulations of the "China Dream" have at times included whoever may be the target audience as witnessed in the cases of "Africa Dream", "Europe Dream", "India Dream" and "World Dream." In conclusion, the "China Dream" in its varied forms may allude to descriptions of a world citizen. If the "China Dream" alludes to inclusion or articulation of a world citizen, why does it then enjoy more appeal in Africa than in any other place? The answer may be discernable in the implementation and manifestation of insurrectionary and conformity acts.[82]

Butler[83] argues that newly introduced social terms or discourse may manifest as "insurrectionary acts." The term "insurrectionary acts" refers to new expressions meant to destabilize the existing status quo suggesting new values beyond normative practice.[84] Usually the new terms are those borrowed from other forms of social practice which, due to acute social problems, "break force" with their old meanings and help to establish a new social order.[85] The newly arrived terms need to be drained of insurrectionary qualities if they are to stand a chance at articulating "new meanings" and values they promise to deliver. The use of "conformity acts" helps to mitigate the insurrectionary qualities of the new expressions. "Conformity acts"

80. Adams, *The Epic of America.*
81. Sørenson, "The Significance of Xi."
82. See Butler, *Excitable speech: A politics of the Performative.* cf. Tembe (2013) for details on the workings of insurrectionary acts and conformity acts respectively.
83. Butler, *Excitable speech: A politics of the Performative.*
84. Lagerway, *Early Chinese religion. Part.1, Shang through Han (1250 BC-220 AD).*
85. Tembe, *Re-evaluating Political Performatives of the PRC: Maoist Discourse – The Historical Trajectory of the* "Laosanpian".

consist of terms that express traditional, local and customary values. Such values are those that constitute a *habitus* of a given society or people. All performatives or expressions may manifest as conformity acts, as long as they have relevance to society and people being addressed at any given time, i.e. the target audience.[86] Using the above analogy, the expression "China Dream" may initially manifest as an insurrectionary act when used in foreign shores, but when articulated using replicative techniques as witnessed in the cases of "Africa Dream", "Europe Dream", "India Dream" and the "World Dream", the term "dream" takes prominence and locks into local frames of reference and culture.[87] In such a scenario, local intentions and ideals take precedence over Chinese ones.[88] In short, "conformity acts" refer to the use of familiar modes that reflect local culture and traditions and therefore are congruent with the frames of reference of all members of society being addressed.[89]

Replication of "China Dream" into "Africa Dream"

Boc[90] points out that the rise of the maxim "China Dream" is regarded by the majority of China scholars as an attempt to counteract Western "discursive hegemony" by strengthening China's "discursive power." Such views bear weight in as far as the attempts to export Chinese political rhetoric into the dominant international sphere, but they fail to account for the appeal of the maxim to nations of emerging and developing economies, especially Africa. According to Chen and Chang,[91] it is imperative that the impact of soft power, which manifests as a strategic narrative, be examined with regard to its effect if we are to understand the processes of its construction. Such examination is deemed necessary in view of the successful synergy between the "China Dream" and the "Africa Dream" on the African continent.

---

86. The chapter relies on Austin's *How to do things with words* for definitions of performatives. See Fowles, *Advertising and Popular Culture*, for details on "target audience."

87. See above Fowles, *Advertising*; Bourdieu (1998); Bohannan (1995); Lagerwey, (2009) for details on local frames of reference.

88. See Lakoff and Johnson, *Metaphors we live by*, for details on the notions of "perceptual metaphors".

89. Tembe, *Re-evaluating Political Performatives of the PRC: Maoist Discourse – The Historical Trajectory of the* "Laosanpian".

90. Boc, "The power of language: Globalizing the 'Chinese Dream."

91. Chen and Chang, "The Power Strategy."

The concept was introduced by president Xi Jinping during his visit to Tanzania in March 2013, when he spoke of the dream of over 1.3 billion Chinese people for great national renewal, and the dream of one billion African people for gaining strength and unity, and achieving development and rejuvenation. China's turn toward a market economy and its growing economic engagement on the African continent, particularly since the 2000s, has been accompanied by a new set of ideological terms.[92] However, in many respects, post-Mao political slogans echo earlier socialist rhetoric. Terms such as "win-win", "harmonious co-operation" and "brotherly assistance" are frequently used in official Chinese discourse toward Africa; these terms have also been adopted by certain African governments themselves to articulate their national ideals within and beyond Africa-China relations forums.[93] Such tendencies reflect the fact that political rhetoric, which has been "made in China", has gained traction in Africa.

The slogan "Africa Dream", as manifested in the Africa-China relations framework and Chinese media, emerged during the promotion of the "China Dream" in Africa. The *Beijing Review*, a weekly periodical which provides foreigners with an official view of the state of China, frequently publishes a piece on "Chinese Dream". These efforts are in line with those of *People's Daily Online*, CCTV Africa, and Xinhua, which spare no effort in emulating the promotion of the "Chinese Dream" to international shores, Africa included. The majority of Chinese foreign media agencies partner with the host country media services. CCTV international and Xinhua have their African headquarters in Nairobi, Kenya, where they have partnered and co-operate with a variety of local media agencies. Zhang Yong, vice-director of the External Communication Department of the *People's Daily* notes that the development of the *People's Daily* is part of the "China Dream." He stressed that the *People's Daily* has the mandate to report and record the "China Dream." The People's Daily Online has since 2011 established a subsidiary company in South Africa. It has also partnered with *The New Age*, a local newspaper in South Africa. In addition, African academics, journalists and students have since 2013 been invited to China to participate in the "China Dream" promotional events. It is within this context that the notion "China Dream" has

---

92. Tembe, "The temptations and promotion of China Dream': calling for Africa's home-grown rhetoric."

93. Ibid.

found fertile ground to manifest and even replicate itself on the African continent in the form of the "Africa Dream."

The primary locus for the transfer of Chinese slogans such as the "China Dream" into Africa are the Africa-China relations forums. In 2013, Wang Xijun, from the Ministry of Foreign Affairs, stated that the "China Dream" is similar to a good dream of people around the world and has the same root and quality as the dream of the African people. He concluded by stating that the consistency of the "China Dream" and the "Africa Dream" determines that two people can work together to realize their dreams. In 2013, the director-general of the African Department of China's Ministry of Foreign Affairs, while addressing a seminar titled "China Dream", stated that the dream is consistent with the beautiful dreams cherished by people of other countries and, in particular, highly consistent with the "Africa Dream." In the same breath, he stressed that the "China Dream" is a blueprint drawn according to the historical trajectory of China. He went further to draw parallels between the "China Dream" and the "Africa Dream."

In such statements, the streamlining of Africa's needs to Chinese political rhetoric and ideals can be detected. It would stand to reason that statements made by government ministers from China carry the CCP-loaded political rhetoric. However, it is concerning when members of the African elite apply rhetorical strategies similar to those applied by Chinese dignitaries. One such example is when the former UN deputy secretary-general, Asha-Rose Migiro, went on record, stating that the "China Dream" has received immense appeal in Africa as it conjures a vision of collective achievement that the continent is striving to reach.[94] She cites poverty alleviation, economic growth, and the attainment of sustainable development as the African ideals expressed within the notion of the "China Dream."

The tendencies are also perpetuated by Chinese and African media in both localities. In Chinese newspapers such as *China Daily*, *Xinhua*, and *People's Daily*, articles are carried with titles such as "Africans in China sharing 'Chinese Dream'", "'Chinese Dream' and 'African Dream' resonate", "Academics help shape multitude of dreams", "African media attends seminar on 'China Dream' and 'Africa Dream'", just to mention a few. Members from mainstream media outlets from a variety of African countries – Liberia, Kenya, South Africa, Tanzania, Zambia and Zimbabwe – make frequent visits to

China's national media houses to learn and discuss the latest rhetoric used by China such as in the case of "China Dream" and "Africa Dream." Comments from the majority of African journalists visiting China reflect an understanding of the "Africa Dream" that is framed by the articulations of the "China Dream". Such replication of the "China Dream" expressed as "Africa Dream" is rife in both Chinese and African media. In addition to these promotions of the "China Dream" into the "Africa Dream", lie temptations that are beyond the confines of this chapter. What is certain is the fact that Africa currently serves consciously or unconsciously as a catalyst or a stepping stone to China's efforts at shaping the international system.

Finally, the following questions are an attempt at teasing out the reasons for why the "China Dream" and the "Africa Dream" appeal to African political elite.

- Has the initial quest for the unification of Africa since the first wave of independence from colonialism finally found favor in the spaces provided by Africa-China relations?
- Does the dominant theme of Africa learning from China within the framework of Africa-China relations include lessons on how China united its great nation?
- Does China's rhetoric of a singular African entity with a singular historical trajectory appeal to the African elite?

If the answer to any of these questions is in the affirmative, is it then possible that the ideal of the "Africa Dream" stands a chance of breaking away from its genesis of Africa-China relations, and instead, that it will manifest as a resource for Africa's "power of attraction" with capabilities of shaping the international system?

Conclusion

The growth in trade between Africa and a fast-developing China led to a discussion of "what Africa can learn from China." The discussion and a search for developmental lessons from China seem to have fueled the promotion of Chinese political rhetoric in Africa-China relations. Such promotion may be discerned in the tendency of combining the "China Dream" with the "Africa Dream." The 2015 FOCAC Summit deliberations, which took place in South Africa, went beyond the usual topic of Africa-China trade to cover the topic of "People-to-People Relations." Alongside the 2015 FOCAC Summit, there were scholarly and business side-events, including the launch of a Africa-China magazine, just to mention a few of the events. Both the Chinese and the African political elite seem to have come to terms with the fact that trade and commerce alone are not sufficient for safeguarding the gains of Africa-China friendships. Left out of the equation is the notion of symmetries in the Africa-China relations framework. The current promotion of "People-to-People Relations" will only benefit Africa-China relations if the grassroots perceive the playing field as level, accompanied by symmetric discourses from both parties.

Moreover, the heightened levels of Africa-China relations seem to have offset the traditional balance of international powers in Africa and elsewhere, especially judging by the number of studies commissioned by the European and American institutes' representatives in Africa regarding China's impact on the continent. Such tendencies are a reflection of the magnitude and effect of China's engagement in Africa that have now gone from politics of trade to laying foundations for shaping the world.

If Africa is to learn anything from China, it is that the continent should use the opportunity presented by the existence of frameworks, such as the FOCAC and BRICS, to establish robust strategies for producing the "power of attraction", which may enable Africa to negotiate from a position of strength in the international system. The African continent should use the spaces provided by current global paradigm shifts to formulate its "power rhetoric" and to argue from a position of strength, leveraging on the fact that the continent is in possession of globally sought-after minerals and natural resources.

Recommendations

- Africa needs to build a soft power and strategic narrative based on the power it possesses through the existence of minerals and natural resources on the continent.
- Africa should build strategic narratives around the AU Agenda 2063 articulation of Country Mining Visions (CMVs) and Regional Mining Visions (RMVs) that go beyond driving national and regional attraction tools to encompass those meant for shaping the international system.
- Africa should deliberately work hard at combining tangible and intangible resources in an effort to create a strategy that favors its

international standing. Reliance on tangible resources, which constitute "hard power" or "coercion", does not deliver strategies and appeal that is necessary to propel Africa into significant international spaces.

- In line with riding the Africa-China relations, Africa may emulate strategies used for the promotion of Chinese culture in Africa to establish a footprint in China and the world.

-

Bibliography

Adams, James. *The Epic of America.* Simon Publications, 2001.

Apter, David and Tony Saich. *Revolutionary discourse in Mao's republic.* Cambridge, Massachusetts: Harvard University Press, 1994.

Austin, John Langshaw. *How to do things with words.* William James Lectures. 2nd ed. Vol. 1955. Oxford, England: Clarendon Press, 1975.

Baker, Hugh. *Chinese family and kinship.* Macmillan: London, 1979.

Bart-Williams, Mallence. "Change your channel" TEDx, Berlin, Salon, January 26, 2015.

Bebbington, Anthony. *Promoting Development by Proxy: The Development Impact of Government Support to Swedish NGOs.* SIDA, Swedish International Development Cooperation Agency. Stockholm: Sweden 1995.

Bello, Ola. "Towards Agenda 2063: Re-Inventing Partnership on Extractive Governance." Governance of Africa's Resources Programme. *Policy Briefing 123.* South African Institute of International Affairs: January, 2015.

Boc, Anny. "The power of language: Globalizing the 'Chinese Dream.'" *East-Asian Affairs. The china monitor,* 3–4. Centre for Chinese Studies, Stellenbosch University, Stellenbosch: South Africa, 2015.

Boden, Jeanne. *Mindmapping China – Language, discourse and advertising in China.* Academic and Scientific Publishers, 2009, 2010.

Bodomo, Adams. "Africa-China Relations: Symmetry, Soft Power and South Africa" The China Review, Vol. 9, No. 2 (Fall 2009), 169-178.

Bohannan, Paul. *How culture works.* New York Free Press, 1995.

Butler, Judith. *Excitable speech: A politics of the Performative.* New York, London: Routledge, 1997.

Bourdieu. Pierre and John B. Thompson. *Language and symbolic power* [Ce que parlerveut dire. English]. Cambridge: Polity Press, 1991.

Bourdieu. Pierre. *Practical Reason: On the theory of action*. Stanford University Press, 1998.

Brown, Kerry. *The EU-China Relationship: European Perspectives: A Manual for Policy Makers*. World Scientific, 2014.

Chachavalpongpun, Pavin, ed. *Entering Uncharted Waters? ASEAN and the South China Sea*. Institute of Southeast Asian Studies, 2014.

Che, Wai-Kin. *The Modern Chinese Family*. R & E Research Associates, INC. Palo Alto, California, 1979.

Chen, Zhimin and Lulu Zhang. "The Power Strategy of Chinese Foreign Policy: Bringing Theoretical and Comparative Studies Together." *NFG Working Paper Series, No. 3*, NFG Research Group "Asian Perceptions of the EU". Berlin: Freie Universität Berlin, February 2013.

Chitty Naren, "The Chinese Dream and international community" China.Org.Cn. Accessed July 19, 2016 http://www.china.org.cn/china/Chinese_dream_dialogue/2013-12/06/content_30821730.htm

"International Attention of Future Reform Agenda," *China Daily*. Accessed March 4, 2016. http://usa.chinadaily.com.cn/2013-11/07/content_17089884.htm.

Compton, Boyd. *Mao's China – Party Reform Documents, 1942 – 44*. University of Washington Press. Seattle and London, 1952.

Copeland, Daryl. "Hard Power vs. Soft Power." Accessed March 3, 2016. *The Mark News*, 2010.

Creemers, Rogier. "The Chinese Dream Infuses Socialism with Chinese Characteristics with New Energy." China Copyright and Media, The law and policy of media in China. May 6, 2013. Accessed June 2, 2016. https://chinacopyrightandmedia.wordpress.com/2013/05/06/the-chinese-dream-infuses-socialism-with-chinese-characteristics-with-new-energy/

Dent, Christopher M. *China and Africa Development Relations*. Routledge, 2010.

Derrida, Jacques. "Signature Event Context," *Glyph*. Johns Hopkins Textual Studies 1: 172–97, 1977.

Ding, X.L. *The Decline of Communism in China: Legitimacy Crisis, 1977 – 1989*. Cambridge University Press, 2006.

Dirlik, Arif. "Mao Zedong in Official Discourse and Historiography," *China Perspectives*, 2: 17-27, 2012.

Dittmer, Lowell and Hurst, William. "Analysis in Limbo: Contemporary Chinese Politics Amid the Maturation of Reform." Issues and Studies.Volume 39, Issue 1, pp. 11-48. March 2003.

Fengyuan, Ji. *Linguistic Engineering: Language and Politics in Mao's China.* Honolulu: University of Hawai'i Press, 2004.

Fowles, Jib. *Advertising and Popular Culture. Foundations of Popular Culture.* United Kingdom, 1996.

Giskin, Howard and Bettye Walsh. *An Introduction to Chinese Culture through the Family.* Albany: State University of New York Press, 2001.

Goldstein, Lyle J. *Meeting China Halfway: How to Defuse the Emerging US-China Rivalry.* Georgetown University Press, 2015.

Grant, J. Andrew, W. R Compaoré, and Matthew Mitchell. *New Approaches to the Governance of Natural Resources: Insights from Africa.* Springer, 2014.

Horsburgh, Nicola, Astrid Nordin, and Shaun Breslin.*Chinese Politics and International Relations: Innovation and Invention.* Routledge, 2014.

Hsia, T. 1961. *Metaphor, Myth, Ritual and the People's Commune.* Studies in Chinese communist terminology No. 7. Berkeley: Center for Chinese Studies, Institute of International Studies, University of California.

Jin Kai. "The China Dream Vs. The American Dream" The Diplomat, September 20, 2014. Accessed 22 June 2016. http://thediplomat.com/2014/09/the-china-dream-vs-the-american-dream/.

Jing, Men. "World Financial Crisis: What it Means for Security – Will the Financial Crisis Make China a Superpower?" Accessed March 1, 2016.*NATO Review*, 2009.

Johnston, Alastair and Robert Ross, eds. *Engaging China: The Management of an Emerging Power.* Routledge, 2005.

Lakoff, George and Mark Johnson.*Metaphors we live by.* University of Chicago Press, 2003.

Lagerwey, J. and Kalinowski, M. *eds. Early Chinese religion.* Part.1, *Shang through Han* (1250 BC – 220 AD). Leiden. Boston: Brill, 2009.

Luo, Yi and Hua Jiang. "A Dialogue with Social Media Experts: Measurement and Challenges of Social Media Use in Chinese Public Relations Practice." *Global Media Journal*– Canadian Edition. Volume 5, Issue 2: 57 – 74, 2012.

Li, Kwok-Sing and Mary Lok. *A glossary of political terms of the People's Republic of China.* Translated. Hong Kong: Chinese University Press, 1995.

Mazrui, Ali A., Kenneth Bradley, and D. Taylor, *The Anglo-African Commonwealth*, 2013.

McClory, Jonathan. "The Soft Power 30 World Rankings." Commores, 2015. Accessed November 2, 2015.

Munro, Donald. "The Imperial Style of Inquiry in Twentieth-Century China: The Emergence of New Approaches." *Michigan monographs in Chinese studies*, 72. Ann Arbor: Center for Chinese Studies, University of Michigan, 1996.

Nye, Joseph. *Bound to Lead: The Changing Nature of American Power.* New York: Basic Books, 1990.

Nye, Joseph. *Soft Power: The Means to Success in World Politics*, 2010.

Nye, Joseph. *The Future of Power.* New York: Public Affairs, 2011: 84.

Nye, Joseph. "China's Soft Power Deficit: To catch up, its politics must unleash the many talents of its civil society." *The Wall Street Journal*, 2012. Accessed March 1, 2016.

Obbema, Fokke. *China and the West: Hope and Fear in the Age of Asia.* I.B. Tauris, 2015.

Organization for Economic Cooperation and Development (OECD). *Policy Priorities for International Trade and Jobs.* OECD Publishing, 2012.

Pickle, Linda. "Written and spoken Chinese: Expression of culture and heritage." In H. Giskin and B. Walsh. *An introduction to Chinese culture through family.* Albany: State University of New York Press, 2001.

Qiu, Huafei. *Contemporary Chinese Foreign and International Relations.* Beijing: Current Affairs Press, 2013.

Qiushi. Accessed March 3, 2016. http://www. chinacopyrightandmedia.wordpress.com.

Roselle, Laura, Miskimmon Alister, Ben O' Loughlin. "Strategic narrative: A new means to understand soft power." *Media, War and Conflict*, Vol. 7, 1 (2014): 70–84. New York: Sage Publications. http://www.mcwsagepub.

Schoenhals, Michael. *Doing Things with Words in Chinese Politics: Five Studies.* Berkeley: Center for Chinese Studies, Institute of East Asian Studies, University of California, 1992.

Selden, Mark. *China in revolution: The Yenan way revisited.* Armonk, N.Y: M.E. Sharpe, 1995.

Shambaugh, David. China's Soft-Power Push – The Search for Respect. *Heinonline.* 94 Foreign Aff. 99. July/August 2015.

Shinn, David and Joshua Eisenman. *China and Africa: A Century of Engagement.* Philadelphia: University of Pennsylvania Press, 2012.

Spence, Jonathan. *The Search for Modern China.* New York. Norton, 1999.

Sun, Baohong. "China's Success Story and Its Relevance to Africa." MFA PRC. Accessed July 25, 2016. http://www.fmprc.gov.cn/mfa_eng/wjb_663304/zwjg_665342/zwbd_665378/t1158751.shtm

Sørensen, Camilla T. N. "The Significance of Xi Jinping's 'Chinese Dream' for Chinese Foreign Policy: From 'Tao Guang Yang Hui' to 'Fen Fa You Wei.'" *Journal of China and International Relations*, Vol. 3, No. 1 (2015).

Tembe, Paul. *Re-evaluating Political Performatives of the PRC: Maoist Discourse – The Historical Trajectory of the* "Laosanpian". Centre for China Studies, Chinese University of Hong Kong. Hong Kong: (S.A.R.), PRC, 2013.

Tembe, Paul. "Misconceptions and omissions in the Africa-China discourse." *Centre for Chinese Studies Commentary.* Stellenbosch: Centre for Chinese Studies Stellenbosch University. July 6, 2015.

Tembe, Paul. "The temptations and promotion of 'China Dream': calling for Africa's home-grown rhetoric." Policy Briefing. Special FOCAC Edition. Stellenbosch, South Africa: Centre for Chinese Studies Stellenbosch University, August 2015.

Tiechuan, Hao. 2013. "Xi Jinping's Explanation of the Chinese People's Dream", China Daily, 16 January. Accessed on March 17, 2016. http://www.chinadaily.com.cn/hkedition/2013-01/16/content_16123041.htm

Tiezzi, Shannon. "The New Africa-China Relations: 4 Trends to Watch." *The Diplomat*, December 6, 2015. Accessed March 2, 2016.http://thediplomat.com/2015/12/the-new-Africa-China-relations-4-trends-to-watch/.

Wang, Zheng. "The Chinese Dream: Concept and Context." *Journal of Chinese Political Science.* March 2014, Volume 19, Issue 1, pp. 1 – 13.

Wang, Zheng. "Never forget national humiliation" The Focus: Postcolonial dialogues. The Newsletter | No.59, Spring 2012.

Xiaoping, Deng. *The Selected Works of Deng Xiaoping (1975-1982).* Translated by The Bureau for the Compilation and Translation of Works of Marx, Engels, Lenin and Stalin under the Central

Committee of the Communist Party of China. Beijing: Foreign Languages Press, first edition, 1984.

Yang, Wenchang. "My Views about *"Tao Guang Yang Hui"*. *Chinese People's Institute for Foreign Affairs*, The 102nd Issue Winter, 2011.

Yi, Xiaoxiong. "Chinese Foreign Policy: "Understanding China's Peaceful Development"." *The Journal of East Asian Affairs*, Vol. 19 No. 1 (Spring/Summer 2005), pp. 74-112.

Yu, Au Loong. *China's Rise: Strength and Fragility*. Issue 54 of the IIE Notebooks for Study and Research. Merlin Press in association with Resistance Books and IIRE, 2012.

Zhang Wei-wei. "Social Media Use Among Youth and Innovation of Moral Education Work with University Students in China." *China Youth University of Political Studies, Beijing, China*. Sino-English Teaching, July 2016, Vol. 13, No. 7, 521 – 527.

Zhu Weilie. "On Diplomatic Strategy and "Keeping a Low Profile and Taking a Proactive Role When Feasible". *Global Review, Vol. 6 No. 3 May/June 2010.*

《成语典故与智慧》新锐编著创意年文化事业有限公司　2005 台北.

《成语九章》倪宝元姚鹏慈著浙江教育出版社 1990.1

《从为人民服务到三个代表》　2004.陕西省社会科学院文史研究所. 中国文联出版社.

Chapter Four. Of Looking East- Implications and Lessons for Africa: A Critical Analysis of Africa-China Relations

═══════════════❖═══════════════

Heather Chingono

Introduction and State of Affairs in Africa

The history of Africa's development and advancement has been characterized by dismal experiments, failed planning and impractical orthodoxies. Such experiences have left the African continent with policy confusion and operationalizing at the mercy of powerful states in the world economy. The internal ruling elites in Africa have again failed to tackle successfully the vicious challenges of the ever-rising expectations (quite rightly) of their citizens that range from the elimination of poverty to living in politically stable havens. Performance on their part has not been so convincing especially in policy formulation[1] and execution which have suffered from the clash of the two major development orthodoxies by the *dependistas* and the liberalists. Also worth noting, in the interim, is that these mounting existential conditions of rising poverty levels and continued bad governance, have arguably been buttressed by the vagaries of the international system that rewards Africa a peripheral position in the political economy despite the continent's stupendous resources. However, the internal processes of Africa have themselves contributed

---

1. Dambisa Moyo, 2009. *Dead Aid: Why Aid is not Working and How there is Another Way for Africa.* (Penguin Books2009)

a fair share towards slowing economic growth in Africa, as both leaders and citizens seem to be operating in a blinkered fashion, or worse still, in a vacuum.

Africa as a continent has critically been experiencing very low levels of industrialization. As one author asserts, "the plan of almost every newly independent African country is to incorporate proposals for industrial growth."[2] However, most African countries lack domestic capital and the technical know-how to achieve industrial growth. Efforts by Zambia for instance to expand the output of copper, which constitutes 90 percent of its exports,[3] in order to finance the import of machinery and equipment for industry as espoused by the Western liberal theories, did not yield any meaningful benefit at one point in history. The essence of industries is to create jobs and add value to raw materials but because Africa lacks these attributes, economic development has slowed. The continent remains shackled by high levels of unemployment and poverty. Ivory Coast and Ghana for instance produce 53 percent[4] of the world's cocoa but the majority of chocolates sold in these countries are imported from United Kingdom (UK) and Switzerland, which are non-cocoa-producing countries. Furthermore, most African countries have plenty of wood as the continent possesses 60 percent of the world's timber reserves but most of the furniture in these countries is actually imported. Crude-oil-producing countries like Nigeria export more than 80 percent of its oil but cannot refine enough for local consumption. Owing to a combination of poor governmental policies, wars and conflict, poverty and hunger, disease, economic disparities, poor infrastructural development, but most importantly, failure to learn and embrace the paths that other experienced states have treaded among other impediments, the prospects of Africa's economic development remain a pipe dream.

Civil and inter-state wars are the order of the day with most of these being fuelled by the presence of rich natural resources and high levels

---

2. Seidman, Ann.1977.Problems of Industrialization in Africa. *Issue: Quarterly Journal of Opinion*, Vol. 7, No. 4: 23–25.

3. Grinker, Richard Roy, Stephen C. Lubkemann and Christopher B. Steiner, eds. 2010.*Perspectives on Africa: A Reader in Culture, History and Representation* (Second edition). West Sussex: John Wiley and Sons Ltd.

4. Ighobhor, Kingsley. 2013. *A New Burst of Energy in Industrial Activity.* Accessed 15 December, 2014.http://www.un.org/africarenewal/magazine/august-2013/new-burst-energy-industrial-activity

of unemployment that translate into disgruntlement. The continent has not managed to significantly address some of the challenges it is facing. Civil wars raging in the Central African Republic and the Republic of Sudan, to insurgencies in the Sahel and Nigeria, and piracy in the Gulf of Guinea over the past few years have not only been detrimental to ensuring stability, but are also a quick reminder that Africa is far from exercising capability in resolving its own internal conflicts. All these security-related situations do not resonate well with prospects for economic development. Currently, a number of countries are considered hotspots in Africa, such as the Democratic Republic of Congo experiencing a war against rebel groups; Egypt marked with a popular uprising against the government; Libya, Mali, Somalia and Nigeria where there are wars against Islamist militants; and conflicts in both Sudan and South Sudan. Such conditions render prospects of economic development very murky.

Furthermore, economically, some of the continent's woes are emanating from the broader capitalist tendencies of the world and this has resulted in volatility of stock markets, high rates of inflation in individual countries and structural unemployment. To further compound the problem, as of today, countries like Zimbabwe do not have a national currency, while Ghana's *cedi,* the country's currency, is continually in free-fall. But while blame may be laid on the complexities of the international system, it is imperative to note that some of these issues are compounded by concerns such as corruption and the embezzlement of funds by bureaucrats. However, it is important to note that African countries cannot avoid the broader capitalist way of life, nor the demands posed by globalization. It will be detrimental for the continent to practice isolationist policies. The continent is also bedevilled with serious problems concerning the overall distribution of wealth among citizens, consequently resulting in the majority of citizens living below the poverty datum line. It is therefore important for Africa to draw lessons from other states on how such issues can be dealt with.

Most of these African states specialize in importing goods and services over and above the over-dependence on foreign generosity. It becomes difficult to assert and evaluate whether such a country is developing or not as it is heavily dependent on aid from overseas. It has to be noted that 80 percent of the annual Malawian budget is donor-funded. The low per-capita incomes of Africans and reduced savings in the economy are all signs that show how the African continent is struggling with underdevelopment. The natural resources of these underdeveloped economies are either unutilized or underutilized and sometimes are usually poorly harnessed.[5] This stems from a lack of technical expertise, a lack of capital and poor levels of technological advancement. The methods of production will be carried out primitively with very low levels of production both in agriculture or industries. The lack of technical know-how, poor scientific advancement, obsolete equipment, coupled with poor entrepreneurship, result in poor-quality products.[6] Some of the African states have adopted indigenization and economic empowerment policies but these have yielded few tangible results as they have been done dismally, selfishly and without expertise. In support of what has been highlighted before, lucidly, understandably, the development model that Africa is using is fraught with weaknesses. Whereas some developing states like China have relied on introspection and people-centered developmental models, African states have prioritized begging from the much richer and developed states. However, the only challenge with this African mindset is that not only is it an unsustainable strategy but it has rendered the prospects of development fallacious.

It is clear from the above discussion that the state of economic affairs within Africa is not satisfactory. Africa needs intervention strategies to address this dire state of affairs. The question is what can Africa use as leverage in order to remove itself from the shackles of poverty? In its quest to attain high levels of economic development, concurrently gaining international recognition, Africa needs to engage vehemently with other states on the international scene but most importantly draw lessons from other states' past experiences. It is indisputable that Africa has been courting several states and that noticeable and entrenched relations between China and Africa are being recorded. These relations are quite broad as they include trade, aid, cultural exchanges, Foreign Direct Investment (FDI), intellectual fertilization and training exchanges amongst other issues. Whilst it is clear that mutual exchange is one pivotal element in this relationship, it has not been without controversies and contestations. Perspectives on this relationship have drawn decidedly mixed views, to the extent

---

5. Kumar, Maulik. 2014. What are the Socioeconomic Features of Underdevelopment Countries? *Economics Journal* Vol 4, 3: 56–72.
6. Ibid: 2014.

of dividing the world into two: what scholarly work is referring to as a case of panda huggers versus dragon slayers. Nevertheless, what is significant is that Africa has always hoped for a long time that this relationship can also address some of its developmental woes. It means Africans themselves have expectations from this relationship: that there should not only be material benefits that do not form a sustainable basis for development. It is appreciable and noble that the relationship has been quite beneficial considering the fact that China has invested billions of dollars in the African economies. In 2012 the total volume of Africa-China trade reached $198.49 billion. Nonetheless, what is more important is the fact that Africans need to learn how the Chinese have managed to do it.

Some notes on development could benefit Africans. Furthermore, owing to the different levels of economic development currently being experienced by these two parties, there are a myriad of lessons that Africa can learn from the Chinese experience. FDI, for instance, and rapidly growing exports rather than foreign kindness or aid have been key to China's economic transformation. Africa needs to take cues from China's phenomenal growth strategy. It becomes the thrust of this article to question why Africa is only "looking East" with China as the locus of attention but not learning, emulating and customizing some of the ideas and concepts of development that have successfully characterized the East-Asian experience. Are Africans complacent enough to want to continue their usual stance of going around with an empty bowl begging as they have always done with the West? Do Africans stand to benefit sustainably from taking the Chinese model for reference? However, it is significant to note that since each country or region has its own unique distinctive backgrounds and features, Africans cannot embrace the model indiscriminately.

China and Africa: Areas of Commonality

The Chinese and Africans have a lot in common which makes it possible for the latter to follow in the footsteps of the former in regard to economic development. It is incontestable that Africa needs also to travel on the tried and tested path of those that have gone before. The presence of cheap labour, availability of "masses and masses" of land coupled with abundant natural resources, similar historical experiences, comparable development potential and prospects, similarities in the role played by the government in developmental issues, and styles of governance among other very important issues, provide ample evidence that Africa can still go the route that China has gone because of abundant areas of commonality.

It is evident that both parties have suffered invasion, bullying and humiliation from the Western colonialists and other imperialists in history. This has made Africans identify more with China than any other parts of the world as a "big brother." In contrast to Western nations, many of whom were former colonial powers, China is viewed by African leaders as an equal, not as an imperialist partner. However, the major difference is that the Chinese have not retrogressed economic transformation by whining and complaining about the colonial era that has since departed, as Africa is still doing. If Africa could put this kind of a mentality aside, then they could benefit from concentrating and expending their energies on issues of economic development. The Chinese clearly appreciate their history of how Japan came to colonize them as a nation but they have not used this to the detriment of their own development. In fact, they took strides to emulate one or two lessons from Japan's developmental experiences and they have since overtaken Japan in terms of gross domestic product (GDP) levels by becoming the second-best country after United States (US).

Additionally, the levels of economic development characterizing both Africa and China reflect high levels of potential and, what is more important, they currently both fall in the group of developing countries. Historically, they have both come from poor backgrounds meaning that they have endured the same experiences in terms of low levels of development. With that in mind, it is worth remembering that just thirty years ago, countries such as Malawi, Burundi and Burkina Faso were economically ahead of China on a per-capita income basis. However, the past three decades have been an era to reckon with in China, and a lot of literature has been penned in a bid to explain the phenomenal development/growth[7]being experienced by China. What is clear is that both China and Africa are lagging behind in terms of technological advancement compared to the West, as they are still in the manufacturing-sector mode. However, the zeal that both parties have in transforming economically is more important. All low-income countries have the potential for dynamic economic growth because it has happened repeatedly: a poor, agrarian economy transforming itself

---

7. Dambisa Moyo, 2009. *Dead Aid: Why Aid is not Working and How there is Another Way for Africa*: Penguin Books.

into a middle-or even high-income urban economy in one or two generations.[8] Stripped to the bare bone, China is a significant role model for African states for the same reasons as noted above. This status-quo makes Africa and China suitable partners to engage in mutually beneficial trade that has long-term effects on Africa's development drive and for Africa to take cues from such engagements.

The vast markets, cheap labour and abundant natural resources that these two parties possess are pivotal, as they provide the strong developmental momentum and broader space for growth. The strategy that was used by Japan, of using labour-intensive industries such as textiles and cheap electronics to drive its economy until the rising labour costs eroded its comparative advantage, is the same approach that has been used by China owing to the cheap labour with which it is endowed. Similarly, Africa has huge markets and cheap labour and it could still tread in the same manner. China is also currently beginning to lose its comparative advantage in labour-intensive industries, allowing for the possibility of other developing countries such as those in Africa to take its place.[9]

It is also of paramount significance to note that both China and Africa are not keen on implementing the Western type of democratic political systems. The majority of African states, as in the case of China, do not support the perspective that democratic political reforms precede economic development. As Moyo[10] succinctly puts it:

> What poor countries at the lowest rungs of economic development need is not a multi-party democracy, but in fact a decisive benevolent dictator to push through the reforms required to get the economy moving. In other words, rushing to elections before economic growth has got underway is a recipe for failure.

Furthermore, these two parties' governments favour command economies – an economy where the government plays a pivotal role in the market. The Chinese market economy is heavily driven by a benevolent government that puts the interests of ordinary citizens

---

8. Lin, Yifu.2015. Africa's Path from Poverty. Available on: http://www.project-syndicate.org/commentary/africa-development-route-by-justin-yifu-lin-2015-02Accessed 22 February 2015

9. Ibid: 2015

10. Dambisa Moyo, 2009. *Dead Aid: Why Aid is not Working and How there is Another Way for Africa*: Penguin Books 2009.

right before their own selfish interests. Moreover, areas of comparative advantage such as agriculture and mining-dominated economies are a characteristic of these two economies. They are both endowed with natural resources such that if Africa were to take its cue from how the Chinese manage their natural resources, then the theory of "natural resource curse" can never be a reality in the African continent. To date, geologists in China have found 172 kinds of minerals in China and confirmed reserves of over 159 different kinds, among which twenty of these are front-ranking in the world.[11] The African continent possesses a generous endowment in natural resources, namely hydrocarbons, minerals and timber, which remain mostly untapped due to decades of political instability, poor infrastructure and lack of investment.[12] In regional terms, Africa possesses the world's third largest oil reserves, an estimated 9.5 percent of global known deposits in 2007 and it boasts the fastest growth rate in identified oil reserves, which doubled in the past two decades.[13]

The Chinese Path to Development: Key Cues for Africa

The concept of imitating development is not new. Countries have always wanted to learn from one another's finest experiences. This paper is not emphasizing that Africa should replicate the Chinese model of development per se, but it is arguing for the continent to adopt, contextualize and re-modify aspects to suit a particular country's own specific conditions. The specific practices of the Chinese model may not have universal significance, but the ideas or concepts behind these practices may be generally applicable. A country therefore needs to select a path of development that is based on its own realities. Put simply, Africa is set to benefit from taking the Chinese model for reference, but it should not adopt the model indiscriminately.

The areas from which Africa could draw lessons from include the Chinese model of playing politics, its stance on corruption, work ethic, labour reforms, views on FDI, which are intricately related to the concept of indigenization, private-public partnerships, legislation

11. Zhou D., M Ming and Li Na. 2012. *China*. Beijing Open Press, Beijing.
12. Alden, Chris and Ana Cristina Alves. 2009. *China and Africa's Natural Resources: The Challenges and Implications for Development and Governance*. South Africa Institute of International Affairs; Occasional Paper 41, September.
13. Ibid: 2009

guiding investments, the culture of saving, leadership cues and the general areas of development. It is important for African leaders to put their citizens first and to promote reforms step by step while the government plays its role of ensuring that its people are well-catered for. Such practice resonates very well not only with the Chinese leaders' rhetoric but also with their implementation. The African countries can draw on such ideas and combine them with their own reality to explore the African model. Aside from putting people first, there are quite a number of issues that Africa can emulate from China.

The Chinese have a tough stance on issues of corruption. As Moyo[14] reiterates,

> If the world has one picture of African statesmen, it is one of rank corruption on a stupendous scale. There hardly seem any leaders who have not crowned themselves in gold, handed over state businesses to relatives and friends, diverted billions to foreign bank accounts, and generally treated their countries as giant personalized cash dispensers'. According to Transparency International, Mobutu is estimated to have looted Zaire to the tune of US $5 billion; roughly the same amount which was stolen from Nigeria by President Sani Abacha and placed in Swiss private banks (later US$ 700 million of the loot was returned to Nigeria).

Additionally, on December 22, 2014, the Tanzanian President, Jakaya Kikwete, fired a government minister of the Land and Housing ministry, Professor Anna Tibaijuka, for taking $1 million from a businessman as a donation for a school. However, instead of allowing the money to be deposited directly into the school account, it was deposited into Prof. Tibaijuka's account. Further investigations into cases of corruption in Tanzania by a parliamentary watchdog revealed that $120 million had been taken from an escrow account, paid to an energy firm and then given to various government ministers. As a result, the minister for energy and minerals, Mr. Sospeter Muhongo, was dismissed. Much earlier, on December 16 2014, the country's attorney-general, Frederick Werema, resigned over his role in this multi-million-dollar energy-sector graft scandal. However, what has since become worrisome in Africa is that it is not only the leaders and senior government officials involved but the moth of corruption has

---

14. Dambisa Moyo, 2009. *Dead Aid: Why Aid is not Working and How there is Another Way for Africa*. Penguin Books.

cascaded to lower levels. Many government workers and even those within the private sector have siphoned billions of dollars over the years as corruption has become normal in these states. Corruption is the moth that kills an economy and stamping out corruption will provide a conducive environment for national development. Africa needs to embrace lessons from the way in which China deals with issues of corruption, as these corrupt governments interfere with the rule of law and the establishment of transparent civil institutions, making both domestic and foreign investments in poor countries unattractive. How is economic development ever going to be attained in a country that has an unattractive record with FDI because of cases of corruption?

Recently, China has intensified its anti-corruption efforts by conducting thorough investigations into major corruption cases and it has worked hard to resolve problems of corruption that directly and indirectly affect the people. It is determined that all those who violate the China Communist Party (CCP) code of conduct and general state laws will be brought to justice, regardless of how much power they wield or their position in government. In the past two years, nearly 90,000 officials at all levels were investigated and penalized, including sixty-eight officials at deputy ministerial level and above.[15] In 2014 alone, over 70 000 Chinese officials were punished for violating the eight-point anti-graft rules. The offenders were involved in over 50 000 violations and more than 20 000received serious party and government penalties. The offences included the violation of rules concerning the construction of government buildings, use of government vehicles and overseas travel financed with public funds, including the sending or accepting of gifts, excessive spending on receptions, extravagant weddings or funerals, and their discipline violations.[16] While China can manage and provide deterrents to these kinds of crimes, Africa seems to have normalized an abnormal attribute. This graft is what has made the African economies scream. In a nutshell, Africa should embrace the Chinese stance on corruption as corruption is bleeding their economies; or maybe it would not be so bad if African leaders, like some of their Asian counterparts, reinvested

15. Global Times: Available at http://www.globaltimes.cn/content/ 833674.shtml Accessed on 16 January 2015
16. See http://english.cntv.cn/2015/01/07/VIDE1420632243188253.shtml.

the embezzled money domestically instead of externalizing it to foreign bank accounts.

One other critical issue that has slowed African states' economic growth is their behaviour with regard to saving, versus spending. Since the late 1970s, marking the beginning of market liberalization, China's national savings rate has been at the top of the world and by the early 1990s, the savings rate stood at 35 percent.[17] Furthermore, in 2014, the savings rate increased to 52 percent, while that of the world average was around 20 percent and most significantly, that of the US was about 4 percent.[18] Now the savings balance of Chinese household equals to over $7 trillion, which means more than $5000 per-capita.[19] Although the concept of a higher savings rate reflects the parsimonious habits of the Chinese people, it also shows that there is income growth to a certain extent. Even though some authors go on to argue that such saving results from non-positive factors within an economy such as: (1) poor and undeveloped national social security systems that mean the ordinary citizens need to save money for health care, children's education, provisions for the aged, home purchase and so on; or (2) the fact that there are fewer channels for private investment so that ordinary people have limited options of where to put their cash.[20] Despite all the arguments, what is clear is that if governments work to improve both the social security systems and to develop markets that will ensure an increase in customer spending, simultaneously expanding the channels of private investment, the high savings could be of huge benefit to the country. Social unrest, instability, uprisings and protests characterizing Africa sometimes are a result of poverty, which is exacerbated by both the inability of Africans to save – that is if there is anything for them to save. However, it is important to note that it is not as if the Chinese earn a lot of income in their various endeavours but the enhanced culture of saving has gone a long way in ensuring stability in the country. It is the culture of saving that facilitated China's quick recovery following the financial crisis in 2008. The culture of saving is based on delayed gratification whereby the

---

17. Global Times: Available at http://www.globaltimes.cn/content/833674.shtml Accessed on 16 January 2015

18. Ibid: 2015

19. Ibid: 2015

20. Yang, Dennis Tao, Junsen Zhang and Shaojie Zhou. 2011. "Why are Saving Rates so High in China?" *IZA Discussion Paper* No. 5465, 2011.

Chinese would rather save and invest the little they have in order to enjoy the greater returns in the future; it is more or less related to the Indian system. Savings are important for the gestation of the struggling small to medium enterprises (SMEs) in Africa and if this system were instilled within the African mind-set, it could bring a lot of economic benefit. In Zimbabwe for instance there is a lot of speculation that billions of dollars could be circulating within the informal SMEs. Effectively a combination of savings and other policies such as business incubation could contribute immensely to economic development.

Currently, the major drawback to FDI is the lack of lucidity around the indigenization and economic empowerment policies of states. There is consensus that there is no country without an indigenization policy and that such policies are efficient in making meaningful contributions to economic development. In the US, as early as 1887, the government enacted the Federal Alien Property Act (FAPA) that sought to prohibit the ownership of land by aliens – or by companies more than 20 percent-owned by aliens – whilst in Japan, the Ministry of International Trade and Industry orchestrated an industrial development programme that has now become legendary[21] among other countries. It is unquestionable that every government's ultimate and ideal objective is to ensure that its ordinary citizens are living well above the poverty datum line. Some governments in Africa have adopted indigenization policies as a result. These have been used as a model of development.

However, what has been problematic about the way these policies are being implemented is that sometimes they have been inconsistent and consequently are suffering from a poor track record. Munzwembiri[22] indicates that an analysis of the indigenization policies of African states identifies the Zimbabwean indigenization policy as suffering from a lack of clarity and consistency: "The main deterrent to FDI at the moment is the lack of clarity around indigenization policies and the inconsistency around implementation. Until we

21. Baffour, Ankomah. 2013. *Zimbabwe: New African Special Report.* London: IC Publications, (July 2013): 45.
22. Munzwembiri, Perry. 2014. Zimbabwe at Crossroads as Controversial Indigenization Law Stands in way of Growth. *Eurasia Review: A Journal of News and Analysis.* 2015. Accessed 14 January 2015. http://www.eurasiareview.com/?p=144881

provide clarity and build a consistent track record in implementation we will continue to see subdued FDI inflows into countries like Zimbabwe."

In support of this view, the Inter-Horizon Securities suggests that policy clarity, transparency and key structural reforms must be made in order to enhance the business climate to attract FDI, boost productivity, competitiveness and build confidence. Overall, their views indicate that policy inertia and the lack of a compromised solution to the African countries' indigenization policies are the largest impediments to growth.[23] China as early as the mid-nineteenth century used high import tariffs to develop its industrial base. Evidence shows that around the 1990s, China's average tariff was over 30 percent but it was still welcoming foreign investment. It also imposed foreign-ownership ceilings and local-content requirements that demanded that foreign firms should buy a certain proportion of their imports from local suppliers. The African indigenization policies sometimes lack a clear direction and properly informed regulations by governments governing their conduct. The Chinese government is stringent with rules and regulations governing the conduct of business in their country by foreigners and these rules have partly facilitated their growth. If a foreigner opens a company in China with an initial capital of $100 000, they are entitled to employ only two foreigners and the rest of the workers should be of Chinese origin. It means the Chinese government has successfully managed to encourage productivity and FDI by implementing labour reforms that ensure both their citizens and nascent industries can survive. Such reforms have been done in China since the market liberalization of 1978. Africa needs to sort out a number of things. As one scholar puts it:

> How successful can the indigenization policy be in a country whose economy is stagnated? How much can a country overburdened by external debt attempt to indigenize its economy? A country that is overly dependent on external trade and on a vulnerably narrow spectrum of primary export commodities and where there is a bifurcation between the traditional and modern sectors of the economy with a circumscribed and fractured industrial base cannot be truly indigenized. Africa must therefore see indigenization not merely as taking over of on-going expatriate concerns but as a challenge to transform its present colonial economy to an

---

23. Ibid: 2014

authentically self-reliant African economy with an internally-generated and self-sustaining process of development.[24]

It becomes imperative to state that while the Zimbabwean policy of 51/49 share ownership might be a noble idea, some of the above concerns need to be addressed first before the country embarks on the policy. The Chinese have most importantly made use of public-private partnerships as these have been significant for technology and skills transfer. It is imperative for African states to craft legislation that drives this agenda but this should not be done at the expense of efforts to attract FDI. In actual fact, the Chinese model is based on encouraging foreign investment with the intention of not only growing the economy but also of gaining from foreign technology and expertise. However, this is done on the terms of the CCP government whose intention is to promote economic development prior to political democratic development. The African states should emulate the Chinese foreign policy of not allowing any outside forces or actors to influence their decisions– what they have called the Beijing consensus – but accepting constructive advice on development.

The calibre of leadership that China has enjoyed over the past three decades is the kind of leadership that Africa requires. Generally, there is an outcry among scholars that Africa has challenges associated with leadership with a majority of scholarly work referring to this as the "leadership crisis". However, widely held views in this scholarship are that failure by the African leaders to adhere to Western liberal democracy tenets has translated into low levels of development. This is not exactly the situation in Africa as confirmed in other Asian states that have registered phenomenal growth under autocratic benevolent leaders, as Moyo[25] puts it. Economic growth is still possible under other types of governance. However, leaders, whether democratic or not, should be of great stamina and resilience in terms of driving an economy towards good governance by condemning corruption, red-tape, complacency, and poor work ethic among their own leaders. The Chinese leaders have progressively over the years managed to hold on to the fundamental principle of putting people first before their own

24. Mazrui Ali and Christophe Wondji.1999. *General History of Africa Since 1935*: University of California
25. Dambisa Moyo, 2009. *Dead Aid: Why Aid is not Working and How there is Another Way for Africa*: Penguin Books.

interests. They have accorded a lot of respect to the principal position of the people (*laobaixing*) in the crafting of national development policies. A study on global attitudes of countries carried out by Pew Research Centre in 2014 reflected that in most of the African states surveyed, the general populace tended to believe that Beijing respects personal freedoms of people. The leaders have prioritized the creativity and innovation emanating from their natives, consequently ensuring a people-centred developmental model. This explains why the Chinese government has managed to move over 300 million of its citizens from living below the poverty datum line in a space of 30 years while decades have passed for Africans without meaningful economic growth. Countries such as Rwanda under the leadership of President Paul Kagame can be commended for adopting a tough stance on his ministers and members of parliament. He has categorically stated that none of these and their immediate families should go outside to access health care, as their major task is to revamp the local ones for the benefit of the people and themselves. In addition, they are not allowed to abuse government automobiles and mobile phones by amassing excessively high, unjustifiable and unreasonable bills.

The Chinese economic developmental model is a combination of the socialist system and the market economy under the robust guidance of an effective and practical government as it is guided by "Five-Year Plans." The country is currently undertaking its twelfth Five-year Plan (2011–2015) which stresses comprehensive, coordinated and sustainable economic development.[26] This includes industrial upgrading and the promotion of domestic consumption. These priorities explain why certain sectors, including energy, automotive, IT infrastructure and biotechnology, also receive a high degree of focus. The Five-Year strategic plans implemented from as early as 1953 usually differentiate the areas and the industries for development; for example, East of China was picked as the experiment area to promote the export-based economy in the early 1980s. However, development in Africa is unplanned and lacks systematization. The focus is *all over* and the consequent result is lack of growth caused by policy confusion. Zimbabwe has currently adopted this strategy by coming up with its first Five-Year Strategic Plan (2013–2018), referred to as Zimbabwe Agenda for Sustainable Socio-Economic Transformation (ZIMASSET). This plan cross-cuts

---

26. Zhou D., M Ming and Li Na. 2012. *China.* Beijing Open Press, Beijing.

along clusters that include food security and nutrition; social services and poverty eradication; infrastructure and utilities; value addition and beneficiation with two sub-clusters – Fiscal Reform Measures and Public Administration, and Governance and Performance Management – to buttress the clusters.[27] The government has to work harder in order to avoid policy inertia.

Linked to this discussion, and of importance, is that governments play an important part in placing leverage on the basic role of the market to allocate resources while simultaneously improving the system of government macro-regulation. In comparison, economic developmental models of African states are weak and unsustainable and the governments are not firm enough in ensuring that development is made the priority. In principle and on paper, the main agenda is economic development but the activities implemented do not harness the requisite resources into meaningful development. Since the late 1970s, the Chinese have persevered unwaveringly in their quest to liberalize their market. What is unique and admirable with the way they have done it, is that the process has unfolded in an orderly manner from the rural areas to the cities and not a single part of China has been left out. This great undertaking of reform and opening up has brought about China's historic transformation from a highly centralized planned economy to a robust socialist market economy; from a closed or semi-closed state to all-round opening up. The socialist market economy is playing an increasingly important role in the allocation of resources and the macro-economic system is being refined; the public and non-public sectors of the economy, including individually-owned businesses and private companies, compose a complementary economic structure.[28]As a result of strengthening and improving the macro-control, the Chinese economy was the first to recover after the 2008 global financial crisis. Before 1978, China's economy was dominated by the public sector, with state-owned and collective-owned enterprises representing 77.6 percent and 22.4 percent respectively of all enterprises.[29]

The Chinese government has also upheld the basic economic system in which public ownership is the mainstay of the economy and economic entities of diverse ownership develop together. While

---

27. ZIMASSET Policy Document.
28. Zhou D., M Ming and Li Na. 2012. *China.* Beijing Open Press, Beijing.
29. Ibid:2012

consolidating the public sector, China is encouraging supporting and guiding the development of the non-public sector, including individually owned businesses, private companies and foreign-investment enterprises. Furthermore, the Chinese model has sought to integrate urban and rural development with an ultimate objective of bringing a balance between urban and rural development, consequently narrowing the gap between these two entities. Effectively, the different systems contributing to economic development are not functioning single-handedly. The industry functions to support agriculture while the cities support rural areas in the quest to modernize on an equal pedestal. This is a way of dealing with the heavy inequalities between people, which Karl Marx heavily bemoans. Yet, the problem of the increased gap between the rich and the poor is dotted all over the African continent.

China has diligently tried to give priority to scientific and technological innovation in the overall national development and to take steps to promote innovation that catches up with global advances. They import technology for the purpose of learning and re-modifying it for their market, while African states have imported technology and used it until it has become obsolete without trying to learn about modifying this to the specific needs of their own countries. This has made the acquiring of technology for Africans rather expensive and pointless.

Issues of politics, especially governed by self-centred interests, have been prioritized more than issues of economic development in Africa. It is not that politics is not a fundamental pillar in the economic development matrix, but over-emphasis of this issue at the expense of developmental concerns has proved to be detrimental to development in Africa. Resources in Africa have been squandered because of political bickering and voting processes by political parties. Some African countries have spent as much as over a billion dollars, either from their budgets or from donors, on elections once in every four or five years, yet their citizenry will be languishing in poverty. But who gives the Chinese aid, even though they are so many, being a quarter of the world population? Who feels sorry for the Chinese? And why can't the Africans take cues from the Chinese regarding their work ethic, as opposed to the "begging bowl" theory promoted by Africans.

Africans should also emulate the way the Chinese adhere to and preserve their history and culture as it relates to development. Many of the ideas guiding economic development in China are trickling down from past revolutionary leaders' rhetoric such as Chairman Mao Ze Dong and Chairman Deng Xiao Ping among others, historical philosophies especially the Confucian ideology, and most importantly their history and realities in general. China has a large amount of written history to learn, much of which is still quite alive and relevant. The reason why development in the urban areas is supposed to benefit those in the rural areas is because the Chinese have always paid attention to income equality, which can be traced back to Confucius. The past Chinese governments have formulated and improved the economic development under the guidance of the Marxist world-outlook and methodology with regard to development. However, as mentioned earlier, of significance is that they have combined the Marxist ideas with their own basic reality of China. Africa has to adjust these ideologies and various policies according to the various changes taking place in their own environments and their cultures. The policy of market liberalization adopted in the late 1970s came at a time when there was a need for China to grapple with the complexities of globalization and it has been a success story for China. It is therefore imperative for Africans to take heed of the dynamics of the international scene and to transform their policies accordingly. A fine example is the red-tape and bureaucracy that mars the process of foreign investment in Africa where it can take years to have an investment application approved. While most countries in the world are moving towards the market economy, which emphasizes foreign investment, some African states still exercise very stringent, retrogressive and primitive regulations that are not attractive for FDI.

As reiterated earlier, there is nothing amiss with countries following in one another's footsteps in terms of economic development, as China has not been an exception. China has drawn on experiences from other states. In the 1950s China borrowed ideas from the Soviet Union that proved to be unsuccessful. Even though a myriad of challenges and setbacks were experienced, they persevered through obtaining lessons from other successful experiences. They went on to borrow from a number of Western countries but most of their ideas came largely from Japan. The key is to capture the window of opportunity for industrialization arising from the relocation of light manufacturing from higher-income countries. Lin[30] traces how Japan

---

30. Lin, Yifu.2015. *Africa's Path from Poverty*. Available on:

seized such an opportunity following the World War II, allowing South Korea, Taiwan, Hong Kong, Singapore, Malaysia and Thailand to follow in Japan's footsteps. He states that currently China is the one going down this road and Africa is likely to jump onto the bandwagon after China, as countries such as Ethiopia have already started making progress in this direction and have recorded successes. The market economy, which is the main direction of economic reform in China, is originating from the West but the Chinese ensured that these same principles be included in their own economy in a way that benefits their citizens and is done on their own terms, leveraging on areas in which they have comparative advantage.

The fact that China began its market liberalization in the late 1970s with strengthened institutions is a pivotal strategy for sustained economic development. China's experience points to the importance of combining pragmatic, evidence-based policy making with capable public institutions and a strong leadership that is committed to poverty reduction.[31] Effective public administrative and decision-making processes are also essential for ensuring the state is an effective tool for economic development. It is clear that the combination of sound policy-making practices with strong state institutions is key to a country's recipe of development and this stresses the importance of Deng Xiao Ping's catchphrase of "searching for truth from facts". However, an intimate analysis of African institutions reflects that much has to be done in revamping the very weak institutions that have further been crippled by cases of corruption, nepotism and maladministration.

In her book, *Dead Aid*, Moyo[32] provides African economies with four options of sources of funding which she believes are not as detrimental as aid:

First, African governments should follow Asian emerging markets in accessing the international bond markets and taking advantage of the falling yields paid by sovereign borrowers over the past decade. Second, they should encourage the Chinese policy of large-scale

---

http://www.project-syndicate.org/commentary/africa-development-route-by-justin-yifu-lin-2015-02Accessed 22 February 2015

31. Ravallion, Martin. *Are there Lessons for Africa from China's Success against Poverty?* World Bank Publishers, 2008.

32. Dambisa Moyo, 2009. *Dead Aid: Why Aid is not Working and How there is Another Way for Africa.* Penguin Books.

direct investment in infrastructure.... Third, they should continue to press for genuine free trade in agricultural products.... Fourth, they need to foster the spread of microfinance institutions of the sort that have flourished in Asia and Latin America....

A careful analysis of Moyo's prescriptions reflects that three out of four of the ideas are borrowed from the East and among these, one originates from China. While it can still be debated on how these prescriptions can be implemented in Africa it is not debateable whether these can work. Also, what is clear, is that there is so much that Africans can learn from the Asians at large and from the Chinese specifically.

Quest to Learn from the Chinese: Major Drawbacks for Africa

There are a couple of challenges that Africa may face in its quest to follow in the footsteps of rising China. In memoirs written by one of Deng Xiao Ping's interpreters, he indicates that as the Chinese reform was progressing very well, the chief architect, Chairman Deng Xiao Ping, advised J.K Rawlings in a discussion:

> We have found our own way...pay a visit to Xiamen, one of the most special economic zones. Don't just copy China's model. You have to walk your own path. If there is any relevant Chinese experience for you, I'm afraid it is only one thing: "seek truth from facts" (Maoism). You must formulate your own policies and plans according to the actual situation of your own country. During the process, you must learn the lessons in a highly timely fashion – to keep the good things and correct the wrong ones. This perhaps is the most relevant experience for you.

The challenge for Africans is therefore to use the Chinese model as a benchmark to develop their own model. However, lack of capacity, innovation, a misplaced work ethic and the will to do such, have acted as impediments to achieving these in Africa. There have been so many clamours for promoting Pan-Africanism coupled with finding home-grown solutions for local problems, but these have been to no avail in terms of making a meaningful economic contribution to the continent.

Furthermore, Africans harbour some feelings of scepticism towards the Chinese when doing business among other engagements. Most of the attitudes are influenced by literature that has been penned so far portraying Africa-China relations in a very negative way. In most of this literature, the Chinese have been demonized and a picture of patron-client is painted, or put in other words –a horse-rider relationship. The presence of China in Africa is being regarded as a new form of colonialism with detrimental effects to the long-term economic development of Africa as there seems to be unequal exchange between the two parties. The Chinese companies are accused of paying little regard to environmental costs, flooding African markets with cheap Chinese products and massive exploitation of Africa's resources. On that basis, Africa has nothing to emulate from the Chinese developmental model. Common to the arguments are sentiments like Africa risks relinquishing its natural resource wealth without having leveraged sufficient Chinese assets in return. Despite favourable Chinese loans, FDI, aid, a large market for African exports, technology transfer and other advantages that Africa gets in exchange for unprocessed raw materials and oil,[33] it still is not a fair deal for Africans. However, if the criticism of Chinese practices in Africa is meant to improve China's labour relations continuously and foreign policy in general to Africa, growth and development will occur to a certain extent. This is because the Chinese way of doing business and entrepreneurship is better for African economic development than charity. African business-people have also proven themselves capable and would be better off generating growth in the marketplace. It is also indisputable that China is transforming Africa's mentality and mind-set from an aid-dependent continent to a business-focused region. Most Africans still possess an old image of China – "China in the 60s and 70s" which was even poorer than the majority of the African states – despite the strides that China has made over the years.

Importantly, the Chinese model is not completely perfect. The issue of the role of women in politics and other top echelons of society still remains a problem. Women are still excluded in top-level government affairs. At the top level of decision making, no woman has ever been among the nine members of the Standing Committee of the Communist Party's Politburo.[34] Currently, only three out of the

---

33. Haroz, D. 2015. *China in Africa: Symbiosis or Exploitation.* 2011. Available on:
   http://www.fletcher.achivetusAccessed 22 February 2015
34. Bauer, J., Feng Wang, Riley Nancy, Xiaohua Zhao. 1992: Gender Inequality in Urban China. *Modern China* 18, 3 (1992): 333–370

twenty-seven government ministers are women and since 1997, China has fallen to the fifty-third place from being sixteenth in the world in terms of female representation at its parliament, the National People's Congress.[35]

Conclusion

In conclusion, the usual song of how Europe and the West at large caused the underdevelopment of Africa has since become monotonous and retrogressive for economic development in Africa. A way forward in regard to ensuring economic development and prosperity in Africa is being encouraged by leveraging on the existing resources and capabilities within the continent. The situation presently in Africa reflects that FDI investment by the Chinese, among other ways of engagement, is playing a fair share of a role in economic development but there is a need to find the best strategies to harness this into meaningful economic development. The African development agenda is no more immune from the influence of a rising China because of the heavy presence, intensity and impact of the latter in these countries. Clearly it is not enough for Africa to continue engaging China diplomatically, and providing China with huge untapped markets and energy resources without taking a single developmental lesson from its partner. It will be a misrepresentation of facts to state that the specific practices of the Chinese model have universal significance especially for the very diverse African states, but the ideas or concepts behind these practices may be generally applicable considering that the two share almost similar histories and possess other common attributes. The African states should draw on these ideas and combine with their own reality in exploring the African model. The hypothetical conjecture being propounded by this article is that the current state of underdevelopment in Africa can partly be understood as a manifestation of failure by Africans to take cues from the Chinese developmental model. The fact that China as a state has not relied on aid should be a good lesson for Africans, to desist from having their public budgets fattened by donor funds. The Chinese development and growth model can serve as a blueprint for African states, even though Africa does not have to emulate everything.

---

35. Tatlow, Didi Kirsten. 2010. *Women Struggle for a Foothold in Chinese Politics.* New York Times, 24 June, 2010.

It is possible for the African continent to make strides from utilizing the Chinese model on condition that it improves its appropriate policy-implementation strategy and environment too. Africans also need to address issues like corruption, their work ethic and mentality to alter their state of desperation to a state of self-belief. The leaders' attitudes are also an important force in this debate: leaders should be modest about accepting their flaws and correct them for the purpose of progress. The quest to maintain stability should be a priority as these leaders desist from pursuing selfish interests at the expense of national, regional and continental development. Most importantly, the model should be tailor-made by governments to suit the conditions in respective African states, as development is affected by education, ideology, political policies, climate and natural resources among others. Africa is not ready for development that is all-encompassing (including economic, social, political and environmental justice at the same time), but they could progress better by borrowing from the Chinese model which partially sacrifices social and political justice to drive economic prosperity, but of course not entirely neglecting these.

Bibliography

Alden, Chris and Ana Cristina Alves. 2009. *China and Africa's Natural Resources: The Challenges and Implications for Development and Governance.* South Africa Institute of International Affairs; Occasional Paper 41, September.

Baffour, Ankomah. 2013. *Zimbabwe. New African Special Report.* London: IC Publications, July: 45.

Bauer, J., Feng Wang, Riley Nancy, Xiaohua Zhao. 1992. "Gender Inequality in Urban China." *Modern China* 18, 3: 333–370.

Bertocchi, Graziella and Fabio Canova. 2002. "Did Colonization Matter for Growth? An Empirical Exploration into the Historical Causes of Africa's Underdevelopment." *European Economic Review* 46, Issue 10 (2002): 1851–871.

Beveridge, A. Andrew. 1974. Economic Independence, Indigenization and the African Businessman: Some Effects of Zambia's Economic Reforms." *African Studies Review* Vol. 17, No.3 December: 477–490.

Global Times: *China's Crackdown on Corruption in 2013.* Available at: http://www.globaltimes.cn/content/833674.shtml Accessed on 16 January 2015

Grinker, Richard Roy, Stephen C. Lubkemann and Christopher B. Steiner, eds. 2010.*Perspectives on Africa: A Reader in Culture, History and Representation* (Second edition). West Sussex: John Wiley and Sons Ltd.

Haroz, D. 2011. China in Africa: Symbiosis or Exploitation. Available on: http://www.fletcher.achivetusAccessed 19 February 2015.

Ighobhor, Kingsley, 2013. A New Burst of Energy in Industrial Activity. Available on: http://www.un.org/africarenewal/magazine/august-2013/new-burst-energy-industrial-activity Accessed 15 December, 2014.

Kumar, Maulik. 2014. What are the Socioeconomic Features of Underdevelopment Countries *Economics Journal* Vol 4, 3: 56–72.

Lin, Yifu. 2015. *Africa's Path from Poverty.* Available on: http://www.project-syndicate.org/commentary/africa-development-route-by-justin-yifu-lin-2015-02 Accessed 22 February 2015.

Mazrui, Ali and Christophe Wondji.1999. *General History of Africa: Since 1935*: University of California.

Moyo, Dambisa 2009. *Dead Aid: Why Aid is not Working and How there is Another Way for Africa.* Penguin Books.

Munzwembiri, Perry. 2015. "Zimbabwe at Crossroads as Controversial Indigenization Law Stands in way of Growth." *Eurasia Review: A Journal of News and Analysis.* 2015. Available on: http://www.eurasiareview.com/?p=144881 Accessed 22 February 2015.

Ravallion, Martin. 2008. *Are there Lessons for Africa from China's Success against Poverty?* World Bank Publishers.

Seidman, Ann. 1977. "Problems of Industrialization in Africa." *Issue: Quarterly Journal of Opinion*, Vol. 7, No. 4. 23–25.

Tatlow, Didi Kirsten. 2010. Women Struggle for a Foothold in Chinese Politics. *New York Times*, 24 June.

Taylor, Ian. 2007. "Unpacking China's Resource Diplomacy in Africa." Centre on China's Transactional Relations, Working Paper No.19, 2007. Available on: www.cetr.ust.hk/materials/work 20/02/2014 Accessed 19 December, 2014.

Wilson, Ernest J.1990. Strategies of State Control of the Economy: Nationalization and Indigenization in Africa. *Comparative Politics*, Vol. 22, No.4. City University of New York, July.

Yang, Dennis Tao, Junsen Zhang and Shaojie Zhou.2011: Why are Saving Rates so High in China? *IZA Discussion Paper* No. 5465, 2011.

Zhou D., M Ming and Li Na. 2012. *China.* Beijing Open Press, Beijing.

Zimbabwe Agenda for Sustainable Socio-Economic Transformation Policy Document, 2013-2018. Zimbabwe Government Printers.

Reports

Pew Research Center 2014: *China's Image*: Available at: http://www.pewglobal.org/2014/07/14/chapter-2-chinas-image/:Accessed 12 January 2015.

Global Times: *China's Crackdown on Corruption in 2013*: Available at: http://www.globaltimes.cn/content/833674.shtml Accessed on 16 January 2015.

Chapter Five. Promoting the Development of the African Continent through the Integration of Modern Science and Technology and the African Culture

=============== ❖ ===============

Antoine Roger Lokongo

Introduction

To explain what we mean by the statement that "African culture and science have always been good bedfellows", we have to go back to Ancient Egypt. Ancient Egypt is not only fascinating, but it is one of the most ancient civilizations established by black Africans or pioneers of civilization. It predates the Greeks and Romans and extends as far as the Middle East, India and Latin America, as Senegalese scholar Cheik Anta Diop has proven in his ground-breaking work.[1] It has also been scientifically proven by recent archaeological findings that Egyptian religion forms the roots of the Jewish, Christian and Islamic religious tree.[2] In fact, the Ten Commandments in the Bible are actually a copy from Chapter 125 in the *Egyptian Book of the Dead,* which one can read inside the pyramids in Egypt today:

I have not done what the gods abominate

---

1. Diop, *African Origin of Civilization.*
2. Acharya / Murdock, "Archaeologist: Egyptian religion forms roots."

I have not committed murder
I have not given the order for murder to be committed
I have not encroached upon the fields of others
I have not carried away the milk from the mouths of children
I have not uttered lies
I have not committed adultery
I have terrorized none.
I have not blasphemed
I have not increased my wealth except through such things are
[justly] my own possessions...[3]

What a beautiful worldview or moral code that stresses harmony between the metaphysical world, the living world, care for others, including human rights in general, women's rights, children's rights in particular and care for the environment! Chapter 125 in the *Egyptian Book of the Dead* constitutes the roots of *ubuntu*: "I am because we are." Yet our erstwhile colonizers claim to have come to teach us humanity, spirituality and morality. We had it all!

This makes Africa the cradle, the source of the real Judaism, Christianity and Islam, which are therefore part of the African heritage originally; but which were repackaged and brought back to Africans in a dualist way. The aim was not only to divide the African's body from his soul but also to divide Africans between themselves: "divide and rule". That is why, today, Africa is divided not only into Portuguese-speaking, French-speaking and English-speaking countries, but also into Christian and Muslim countries. And after being forced to adhere to Islam and Christianity by the sword or by a whip called *Chicotte*[4] in the case of Congo, Africans were still divided into many religious denominations: Catholic and Protestant Christians, Salafi, Sunni, Shia, Suffi, Wahabbis, Muslims, you name it. That was just an anecdote. Africa is for sure not only the cradle of humanity but also the cradle of spirituality. There are no probabilities here!

---

3. Osman, "The Ten Commandments."
4. *Chicotte* is a Portuguese word for a whip or *fimbo* in the Lingala language: a whip made from the dried hide of a hippopotamus and encrusted with nails, applied to a victim's bare buttocks. Its blows left permanent scars. See Hochschild, *King Leopold's Ghost*, 199-259.

Ours is also the continent where not only humanity began but also where art did so. [5] One single proof of that are the African rock arts from the desert of Libya in the north to the desert of Namibia in the south, east, west and central, which share common naturalistic features. Interestingly, rock arts in South Africa bear the same pictorial resemblance with Chinese characters. According to the *Economist*, Africa may have 200,000 rock-art sites, more than any other continent. The oldest known site, in Namibia, is between 18,000 and 28,000 years old. Several African universities now have programmes to decipher the paintings and carvings. They are being helped by the Kenya-based Trust for African Rock Art (TARA), which seeks to discover and digitally archive as much of the art as it can for future scholars.[6] This is the truth which Western media, including the *Economist*, have to reckon with since Europeans could not have discovered Africa as one does not discover what has already existed for thousands of years and Africa boasts rich pre-colonial cultures. This is what this article aims to demonstrate.

Let me now explain why Ancient Egypt was also the cradle of science and why we lost scientific power.

Ancient Egypt's Scientific Achievements and Rich Cultural Heritage Prior to the Colonial Period

These achievements and heritage not only stand as a paragon of excellence, hard work and progress, but they should also challenge our consciences, especially those of our leaders and decision-makers. We Africans wear the best clothes which will probably not be made in Africa for a long time to come; we drive the best cars which will probably not be made in Africa for a long time to come; our leaders fly in the latest expensive and luxurious jets (Mobutu used to send his pilot to France just to buy wedding cakes) which will probably not be made in Africa for a long time to come; and I can go on and on. As the late president of the Democratic Republic of Congo (DRC), Laurent Kabila, said, "in Congo we import even our neck ties."

---

5   Rock Art Research Institute, The Rock Art of Africa, The University of Witwatersrand, https://www.wits.ac.za/science/schools/geography-archaeology-and-environmental-studies/research/rock-art-research-institute/about-rock-art/rock-art-of-africa/

6   "African rock arts: The continent's true history", *The Economist*, 1 May 2008.

Our ancestors' scientific achievements include metallurgy, building of infrastructure and temples, architecture, rock art in South Africa that resemble Chinese writing characters, navigation and shipbuilding technology, glassmaking, paper and writing, irrigation and agriculture, plant medicine and alchemy, furniture, rope making for mummification, and the Dendera light representing Ancient Egypt's electrical lighting technology.

Metallurgy: Our ancestors in Ancient Egypt and everywhere else in Africa used their own technology to process minerals to make tools, weapons, nails, thrones, golden stools (in Ghana), crowns and jewellery. In other words, this was advanced metallurgy and steel-making,[7] following copper, iron, gold and mercury extraction.[8] Today we cannot even transform our minerals on the spot – including the manufacture of arms to defend political and economic sovereignty – thereby creating jobs and markets for our people on national, regional, continental and international levels and to improve their living standards. We can no longer afford to remain consumers forever of finished goods manufactured by others with Africa's own resources cheaply looted through Western-controlled mechanisms, including the International Monetary Fund (IMF), the World Bank, the United Nations(UN), Western non-governmental organizations (NGOs) or Western-controlled Catholic and Protestant churches. Very often, when our governments sign deals, especially in mining contracts, the investor enjoys 99 percent of the stakes while the state enjoys only 1 percent "plus commission." For instance, oil, gas and mineral exports from Africa, exported to countries including the United States (US), were worth $382 billion in 2011 alone – more than eight times the value of official development aid received by African countries.[9] Can you believe that, now in the DRC, records of all the coltan used for the manufacturing of computers and mobile phones, and the registration of births, marriages or deaths are by hand in a register. Only a few state offices make use of computers.

We have to ask ourselves two fundamental questions: What does the term investment mean? What does globalization mean? Take the

---

7. Shore, "Steel-Making in Ancient Africa," 157–162.
8. "Ancient Egyptian Science and Technology."
9. "Transparency: increasing resources for development," *ONE Policy Brief Report*, June 6, 2013, accessed August 18, 2014. www.one.org/c/international/policybrief/4696/.

DRC again. In the last sixteen years, Congo's natural and mineral resources have been systematically looted by the same powers used Rwanda and Uganda to kill 8 million people in Congo and use rape as a weapon of war. However, the same powers are coming back to the Democratic Republic of Congo as investors. What does the term "investor" mean in this case? You loot the wealth of Africa and you come back to Africa with Africa's money as an investor. Secondly, if America and its allies from the North Atlantic Treaty Organization (NATO) can bomb Iraq and Afghanistan back to the stone age and then award contracts to American companies to "rebuild" these countries, is that what "globalization" is all about? At the same time, a recent study by Global Financial Integrity (GFI) found that total illicit financial outflows from Africa were estimated at $ 854 billion during the period 1970–2008, which led President Thabo Mbeki to castigate what had clearly gone wrong: that is, the quality of leadership on our continent.[10]

Infrastructure and architecture: The Pharaoh's tombs or the pyramids[11]– especially Pharaoh Tutankhamun's rock-cut tomb in the Valley of the Kings, the Pyramids of Giza and the Great Sphinx – are among the largest and most famous buildings in the world, as well as the obelisks and other monuments built in the Nile valley, Ethiopia and Sudan. The more than eighty pyramids cover thirteen acres and are made of 2.25 million blocks of stone. Later, in the twelfth century and much further south, there were hundreds of great cities in Zimbabwe and Mozambique, notably the Great Zimbabwe.[12] There, massive stone complexes were the hubs of cities. One included a 250-meter-long, 15000-ton curved granite wall. The cities featured huge castle-like compounds with numerous rooms for specific tasks, such as iron-smithing. In the thirteenth century, the empire of Mali boasted impressive cities, including Timbuktu, with grand palaces, mosques and universities.[13]

---

10. Isilow, "Africa loses billions of dollars to illicit financial outflows," *Euro Asia News*, May 23, 2014, accessed http://euroasianews.com/africa-loses-billions-to-illicit-financial-outflows/.

11. Lumpkin, "The Pyramids: Ancient Showcase," 67–83.

12. Ndoro, "Your Monument, Our Shrine."

13. Van Sertima, "The Lost Sciences of Africa: An Overview," In Ivan Van Sertima, ed., *Blacks in Science. Ancient and Modern*, (New Brunswick: Transaction Books), 7–26.

All these prove that our ancestors were experts in mathematics, as they could accurately calculate distances and angles[14] and they could build their infrastructure, based on their own engineering. A 20000 counting-tool, called *Ishango Bone,* discovered in the DRC[15] in addition to the Yoruba counting system invented some 8000 years ago,[16] proved that our ancestors had developed their own numeration system. There was also expertise in astrology in Bakuba Empire in Congo,[17] and a developed and sophisticated agricultural system in ancient Congo.[18]

Today we cannot even build a wall without paying for foreign expertise, despite the fact that many African engineers graduate from our universities and abroad every year!

Navigation and shipbuilding technology: Sydella Blatch argues that we should unlearn what we have always been taught, namely that Europeans were the first to sail to the Americas.[19] Several lines of evidence however suggest that ancient Africans sailed to South America and Asia hundreds of years before Europeans.[20] Thousands of miles of waterways across Africa were trade routes. Many ancient societies in Africa built a variety of boats, including small, reed-based vessels, sailboats and grander structures with many cabins and even cooking facilities. The Mali and Songhai built boats 100 feet long and thirteen feet wide that could carry up to eighty tons.[21] Currents in the Atlantic Ocean flow from this part of West Africa to South America. Genetic evidence from plants and descriptions and art from societies inhabiting South America at the time suggest small numbers of West Africans sailed to the east coast of South America and remained there.[22] Contemporary scientists have reconstructed these ancient vessels and their fishing gear and have completed the transatlantic voyage successfully. Around the same time as they were sailing to South America, in the thirteenth century, these ancient peoples also sailed to China and back, carrying elephants as cargo.

---

14. Woods, *Science in Ancient Egypt.*
15. Muhagir, "Ishango Bone."
16. Zaslavsky, "The Yoruba Number System," 110, 125.
17. Jesman, "Background to Events," 388. See also: Jan Vansina "Recording the Oral History."
18. Vansina. *Paths in the Rainforests,* 71–123.
19. Blatch, "Minority Affairs."
20. Van Sertima, *They Came Before Columbus.*
21. Van Sertima, see note 11 above.
22. Ibid.

Glassmaking: Egyptian knowledge of glassmaking was advanced. The earliest known glass beads from Egypt were made during the New Kingdom around 1500 BC and were produced in a variety of colors, often beautifully patterned.[23]

Paper and Writing: The word "paper" comes from the Greek term for the ancient Egyptian writing material called papyrus, which was formed from beaten strips of papyrus plants. Papyrus was produced as early as 3000 BC in Egypt, and sold to ancient Greece and Rome. The establishment of the Library of Alexandria limited the supply of papyrus for others. As a result, according to the Roman historian, Pliny,[24] parchment was invented under the patronage of Eumenes II of Pergamon to build his rival library at Pergamon. Egyptian hieroglyphs, a phonetic writing system, served as the basis for the Phoenician alphabet from which later alphabets were derived. With this ability, writing and record keeping, the Egyptians developed one of the first decimal systems. The city of Alexandria retained pre-eminence for its records and scrolls in its library. That ancient library was damaged by fire when it fell under Roman rule, and was destroyed completely by 642 CE. With it, a huge amount of antique literature, history, and knowledge was lost.[25] Greek philosophers came to Egypt to study philosophy, literature, letters, writing, mathematics, astronomy, history, chronology and Arabs came to study medicine there. The Senegalese scholar, Cheikh Anta Diop, has proved that the ancient Egyptian civilization is not only black African, but also the origin of "Western" civilization, and especially the initiator of Greek civilization.[26]

Cheikh Anta Diop was proven to be right! First by Herodotus (the Greek historian, 484 – 425 BC) who called Africans "those wisemen occupying the Upper Nile, men of long life, whose manners and customs pertain to the Golden Age, those virtuous mortals whose feasts and banquets are honoured by Jupiter himself."[27]

Stephanus of Byzantium (author of *Ethnica*, a sixth century AD geographical dictionary), voiced the universal testimony of antiquity when he wrote, "It [Africa] was the first established country on earth

---

23. "Ancient Egyptian Science and Technology."
24. Natural History records, xiii.21.
25. "Ancient Egyptian Science and Technology."
26. Okafor, "Diop and the African origin,"252–268.
27. Read, *Children of Saba.*

and (its peoples) were the first to set up the worship of the gods and to establish laws."[28]

Irrigation and Agriculture: Irrigation as the artificial application of water to the soil was used to some extent in Ancient Egypt, a hydraulic civilization (which entails hydraulic engineering). In crop production, it is mainly used to replace missing rainfall in periods of drought, as opposed to reliance on direct rainfall (referred to as dryland farming or as rain-fed farming).[29] There is evidence of the ancient Egyptian pharaoh Amenemhet III in the twelfth dynasty (about 1800 BCE) using the natural lake of the Fayum as a reservoir to store surpluses of water for use during the dry seasons, as the lake swelled annually from the flooding of the Nile.

To lift the water from the canal they used a *shaduf*. A *shaduf* is a large pole balanced on a crossbeam, a rope and bucket on one end and a heavy counter weight at the other. The pulling of the rope helped to lower the bucket into the canal. The farmer then raised the bucket of water by pulling down on the weight. He then swung the pole around and emptied the bucket onto the field. Animals were very important to Egyptian farmers. Animals helped them with jobs like trampling in seeds, pulling the plough, eating unwanted grain or wheat and providing the Egyptians with food and drink. They kept animals such as cattle, goats, pigs, ducks, cows, and geese.[30]

Plant medicine and alchemy: According to Sydella Blatch, before the European invasion of Africa, medicine in what is now Egypt, Nigeria and South Africa, to name just a few places, was more advanced than medicine in Europe.[31] Some of these practices involved the use of plants with salicylic acid for pain (as in aspirin), kaolin for diarrhoea (as in Kaopectate), and extracts that were confirmed in the twentieth century as having the ability to kill Gram-positive bacteria.[32] Other plants used had anti-cancer properties, caused abortions and treated malaria –and these have been shown to be as effective as many modern-day Western treatments. Furthermore, Africans discovered ouabain, capsicum, physostigmine and reserpine. In addition, African

---

28. Ibid.
29. Wendorf, "An Ancient Harvest on the Nile,"58–64.
30. "Ancient Egyptian Science and Technology."
31. Blatch, "Minority Affairs." See also Frederick Newsome, "Black Contributors,"127–139.
32. Van Sertima, "The Lost Science of Africa."

cultures preformed surgeries under antiseptic conditions universally when this concept was only emerging in Europe.[33] Medical procedures performed in ancient Africa before they were performed in Europe include vaccination, autopsy, limb traction and broken bone setting, bullet removal, brain surgery, skin grafting, filling of dental cavities, installation of false teeth, what is now known as Caesarean section, anaesthesia and tissue cauterization.[34]

Furniture: The Egyptians developed a variety of furniture. There in the lands of ancient Egypt is the first evidence for stools, beds, and tables (such as those found in tombs similar to Tutankhamen's). Recovered Ancient Egyptian furniture includes a bed – from the third millennium BC – discovered in the Tarkhan Tomb; a 2550 BC gilded set from the tomb of Queen Hetepheres; and a 1550 BC stool from Thebes.[35]

Rope making factories for uses such as mummification.[36]

Astronomy: According to Sydella Blatch, several ancient African cultures birthed discoveries in astronomy. Many of these are foundations on which we still rely, and some were so advanced that their mode of discovery still cannot be understood.[37] Egyptians charted the movement of the sun and constellations and the cycles of the moon. They divided the year into twelve parts and developed a year-long calendar system containing 365 and a quarterdays.[38] Clocks were made with moving water and sundial-like clocks were used.[39]

A structure known as the African Stonehenge in present-day Kenya (constructed around 300 BC) was a remarkably accurate calendar.[40] The Dogon people of Mali amassed a wealth of detailed astronomical observations.[41] Many of their discoveries were so advanced that some

33. Ibid.
34. Woods, "Science in Ancient Egypt." See also, Newsome, "Black Contributors,"127–139.
See also Finch, "The African Background of Medical Science,"140–156.
35. "Ancient Egyptian Science and Technology."
36. Ibid.
37. Blatch, "Minority Affairs."
38. Woods, "Science in Ancient Egypt."
39. Ibid.
40. Lynch and Robbins, "Namoratunga," 766–768.
41. Adams, "African Observers of the Universe," 27–46.

modern scholars credit their discoveries instead to space aliens or unknown European travellers, even though the Dogon culture is steeped in ceremonial tradition centered on several space events. The Dogon knew of Saturn's rings, Jupiter's moons, the spiral structure of the Milky Way and the orbit of the Sirius star system. Hundreds of years ago, they plotted orbits in this system accurately through the year 1990.[42] They knew this system contained a primary star and a secondary star (now called Sirius B) of immense density and not visible to the naked eye.

The Dendera light representing Ancient Egypt's electrical lighting technology: Beneath the Temple of Hathor at the Dendera Temple complex located in Egypt, there are inscriptions depicting a bulb-like object which some have suggested is reminiscent of a "Crookes tube" (an early light bulb). Inside the "bulbs", a snake forms a wavy line from a lotus flower (the socket of the bulb). A "wire" leads to a small box on which the air god is kneeling. Beside the bulb stands a two-armed djed pillar, which is connected to the snake, and a baboon bearing two knives. In *The Eyes of the Sphinx,* Erich Von Daniken suggested that the snake represented the filament, the djed pillar was an insulator, and the tube was in fact an ancient electric light bulb.[43] The fact remains that the Dendera light resembles the modern light bulb.[44]

Glorious Past; Unenviable Present

Now, after surveying all these feats of science and culture, the following question arises: How come a people, the African people, with a glorious past, a rich civilization and culture, scientifically and technologically, find themselves today at the bottom of the ladder of development without jobs and without prosperity, despite the African growth that is being talked about?

Once more, let us use our most ancient Egyptian civilization as a case study to address this fundamental question. We propose three answers:

(1) Internal divisions weakened Egypt and facilitated its invasion by the Arab Turks, the Persians, the Greeks, the British and the French successively.

---

42. Ibid.
43. Hill, "The Dendera Lightbulb."
44 "Ancient Egyptian Science and Technology."

(2) The penetration of foreign philosophy and religious thoughts eroded the Egyptian traditional culture, religion and art.

(3) The Egyptian language and script got mixed with the Roman and Greek languages and this eroded the Egyptian culture and undermined Egyptian science and technology.

That is how and that is why we got lost. With the loss of our own way of doing things, we lost our political and economic power. Our culture was uprooted and never replanted, so much so that we became alienated from our own identity. If Africa has to find its own path of development through promoting its own science and technology – because that is where our evolution was cut short –it has to rely on its diverse traditions and cultures which make up the universal African culture. In fact, African culture and science have always been good bedfellows as life in ancient Egypt proved. This is because in the African philosophy, there is no division between the natural and the supernatural, between the physical and metaphysical, between the spiritual and the material world and therefore there is no division between science and culture. There is no dualism. Dualism was brought to Africa by colonial Christianity and Islam which, during the colonial time, induced Africans to pray for better things in heaven while the land, which can be used to produce those better things, was taken away from Africans by the conquerors using force or subterfuge. As Jomo Kenyatta famously said, "When the white men came they asked us to kneel down, close our eyes and join them in prayers. When it was all over and we opened our eyes, we had their Bible and they had our land."[45]

In addition, we are in era of globalization, but as Molefi Kete Asante asks herself: who does not know that foreign diplomats, Peace Corps volunteers, missionaries, NGO workers and other expatriates serve as secret informants for foreign governments, human right groups, or business entities with exploitative intentions?[46]

Africa underwent ten centuries of slavery, as a result of Arab and Western domination, and more than 150 years of colonialism and neo-

---

45 Ali A. Mazrui, *Cultural Forces in World Politics*, London: James Curry, 1990, pp. 1 – 14.

46. Asante, "Resurgence of African World,"231.

colonialism. In fact, some "independent African countries" still have to pay taxes to France to this day.[47]

The fact that we no longer think for ourselves or take our own initiatives was best illustrated by Ugandan journalist Andrew Mulindwa who on January 22, 2012, asked President Thabo Mbeki, that day a guest of honour at the Makerere Institute of Social Research, to comment on the mere flag and anthem independence we received without changing our conditions and the nature of our relations with our former colonial powers. This is how Mulindwa put it:

> Whether it is in literature, philosophy, politics or art, there is very little output about Africa by Africans. Our freedom today is fought for by Human Rights Watch and Amnesty International, our press freedom is fought for by the Committee to Protect Journalists and Reporters without Borders, our civil wars are ended by UN peacekeepers, our refugees are fed by the United Nations High Commissioner for Refugees (UNHCR), our economic policies are determined by the World Bank and IMF, our poverty is fought by Bono and Jeffery Sachs, our crimes are adjudicated upon by the International Criminal Court (ICC), our liberation is achieved through NATO war planes. I just wanted you to comment on that part of Africa that is happening today.[48]

Like President Thabo Mbeki, we believe that Mulindwa is right. African renaissance is about rekindling the progressive movement in Africa, the kind Africa had in the 1960s, especially in universities. The continental dream of Kwame Nkrumah, Patrice Lumumba, Ahmed Sekou Touré, Amilcar Cabral, Félix-Roland Moumié, Jomo Kenyatta, Julius Nyerere, Kenneth Kaunda (still with us) Steve Biko, Nelson Mandela, Laurent-Désiré Kabila, Muammar Gaddafi, Laurent Gbagbo (unjustly imprisoned) to name but a few, must be kept alive as the like of Robert Mugabe are doing. President Thabo Mbeki rightly pointed out that if we do not do it, nothing will change.[49] NGOs and civil society organizations paid for by our former colonizers will continue to smother us and have us believe that when somebody is urinating over us, we should think that it is raining!

---

47. Koutonin, "14 African countries forced by France."
48. Ibid.
49. Ibid.

The Turning Point; There Must Be a Turning Point!

Africa's current challenges are huge but not insurmountable. With our abundance in human, natural and cultural resources and a young population, it is absolutely possible to pursue our own development path based on our own culture. We can build an Africa that is different from the Africa of previous centuries since our contact with the West, and we can claim the twenty-first century. How can we make the twenty-first century a turning point for our rich continent and even engage and co-shape the international environment to our own advantage; and deal with the rest of the world only in our own terms, together with the Global South in the framework of "South-South, Win-Win" cooperation?

Conclusion and Way Forward

There is an ancient African proverb which says that "To get lost is to learn the way". In order to find the way, we Africans must learn the following:

Using our own language for the development of science: In order to completely achieve our own scientific and technological know-how (we can also learn from others and perfect what we learn from others) and therefore our own economic development, we must use our own language to develop science theory and practice. Although African languages faced the onslaught of colonialism, they still show their resilience. China has achieved its own technological transformation because it is using its own language to develop science and technology. This applies to Japan and other Asian countries. A Chinese boy or girl can explain how PowerPoint works to his parents in Chinese and that ingrained knowledge in his or her own language makes a difference, while an African boy or girl can do so only in Portuguese, French or English. We can learn from others, and we must learn from the experience of others, but we must Africanize this.

The day when we will hear two African economists or scientists discussing their newly found scientific breakthroughs using our own African languages, that is when we will know that we have succeeded. In Africa, we rarely use our own native language to teach science, but we do so to teach the Bible. It is about changing the software in our brains. You can never dissociate one's language from one's identity.

African culture and science and technology must become good bedfellows, especially in the field of African traditional medicine and other fields. Hence the importance of culture as a fundamental element in any

131

development project of any country; at least the best elements of a culture that help the continent move forward. That is the Akan[50] concept of *Sankofa* (meaning "return to the past to move forward").[51] That is exactly what Chinese President Xi Jinping said in his speech at the Korber Foundation in Berlin on March 28, 2014: "History is the best teacher. It records the journey that every country has gone through, and offers guidance for its future development".[52]

African cultural values must be incorporated into the national, regional and continental development plans, including traditional solidarity mechanisms, such as *Likelemba*. The concept of *Likelemba* in Africa in general, and in the DRC in particular, is a system of solidarity savings, whereby several members put a certain sum of money in a "pot"; and every month, the total amount contained in the pot is then donated to one of the participating members. The secret of the success of *Likelemba* is the simpleness of its formula whereby many small amounts, which every member can easily spare, make one big prize. The winner has a fairly large amount with which he/she can do something extraordinary and, hopefully, break out of a financial circle of misery or lifestyle in which he/she might be stuck—especially during family events such as birth, marriage, death, pilgrimage, etc.[53]

In the DRC's rural areas, when a group of people take turns to help one another with work in the fields, this is also called *Likelemba*. This is the African philosophy of life or *"ubuntu"* (African humanness, the spirit of African communities): "I am because we are". Outside the community, I am nobody. The concept of *Likelemba* can also be applied in our relations with other emerging countries such as China, India and Brazil. We can say, China, India, Brazil, we supported you and you have gone ahead (Africa's contribution to your development has been huge); now you have to pull us up with you.

Priority for rural development, grassroots development, community mobilization: Our national, regional and continental development plans must be based on the people's needs and must stress an endogenous kind of development in which the people themselves, not the

---

50. Today, Akan people inhabit parts of Ghana and the Ivory Coast in West Africa.

51. Kanu, "Tradition and Educational Reconstruction,"66–84.

52. Available online at: http://english.cntv.cn/2014/03/29/VIDE1396039077777643.shtml

53. Sourced from http://en.wikipedia.org/wiki/Likelemba

multinationals, would become the main actors in defining their own priorities; starting with agriculture and from the village as the object and subject of rural development. This is because the village constitutes the basic unit of the African traditional society where subsistence agriculture is the main economic activity. Such a development plan therefore has a great political and historical significance.

As Molefi Kete Asante argues, at this stage of our development, we need to develop, first and foremost, rural areas and rural people. These people, and this type of development work, do not need that much from abroad. Therefore, the need for free trade and development to take place in rural areas, the site of the overwhelming majority of the African people, must become a priority, including eco-tourism, hotels and other non-agricultural industries. Africa needs to develop and conceptualize a new and different relationship between the city and the countryside, between urban and rural communities, from that which exists in the developed West, and which we inherited from the West. [54]

As Patrice Lumumba wrote in his last letter to his wife Pauline Opango, "Africa must write its own history, and it will be, to the north and to the south of the Sahara, a history of glory and dignity." Although we do not need to live in smoke-suffocating mud huts and tin houses in the twenty-first century, Molefi Kete Asante further argues that it is disastrous that we should see cities like New York City, London, Berlin, Mexico City, New Delhi, Paris, Brussels, etc., emerging in Africa. The African ecology, the world ecology, and humankind as a whole do not need such a development. We have a precious rare opportunity in Africa as the last continent to plan industrialization, to bring about a new, and healthier (not just physically, but also spiritually) relationship between the countryside and the city. We need to learn from China in this regard. Thanks to Mao Zedong's "To the Countryside" revolution, the major thrust forward in the development of the Chinese economy in the 1980s and 1980s was provided by the development in which there were so many striking innovations. [55]

Empowerment of African women: We have to change certain aspects of our culture, such as those that prevent girls from going to school.

---

54. Asante, "Resurgence of African World," 217–218.
55. Ibid.

African women must be encouraged to study engineering and advanced science, especially African girls who receive scholarships to study in China. In fact, China recently sent a woman into space.

Scientific and technological innovation: When Africans meet, they should not just talk about war and conflict. Africans must stop fighting each other, should unite to only fight the common enemies they have: poverty, under-development and backwardness. They must unite together to solve their problems through scientific and technological innovation, entrepreneurship – especially in rural areas – drawing inspiration from their glorious past, their traditions and cultural heritage.

Africa unite! We have to speak with one voice and refuse to be used one against the other – divide and rule – as Rwanda and Uganda, backed by the US and Britain, have just invaded Congo, killing 8 million people, looting Congo's wealth and using rape as a weapon of war and occupying land; and that war was aimed also at kicking China out of Congo; we have to reject the Washington consensus, rely on ourselves in cooperation with our true friends(China and South America) in order to bust those mechanisms (Churches, IMF, World Bank structural adjustment mechanism, Africom – I call it Africoma because it puts Africa into a coma –civil societies and NGOs, both local and international, all financed from outside, and aid agencies), which have been put in place to keep Africa down always and last in the queue. And as the financial crisis bites, cunning Western powers are adding new mechanisms such as telling African countries "to ensure a better environment for business" and homosexual rights. That is a ploy, because they want to revive their economies, and as the situation in Libya and the Ivory Coast demonstrates, they will not hesitate to use military power to grab African resources in order to revive their economies hit by the global financial crisis.

In fact, African unity is what Western powers fear most. Pan-Africanism is considered by France as a "threat to Western interests in Africa", as a French defense report indicated in October 2012.[56]

According to a Bloomberg report, the possible launch of the African Monetary Union has already stirred the criticism of France!

---

56. "Côte d'Ivoire: French Defense Report Views Pan-Africanism As Threat to West," *Le Nouveau Courrier Online*, October 18, 2012. Accessed August 22, 2014. http://www.biyokulule.com/view_content.php?articleid=5301.

That is because a hoard of cash sits in the Bank of France: $20 billion of African money is held in trust by the French government and earning just 0.75 percent interest. Now economists and politicians from fourteen Central and West African countries say they want their funds returned and an arrangement dating back to the days when France's colonial empire ended. France holds the money to guarantee that the CFA franc, the currency used in the fourteen nations, stays convertible into euros at a fixed exchange rate of 655.957.[57] The compulsory deposits started more than half a century ago, when the then-colonies had to place all their financial reserves in the French Treasury. The deposit requirement has dropped over the decades: today the African members entrust 50percent of their reserves to Paris. That's a lot of money. According to the 2012 annual report of the Bank of France, the amount of African cash it safeguards is larger than the individual gross domestic product of all but two of the nations in the CFA region. CFA originally stood for *Colonies Francaises d'Afrique*, and now means either *Coopération Financière en Afrique Centrale* or *Communauté Financière Africaine*, depending on the country. Member states in the monetary union include Chad, Senegal, Mali, Cameroon, and Ivory Coast.[58]

We have to unite and go the Chinese way as well as the South American way. We need to follow the Chinese way because we have to rely on ourselves instead of continuing to be dependent on our former colonizers; we have to protect our sovereignty and demand a new relationship with them based on our own terms, on mutual respect and win-win cooperation. We have to make France and other Western countries realize that they should stop "cutting the same tree branch on which they are sitting" (African proverb). South American countries are succeeding exactly because they have reached their own consensus instead of trusting the Commonwealth, the Francophonie, "Lusophonie", Washington Consensus and so on. As Noam Chomsky puts it, in the past decade, for the first time in 500 years, South America has taken successful steps to free itself from Western domination, another serious loss for America. The region has moved towards integration, and has begun to address some of the terrible internal problems of societies ruled by mostly Europeanized elites, tiny islands of extreme wealth in a sea of misery. They have also rid themselves of

---

57. Neuwirth, "African Monetary Union."
58. Ibid.

all US military bases and of IMF controls. A newly formed organization, the community of Latin American and Caribbean states (CELAC), includes all countries of the hemisphere apart from the US and Canada. If it actually functions, that would be another step in American decline, in this case in what has always been regarded as "the backyard."[59]

No to corrupt leadership: Some African leaders, not all of them, should stop amassing personal wealth with state funds while paying little attention to the socio-economic needs facing their people.[60] Our government should stop placing Western public relations agents, American European and Israeli advisers in their cabinets. It is a matter of self-respect and dignity! These practices will not work in the long run, because now in Africa and in the Diaspora, there is a very informed populace.

Proud to be an African, pride in our African identity: We must teach our children to be proud of their roots, of their traditions and cultures. They are the Africa of tomorrow. Let us not downgrade our own traditional and cultural values as a matter of mere curiosity for foreign tourists (inferiority complex). Our identity is who we are. Acculturation is the biggest danger facing Africa. Despite all the woes faced by our African continent today, we must always be proud to be Africans. So, despite the ardent psychological warfare waged against Africa through the Western media, public relations and Western academia, we should not be ashamed to be Africans. If we give in to this massive intoxication and manipulation and turn our back on our continent who will make it better for us? Even China our true friend is there to support us. China cannot do everything in our place. China is not the saviour of Africa. The Chinese have come to teach us how to fish, not to give us a fish!

Bibliography

"Ancient Egyptian Science and Technology," *Cristalinks,* 2011. Accessed August 18, 2014.http://www.crystalinks.com/egyptscience.html.

Adams, Hunter H. "African Observers of the Universe: The Sirius Question." In *Blacks in Science: Ancient and Modern,* 27–46. 1983.

---

59. Chomsky, "The Imperial Way."
60. Ayittey, *Africa Betrayed,* 142–152.

Akomolafe, Femi. "On The Claims Of Christianity." *GhanaWeb*, May 27, 2014. Accessed August 18, 2014. http://www.ghanaweb.com/GhanaHomePage/religion/artikel.php?ID=310636.

Anta Diop, Cheik. *The African Origin of Civilization: Myth or Reality.* Chicago: Chicago Review Press, 1989.

Asante, Molefi Kete. "The Resurgence of the African World in the 21st Century." In *Africa in the 21st Century: Toward a New Future*, edited by Ama Mazama, 231. New York: Routledge Taylor & Francis Group, 2007.

Ayittey, George. *Africa Betrayed*, 142–152. New York: Palgrave Macmillan, 1993.

Blatch, Sydella. "Minority Affairs: Great achievements in science and technology in ancient Africa." *American Society for Biochemistry and Molecular Biology (ASBMB)*, February 2013.Accessed August 18, 2014. http://www.asbmb.org/asbmbtoday/asbmbtoday_article.aspx?id=32437.

Chomsky, Noam. "The Imperial Way: American decline in perspective, Part 2." *Asia Times*, Feb 17, 2012.http://atimes.com/atimes/Global_Economy/NB17Dj02.html.

Economist, "African rock arts: The continent's true history", 1 May 2008.

Finch, Charles S. "The African Background of Medical Science." In *Blacks in Science: Ancient and Modern*, 140–156. New Jersey: Transaction Books, 1983.

Hill, J. "The Dendera Lightbulb." *Ancient Egypt Online*, 2011. Accessed August 18, 2014.http://www.ancientegyptonline.co.uk/Denderahlightbulb.html.

Hochschild, Adam. *King Leopold's Ghost*, 199–259. London: Papermac/Macmillan Publishers Ltd, 2000.

Jesman, Czeslaw. "Background to Events in the Congo." *African Affairs*, Vol. 58 (March 2, 1961): 388.

Kanu, Yatta. "Tradition and Educational Reconstruction in Africa in Postcolonial and Global Times: The Case for Sierra Leone." *African Studies Quaterly*, Volume 10, No.3 (2007): 66–84.

Koutonin, Mawuna Remarque. "14 African countries forced by France to pay colonial tax for the benefits of slavery and colonization."

Silicon Africa, January 28, 2014. Accessed August 18, 2014.http://www.siliconafrica.com/france-colonial-tax/.

Lumpkin, Beatrice. "The Pyramids: Ancient Showcase of African Science & Technology." In *Blacks in Science: Ancient and Modern*, 67–83. New Jersey: Transaction Books, 1983.

Lynch B.M. and L.H. Robbins. Namoratunga: The First Archeoastronomical Evidence in Sub-Saharan Africa: *Science*, Vol. 200 No. 4343 (19 May 1978): 766–768.

Mazrui, Ali A. *Cultural Forces in World Politics*, London: James Curry, 1990, pp. 1 – 14 .

Muhagir, M.A. "Ishango Bone: a 20000 years old African mathematical document." September, 1, 2010. Accessed August 18, 2014. *Sudaneseonline.com.*
http://www.sudaneseonline.com/cgibin/esdb/2bb.cgi?seq=msg &board=12&msg=1283356463&rn=0.

Murdock, D.M./Acharya S. "Archaeologist: Egyptian religion forms the roots of Jewish, Christian, Islamic religious tree," *Freethought Nation*, August 28, 2011. Accessed August 18, 2014.http://freethoughtnation.com/archaeologist-egyptian-religion-forms-the-roots-of-jewish-christian-islamic-religious-tree/.

Ndoro, Webber, "Your Monument, Our Shrine: The Preservation of the Great Zimbabwe." *Studies in African Archaeology* 19, 2001. Doctoral Thesis in Archaeology: Uppsala University. Accessed August 18, 2014. http://www.arkeologi.uu.se/digitalAssets/32/32403_3ndoro_4.pdf.

Neuwirth, Robert. "African Monetary Union Stirs Criticism of France." *Bloomberg*, April 17, 2014. Accessed August 22, 2014. http://www.businessweek.com/articles/2014-04-17/african-monetary-union-stirs-criticism-of-france.

Newsome, Frederick. "Black Contributors to the Early History of Western Medicine". In *Blacks in Science: Ancient and Modern*, 127–139. New Jersey: Transaction Books, 1983.

Okafor, Victor Oguejiofor. "Diop and the African origin of civilization: An Afro-centric analysis." *Journal of Black Studies*, Volume 22, Issue, 22 (1991): 252–268.

Osman, Ahmed. "The Ten Commandments and the Book of the Dead." *Out of Egypt. An Educational Forum based on new historical and scientific discoveries,* 2001. Accessed August 18,

2014.http://dwij.org/forum/amarna/2 cmndmts book of the dead.html.

Read, N.K. *Children of Saba (The Epic of Aphrike Trilogy)*, African Books, 2013.

Rock Art Research Intitute, The Rock Art of Africa, The University of Witwatersrand, https://www.wits.ac.za/science/schools/geography-archaeology-and-environmental-studies/research/rock-art-research-institute/about-rock-art/rock-art-of-africa/

Sertima, Ivan Van. *They Came Before Columbus: The African Presence in Ancient America (Journal of African Civilizations)*. New York: Random House, 2003.

Shore, Debra, "Steel-Making in Ancient Africa." In *Blacks in Science: Ancient and Modern*, 157–162. New Jersey: Transaction Books, 1983.

Vansina, Jan. *Paths in the Rainforests: Toward a History of Political Tradition in Equatorial Africa*, 71–123. London: James Currey, 1990.

Vansinaa, Jan, "Recording the Oral History of the Bakuba II." *Journal of African History*, Vol. 1, No. 2, 1960.

Wendorf, Fred. "An Ancient Harvest on the Nile." In *Blacks in Science: Ancient and Modern*, 68–64. New Jersey: Transaction Books, 1983. http://afritorial.com/africas-greatest-story/.

Woods, Geraldine. *Science in Ancient Egypt*. London: Franklin Watts, 1988.

Zaslavsky, Claudia, "The Yoruba Number System." In *Blacks and Science: Ancient and Modern*, 110, 125. New Jersey: Transaction Books, 1983.

Chapter Six. Locating the "Nation" in African Innovation Systems: Implications for Africa-China Economic Relations

==============❖==============

Ogundiran Soumonni

Introduction

The objective of this paper is to interrogate the apparent lack of a strategy on the part of African countries for acquiring technological capabilities (including both technical and related managerial know-how) from foreign direct investment (FDI) and other economic relations with other nations. While many African governments have praised the preferential trade and loan agreements they have with China, there has also been some measure of displeasure within segments of civil society. These perspectives generally point to the disadvantages investments create regarding the lack of credible job creation, poor quality goods, or the crowding out of locally manufactured products from the domestic market, as reported by Kwesi Kwaa Prah.[1] Some commentators even lament the lack of "technology transfer" from China in its dealings with Africa. In both discourses, not enough attention is paid to the value and influence of interests; in that it is not the primary responsibility of the foreign investor to resolve the socio-economic ills of a given country, but that of the host country itself. Indeed, the use of concepts and theories in

---

1   See the section entitled "Frequently Expressed Doubts" in Kwesi Kwaa Prah, *Afro-Chinese Relations*, 3–10.

modern innovation studies and related disciplines, such as absorptive capacity, technological learning, dynamic capabilities, or economic catch-up, among others, reveals that the dominant view in those scholarly communities is that the strategic burden of developing technological competence rests on the host firm, region or country that seeks it. However, the view that technological and industrial capabilities are related to a people's survival, competitiveness, and overall quest for self-determination, is not limited to the influential thinkers in the disciplines listed above, but has already been central to the visions of many African leaders in the modern period, that is, beginning with Haiti at the turn of the nineteenth Century.[2]

Thus, in the context of this book's focus on the Afro-Chinese partnership, the question of what understanding or framing of "Africa" is most germane for bringing about a mutually beneficial and reciprocal relationship between the two peoples cannot be circumvented. While China as a nation-state is generally understood to be a dominant global player and a rising super power, the Africa that engages it, whether through the aegis of the African Union (AU) or as individual countries, cannot, by any measure, be said to have nearly the same degree of internal coherence or commonality of purpose to contend with China's level of preparedness with respect to its international relations. As such, this chapter will begin with a critical exposition of some of the main dimensions, institutions, as well as contending frameworks that seek to guide an "African project", and more specifically, which of these might be more promising for the purpose of scientific and technological development. However, it privileges the historical and cultural bases for African unity or "nationhood" (as articulated by Marcus Garvey, Cheikh Anta Diop, and more recently, Kwesi Kwaa Prah)[3] and employs this understanding

---

2   Haiti was the first country in the Western Hemisphere to abolish slavery and as such, its revolution stands out in world history. Secondly, its establishment, following successful victories over three European slaving nations, also made it the first black republic in the world and for this reason, it represents a victory for the African world. Thirdly, its leading general Toussaint Louverture was born to an enslaved prince from the Allada nation in today's Benin Republic, and its first emperor, Jean-Jacques Dessalines, is widely reported to have consistently referred to himself as an African.

3   See Chapter 3 on "Nationhood" in Tony Martin, *Race First*, 41–66; the Foreword in Cheikh Anta Diop, *The Cultural Unity of Black Africa* 3-4; and

as its conceptual framework rather than the civic and geographic bases (propounded by Léopold Sédar Senghor, Kwame Nkrumah and SKB Asante)[4] for what might be more appropriately termed African "statehood." One reason for this choice is that it is the more comparable one to the modern China that is being referred to by one of its leading scholars, Zhang Weiwei, as being more than just a country or a nation-state, but as a civilizational state, that is, an endogenous civilization that acquires insights from other nations, while maintaining its own "intrinsic logic of evolution" and identity.[5]

The chapter is organized as follows. In the first section, I discuss the analytical framework for the chapter, that is, the emphasis on the historico-cultural understanding of the African reality over the civic one, as the more effective one for stimulating and catalysing the disposition and human resources needed for building technological capabilities. Secondly, I provide an overview of innovation and capability-building efforts in Africa, with a view towards highlighting the various scales at which such a capability might be more effective.

Chapter 5 on "Nations, Nationalism and the National Question" in Kwesi Kwaa Prah, *The African Nation*, 196231.

4   See Léopold Sédar Senghor, who distinguishes between the race (a physical community), a people or ethnic group or civilization (a cultural or metalinguistic community) and the nation or state (a political community) in *Les Fondement de L'Africanité ou Négritude et Arabité*, 9–11. We therefore understand his conflation of the nation and the state as synonymously referring to a political community and his elevation of the latter over other categories, as being clearly indicative of a greater commitment to African "statehood" as in our characterization of that position. For Kwame Nkrumah, in *Class Struggle in Africa*, 88, while a common territory, a common culture or a common language may be features of a nation, in his words: "In some cases, only one of the three applies. A state may exist on a multi-national basis. The community of economic life is the major feature within a nation, and it is the economy which holds together the people living in a territory." Likewise, we see a fusion of the nation and the state in Nkrumah's thinking, with its fundamental basis as the economic relations among the constituent actors, with the ultimate goal being to "advance the triumph of the international socialist revolution, and the onward progress towards world communism". Lastly, see SKB Asante, *Regionalism and Africa's Development*, for his emphasis on modern African states as the basis for regional integration.

5   Zhang Weiwei, Zhang, *The China Wave: Rise of a Civilizational State*.

Here, I employ the National Systems of Innovation framework as originally developed by Chris Freeman[6] but modified in favour of the version in Mammo Muchie's work that goes beyond the existing African states[7], while seeking to prioritize the ontology of the nation over that of the state. Thirdly, I provide a sketch of some salient insights and examples from the literature about the way in which the innovation system in China, in particular, and those of some of the other Newly Industrialized Countries (NICs) in Asia were able to acquire their own technological know-how from foreign firms in a relatively short period of time. Fourthly, I assess some of the ways in which African societies can learn from these experiences and adapt them in their relationship with China as well as other more industrially advanced countries. This aspect of the analysis is carried out with the intention of helping to change the relative emphasis on the part of African countries from trading their natural resource endowments for foreign exchange towards developing strategies for acquiring the much more valuable technological capabilities that can only be accumulated over time in human bodies and minds as proposed by the South Korean innovation scholar, Keun Lee.[8] Finally, in light of the generally positive disposition between African countries and China, I synthesize these considerations and provide some insights and recommendations for both policy and practice, which should contribute to fostering a more healthy and balanced Africa-China partnership predicated on mutual interests, goodwill, and a reciprocal recognition of sovereignty.

Historico-Cultural Basis for the African Nation

When one analyses the history of Africa over the *longue durée*, it becomes obvious that the emergence of its modern states was neither inevitable, nor is there any reason to believe that these states will be eternal in their present form. Indeed, the number of border contestations and threats of secession on the continent, as well as the creation of new states (most recently, South Sudan), confirms the highly contingent and mutable nature of its countries. This version of Africa that is the legacy of its partition at the Berlin Conference (1884 – 1885), and the present-day leadership and developmental challenges, has been defined as "the problematic Africa" by Olabiyi Yaï, who distinguishes it from the understanding that reflects "the sum total of

---

6   Chris Freeman, *The 'National System of Innovation' in historical perspective*.
7   Mammo Muchie, *Re-thinking Africa's Development*, 43–62.
8   Keun Lee, *Schumpeterian Analysis of Economic Catch-up*.

African cultures as sedimented for millennia in philosophies, wisdoms, ways of being and doing things, as well as ways of relating to otherness."[9]

The distinction drawn above also characterizes the ambivalent relationship between Africans and the states in which they are citizens as was insightfully explained by Peter Ekeh, who famously theorized the existence of two public realms in Africa as being characterized by a primordial public (or ethnic domain) and a civic public (associated with governmental administration) – a bifurcation that is historically linked to colonial rule – as opposed to only one public sphere in Europe.[10] The main implication of the existence of these two public realms is that citizens are much more committed to the primordial public, which has the same moral imperatives as the private realm (that is, family and private property), while they typically have an amoral relationship, at best, with the civic public.[11] However, in a more recent assessment of this thesis in light of the socio-political context in Nigeria, Olayinka Akanle argues that even the primordial sphere is no longer immune from being corrupted by much of the ruling class, which similarly exploits the primordial and the civic spheres.[12] He then employs this observation as a premise to articulate the need for more compliance, coherence, and a democratic voice within the civic order.[13] While the primordial public may not be immune from corruption, the current study nevertheless proceeds from the starting point, in line with the proposition by Peter Ekeh, that the primordial public still wields enormous psychological, emotional and social significance over the citizens of the modern republics – a phenomenon that is reflected, in part, by the numerous ethno-national contestations within the borders of those states.

As such, the anchor for constructing an African nation (or nations) ought not to simply be based on its geography or the administrative and governmental structures that are currently in place, but more fundamentally, on the development and articulation of a *leitmotif*, that is, a motive force that would drive its peoples and polities, and that

---

9   Olabiyi Yaï, *Africa, African Diaspora and the Prospect of Global Cultural Dialogue.*
10   Peter Ekeh, *Colonialism and the Two Publics in Africa.*
11   Ibid.
12   Olayinka Akanle, *The Development Exceptionality of Nigeria.*
13   Ibid.

would be rooted in the collective history, culture and consciousness of their identity.[14] One of the most outstanding African historians of the twentieth century, the late Professor Cheikh Anta Diop, spent his life working to elucidate this basis for the creation of an African nation, dating back to antiquity, but more importantly, for the purpose of articulating a common understanding of the "profound cultural unity' of its past, despite the superficial appearance of an irreconcilable cultural heterogeneity.[15] In his words, "Only a real knowledge of the past can keep in one's consciousness the feeling of historical continuity essential to the consolidation of a multinational state."[16] The basis of this cultural unity, in his view, was the history of African matriarchy, which he explains as being a "harmonious" dualism, in which both sexes work to build a society where every member can develop fully based on his or her abilities.[17] Furthermore, the importance of this model for modern Africans is that this matriarchal system had privileged the woman as the mother of the family and therefore, of the nation, thereby normalizing her political role in a meaningful and effective manner, in what is referred to as women's rights in modern parlance.[18] Indeed, the exciting and compelling recent work by Oyeronke Oyewumi similarly contends that the institution of Ìyá (or motherhood in the Yòrubá language) is "historically the most consequential category in social, political, and spiritual organization" among the Yòrubá.[19] She further argues that Ìyá is not even a gender category in its origin, and proceeds to advance the idea of "matripotency" as an indigenous ethos that is based on the supremacy of motherhood and seniority, as opposed to the currently pervasive gender-based attitudes that are based on male dominance.[20]

Special attention is being paid to a few of these substantive and historically rooted constructions of nationhood to emphasize the premise of this chapter, which is that the more effective framework

---

14 For a cogent articulation of the reasons for the failures of regional groupings that are based on African states, which represent little that is organic to the history and culture of their peoples, see Chapter 1, "How We Lost Our Way", 59–61, in Kwesi Kwaa Prah, *The African Nation*.
15 Cheikh Anta Diop, *The Cultural Unity of Black Africa*, 1
16 Ibid., 4
17 Ibid., 108
18 Cheikh Anta Diop, *Black Africa*, 33–35
19 Oyeronke Oyewumi, *What Gender is Motherhood?*, 2.
20 Ibid.

for Africa's equitable engagement in international relations in general, and with China in particular, ought to be based on an organic, primordial conception of the nation, rather than the apparatus of the civic state, whether at the country, regional or continental level. This is important mainly because the notion of Sankofa historiography (critical retrieval) in Akan culture, and its equivalent in other African cultures was central to the self-definition of "pre-modern" nations going back to antiquity. It is important too to highlight that other nations in the world also go to great lengths to ground their ontology in the remote past in so far as they can. Indeed, the prominent Chinese scholars Zhang Weiwei and Wang Hui have been engaged in historically based discourses that interpret the rise of China by advancing notions such as the "civilizational state" and the non-Western "imagining" of the country, which merge the culture of its civilization with the exigencies of the state in the modern world.[21] This modern state therefore maintains features of its millennia of a unifying history and culture among hundreds of states – thus the appellation of the "civilizational state."[22]

In a none too dissimilar manner, Élisée Soumonni has argued that the colonial heritage represents a disintegrating force for Africans; that the basis of any unity built on this basis is fragile, as attested by minimal progress from such initiatives at various levels; and that a more serious study of the precolonial period would reveal much more solid bases – cultural, economic, linguistic, etc. – for their unification.[23] In an earlier classic work, I.A. Akinjogbin had referred to Ẹbí social theory, as the guiding framework for nationhood in Aja and Yòrubá societies prior to the onset of European-led slavery.[24] This concept, which was more practised than theorized about, meant that people viewed the nation as an extended family founded by a common ancestor and as a commonwealth of polities that descend from this founding ancestor, rather than as civic citizens of a given state.[25] Olabiyi Yaï provides

---

21   See Emilian Kavalski's reviews of *The China Wave: Rise of a Civilizational State*; and *The Politics of Imagining Asia*

22   Zhang Weiwei, *The China Wave.*

23   Élisée Soumonni, *L'Héritage Colonial et l'Unité Africaine.*

24   I..A. Akinjogbin, *Dahomey and Its Neighbours*, 16.

25   Ibid. See also the enlightening discussion by Asmarom Legesse in *Oromo Democracy*, 1–14, where he discusses the indigenous democratic political system of the Oromo, which in his view, has been minimized in the more dominant "Ethiopianist" academic school of thought that favors an

further insight in demonstrating that the definition of a nation in these societies, both on the continent and its diaspora, was not primarily the place where a person was born, but that more importantly, it represented his or her identification with the values that this place stood for – that is, the person's membership in the *Ẹbí* or commonwealth.[26] This dynamic can be seen among Afro-Brazilian returnees, who are called the *Aguda* in the present-day Republic of Benin to signify their Brazilian provenance, but who are simultaneously well-integrated into local ethnic nations.[27] Similarly, African descended groups in the province of Bahia in Brazil, for instance, continue to identify with their nations of origin in Africa through the use of such terms as *Nago* to refer to Yòrubá groups, and *Jeje* to refer to Fon groups, even though both were always permeable to individuals from other nationalities.[28]

As a consequence of such an understanding, there was no contradiction in people claiming membership in different nations for various purposes and due to their strong psychological and affective ties, these original identities have been preserved till today. Indeed, it is reported that the Haitian revolutionary and statesman, Jean-Jacques Dessalines, although born in the Caribbean, consistently referred to himself humorously and boastfully as being *"un sauvage africain"* (more accurately interpreted as being "a natural African").[29] He reiterated this claim in order to emphasize his socialization and self-identification as an African, with his reference points being sovereign nations in Africa, rather than the conditions of enslavement and colonial subjugation in the French colony of Saint-Domingue.[30] Furthermore, it is not surprising to note that he owed his lifelong education primarily to the *Ìyá*, that is, the archetypal mother figures in his life – his biological mother, his aunt, Toya, (also called Agbaraya, which literally means

Orientalist and monarchist perspective rather than an Africanist one on the country's diverse peoples. I acknowledge Mr. Amanuel Gebremeskel for directing me to this work.

26 Olabiyi Yaï, *African Diasporan Concepts and Practice of the Nation and their Implications in the Modern World*.

27 Élisée Soumonni, *Some Reflections on the Brazilian Legacy in Dahomey*.

28 See Olabiyi Yaï, *African Diasporan Concepts and Practice of the Nation and their Implications in the Modern World*. See also Élisée Soumonni, *Some Reflections on the Brazilian Legacy in Dahomey*.

29 Berthony Dupont, *Jean-Jacques Dessalines*.

30 Ibid.

Strength of the Mother), his spiritual counsellor, Mambo Grann Gitonn, his wife, Marie-Claire Heureuse Félicité Dessalines, his comrade-in-arms, Marie-Jeanne Lamartinière, and even his oldest daughter and fellow combatant, Marie-Françoise Célimène Dessalines.[31] This particular diasporic experience would, in my view, seem to confirm easily the persistence of the concept and practice of matripotency among African people (as advanced by Oyeronke Oyewumi)[32], who identify with their historico-cultural roots, in spite of the spatial and temporal distance from their ancestral homeland.

Given the preceding background, it is very difficult, even for a keen observer of African countries, to identify any profound moral and historical ontological basis or epistemological construction of citizenship in most of the states, beyond the paraphernalia of flags, the uniforms of security forces and football teams, or the declarations contained in anthems and pledges. While these may help to build national sensibilities to a certain extent, the more profound preoccupation of the African scholars highlighted above is with the development of modern countries or regional groupings that are animated by the organic cultural values of their peoples and the lived reality of their permeable, overlapping and evolving nationalities, as opposed to the current bifurcation between the state and the nation that muddles any coherent sense of a collective vision, as is currently the case.

African Systems of Innovation

One of the most influential paradigms for planning for knowledge-driven economies rather than resource-based ones is the National Systems of Innovation framework, which views innovation in terms of a set of national institutions that interact to facilitate the diffusion and development of new technologies in a manner that enables a given country to acquire, maintain and advance its relative capability for self-development. Nevertheless, scientific and technological knowledge (e.g. technological inventions) require a system of other actors to be diffused throughout an economy or a society and need not necessary depend on a national network of actors. Indeed, even at the level of a

---

31 For a fascinating exposition of twenty-one little known facts about the life of Jean-Jacques Dessalines based on a combination of oral history and written documents, see Bayyinah Bello, *Jean-Jacques Dessalines.*
32 Oyeronke Oyewumi, *What Gender is Motherhood?*

firm or organization, the American economic sociologist, Arthur Stinchcombe, has reasoned that turning an invention into an innovation, that is, one that actually has an impact in either the economic or social sphere, is actually creating a social system that has to nurture technical ideas, make investments in risky situations, and arrange the division of benefits so that both investors and personnel are motivated to develop the competences that are needed to do all these things, and actually do them.[33] Thus, even if we concede that it is easier to specify the collective goal in a profit-seeking firm as primarily being pecuniary, it does not undermine the idea that an innovation "system" is a social one and that the various actors involved are driven to acquire the capabilities needed to accomplish a common objective. However, while a "national system" of innovation in Western countries, for instance, would to a large extent, mirror a "social system" of innovation, following the argument by Peter Ekeh outlined earlier, this is not the case in Africa.

It is of little surprise, therefore, that the European and American scholars who pioneered the modern concept of national systems of innovation, such as, Chris Freeman, Bengt-Åke Lundvall and Richard Nelson, equated the countries that they analyzed with nations. However, Chris Freeman perceptively argued that long before the advent of modern nation-states, both social and technical innovations had a significant impact on economic life, whether they were city-states, principalities or empires.[34] As such, he proposed a view of innovation systems that emphasized the complementarity and interactions between sub-national, national, and supra-national geographical entities as they have evolved over time.[35] Indeed, the inspiration for the concept of national systems of innovation goes back to the German political economist, Friedrich List, who published a three-volume work entitled "The National System of Political Economy" in 1841, wherein he articulated a range of policies and strategies that Germany, in conjunction with other Germanic countries (Austria, Holland and Denmark), might deploy in order to overtake England, which was then the leading industrial and economic power in Europe.[36]

---

33 Arthur L. Stinchcombe, *Turning Inventions into Innovations*.
34 Chris Freeman, *Continental, national and sub-national innovation systems*.
35 Ibid.
36 Chris Freeman, *The 'National System of Innovation' in historical perspective*.

A very insightful article on the role of African states in promoting innovation-based development by Banji Oyelaran-Oyeyinka outlines a series of issues that have caused the vast majority of the states to fail at this mission, namely: the lack of a collective vision by the leadership; little or no attempt to create a coherent system of innovation or even of production; inadequate regulations and the flawed enforcement of these in both the public and private sectors; and an insufficient development of human and infrastructure capabilities that would enable the state to "mid-wife" domestic entrepreneurs in targeted sectors.[37] While this critical appraisal is extremely helpful in identifying the bottlenecks that need to be overcome, the argument in this chapter is that these kinds of challenges faced by the state are not merely bureaucratic or organizational failures, but are more fundamentally reflective of the ontology of the post-colonial state *vis-à-vis* the challenges of the African nation. It therefore becomes apparent that the national systems of innovation approach, as developed and applied by its originators, is not cognate with the amoral and apathetic civic order that Peter Ekeh identified in African states. In that conception then, it stands to reason that only the kind of morality that is engendered by the primordial public, which he defined as ranging from the family to the clan to the ethnic group, can stimulate the kind of motivation, vision and sense of a shared destiny needed to engender the type of knowledge-driven economic and social transformation that African societies need. This point will be further developed later in the chapter.

In spite of the problematic character of their states, we nonetheless welcome the fact that a few African countries, namely, South Africa, Ghana, Nigeria and Kenya, among others, have now adopted the national systems of innovation framework, to varying degrees, as a model for conceptualizing the stated goal of transitioning from resource-based to innovation-driven economies. The South African and Ghanaian strategies have been reviewed a few years after their initial promulgation in what are notably rigorous assessments of the strengths and weaknesses of the various components of their respective systems, and of the linkages between them. This was carried

---

37   Banji Oyelaran-Oyeyinka, *The state and innovation policy in Africa.*

151

out by the government itself in the case of South Africa,[38] and by a collaborative effort between international agencies and the government in the case of Ghana.[39] However, a historical sensibility of the type that is typical of the Western scholars, who have shaped the understanding and formulation of national innovation strategies in their countries, is noticeably absent from the strategies of the various countries. Similarly, the regional strategies, at least in the case of the 2008 Southern African Development Community (SADC) Protocol on Science, Technology and Innovation (STI) and at the continental level, the African Union's STI Strategy for Africa 2024, are all operational documents that do not link themselves with any scientific and technological heritage prior to, or outside of, their organizational mandates.[40] In the emerging community of African researchers and scholars who are working in the field of innovation scholars, Mammo Muchie is one of the few who has problematized the meaning of the word "national" in African systems of innovation, and has gone further to emphasize a number of important considerations, namely, the need to understand the way in which modern institutions and traditional ones evolve with respect to techno-economic networks; the need to ground Africa's learning and innovation culture in its own scientific and technological heritage, past and present; and the need to assert agency in decision-making, rather than acquiescing to policy impositions from elsewhere that may not be in the best interests of its people.[41] He has further systematized these ideas and recently proposed a conceptual framework known as the African-centred Innovation and Development Systems (IDS) to address these questions from a research and policy perspective.[41] This chapter also inscribes itself within this outlook, which with sustained effort can

---

38 See the *Final Report of the Ministerial Review Committee on the Science, Technology and Innovation Landscape in South Africa* by Department of Science and Technology of South Africa.

39 See the *Science, Technology and Innovation Policy Review: Ghana* by the United Nations Conference on Trade and Development (UNCTAD).

40 See the *Protocol on Science, Technology and Innovation* by the Southern African Development Community (SADC). Also see the *Science, Technology and Innovation Strategy for Africa 2024* edited by African Union.

41 See Chapter 3 entitled "Re-thinking Africa's Development through the National Innovation System" in Muchie, Gammeltoft and Lundvall, *Putting Africa First*, 43–62.

begin to exert a more context-sensitive influence in the community of innovation scholars, managers and policymakers.[42] In order to counter the generally ahistorical and relatively marginal role of innovation strategies in economic planning in countries in Africa today, it is useful to provide a brief survey of the views and practices of a few African national leaders in the modern historical period (sixteenth century to early twentieth century). The efforts at nation building, or even more modest attempts at self-determination, based on modern scientific, technological and industrial development was spearheaded by Africans in the Diaspora because of their crucial role and participation in the industrialization of England as demonstrated by Joseph Inikori[43], and more generally, Europe and America, but the conditions of enslavement and subsequent colonization simultaneously underdeveloped their own societies, as Walter Rodney famously contended.[44] However, in addition to the destructive impact of European-led slavery on the demographics and on the development of African people, Élisée Soumonni argued in his commemoration of the Haitian revolution that this forced migration, the largest in all of human history, also had a significant psychological impact on those who endured and inherited the traumatizing memory of these events – a challenge of rehabilitation that must be pursued so that reasons and resources for pursuing a brighter future can be found.[45]

The first governor general and emperor of Haiti, Jean-Jacques Dessalines, though his tenure from 1804 to 1806 was aborted prematurely by an assassination, advanced a number of initiatives based on science and technology. These included a factory for the production of cannon powder and the repair of artillery, the establishment of a healthcare system through the rehabilitation of old hospitals and the construction of new ones, and his endorsement of a scientific assessment of the status of the botanical heritage of the

---

42 See Chapter 2 entitled "Towards a Unified Theory of Pan-African Innovation Systems and Integrated Development" in Adesida, Karuri-Scna and Resende-Santos, *Innovation Africa*, 13–35.

43 Joseph Inikori, *Slavery and the Development of Industrial Capitalism in England*.

44 Walter Rodney, *How Europe Underdeveloped Africa*.

45 For a survey of the impact of the transatlantic slave trade on Africa's evolution, see Chapter 1 entitled "L'impact de la traite négrière transatlantique sur l'évolution de l'Afrique in Franklin Midy, *Mémoire de Révolution d'Esclaves à Saint-Domingue*.

island, which demonstrated that the colonial system had destroyed 90 percent of its flora and a significant, but undetermined percentage of its fauna.[46]

Another figure, who worked for a greater degree of sovereignty for people of African descent in a multiracial society was Booker T. Washington. He founded the Tuskegee Institute in the US state of Alabama as a tertiary institution that would provide an industrial education to black people, which in his view, would engender an increasing level of economic self-determination among them that would be a firmer basis for demanding political rights. In developing his school, he recruited Robert Robinson Taylor, the first black graduate of the Massachusetts Institute of Technology (MIT) to found the architecture program at Tuskegee, where he trained both young men and women to design and construct the dormitories, classrooms, library, and other buildings that they would themselves study.[47] Mr. Washington also employed the famed agricultural scientist, Dr. George Washington Carver, a graduate of Iowa State College (now Iowa State University) to found the plant and soil sciences program at the Tuskegee Institute. There, he famously developed 325 products based on the peanut, 118 food and industrial products from the sweet potato, and hundreds of industrial uses from the pecan, cotton, corn stalks and other food waste, which would all either influence or give rise to new industries such as in the paper, plastics and paints industry, the dehydrated food industry, and the veterinary medicinal industry, among others.[48] Equally importantly, Robin Walker has suggested that underlying Dr. Carver's work, was a political agenda to undermine Southern US cotton oligarchs, thereby freeing many African Americans from the excessively harsh working conditions in that sector.[49]

The connection between Booker T. Washington and the Global Pan-African movement is often under-appreciated, particularly with respect to its impact (both direct and indirect) on those who would either lay the foundations, or lead their countries to independence on

---

46 Bayyinah Bello, *Jean-Jacques Dessalines.*

47 Ellen Weiss, et al., *An African American Architect Designs for Booker T. Washington.*

48 Robin Walker, *Blacks and Science Volume Three,* 51

49 Robin Walker attributes the detection of a political motivation for Dr. George Washington Carver's work to the historian J.A. Rogers in Robin Walker, *Blacks and Science Volume Three,* 51.

the continent itself. Washington provided support to the conveners of the First Pan African Conference, which was held in London in 1900, and inspired the early founders of the African National Congress in South Africa with his program, namely, John Langalibele Dube and Pixley ka Seme, who visited his Tuskegee Institute.[50] Similarly, the great Jamaican Pan Africanist, Marcus Garvey, was also inspired by Washington to build a similar industrial college in Jamaica. Washington invited Garvey to visit his Tuskegee Institute, but upon his arrival in the US in 1916, he found he former had passed away a year earlier, although he did meet Dr. George Washington Carver who impressed him greatly, as attested to by Amy Jacques Garvey.[51] Marcus Garvey would remain in the US for ten years, and lead perhaps the largest worldwide movement of Africans in history, with its primary goal being the establishment of an industrial power in Africa to protect its descendants scattered all over the world.[52] As Cedric Robinson convincingly argued, Booker T. Washington's moderate political stance notwithstanding, Garvey's movement was the logical culmination of the former's program.[53] African leaders who were subsequently inspired, funded, and otherwise supported by Garvey's United Negro Improvement Association (UNIA) included J.E. Caseley Hayford and later, Kwame Nkrumah, of what is now Ghana, Ladipo Solanke and later, Nnamdi Azikiwe of Nigeria, Harry Thuku and later, Jomo Kenyatta of Kenya, and many other African nationalists.

In the contemporary period (1950s up to the present), particularly in the lead up to, and in the aftermath of the independence movements that swept Africa, one of the most succinct visions for the continent's economic basis, particularly with respect to the role of STI, was also articulated by Cheikh Anta Diop. Although better known for his work on ancient African civilizations, the ultimate purpose of that Herculean effort was to attempt to create a common basis for nationhood that stretched back to antiquity. In an important book that was originally published in 1960, entitled "Black Africa: The Economic and Cultural Basis for a Federated State", he reiterates the historico-cultural basis for nationhood, and subsequently enumerates the various sources of

50   Manning Marable, *Booker T. Washington and African Nationalism.*
51   Amy Jacques Garvey, *Garvey and Garveyism.*
52   Tony Martin, *Race First.*
53   Cedric Robinson, *Black Marxism,* 214

energy that can be found in various parts of the continent.[54] He then innovatively combines these energy sources with raw materials that can be found to identify eight natural zones, and very briefly outlines a roadmap to industrialization based on three stages, as follows:

1.) The importation of factories (capital goods) with foreign experts in every category of industry. During this stage, African engineers should be placed in positions of responsibility, such that they can quickly acquire the knowledge and capabilities needed to manage those factories in as short a time as possible as needed to replace the foreign engineers.[55] Indeed, in an article written seventeen years after he first published "Black Africa", Diop bitterly challenged the Senegalese government's approach to foreign technical assistance on the grounds that it was too expensive, the University of Dakar's doctoral graduates remained dependent on their accreditation from French university boards, and French jurists were employed to arbitrate in national matters, among other complaints, all of which in the final analysis, he considered to be humiliating and intolerable.[56]

2.) After this original infrastructure has been installed, assembly plants for various machines such as automobiles, planes and tractors, should be established. This should occur simultaneously with the acquisition of foreign patents for the manufacture of modern technologies in electronics, aeronautics, and so on.[57] In a keynote lecture on Africa's energy challenge, addressed to an International Symposium on African Science, Technology and Development that was held in Kinshasa in the present Democratic Republic of Congo (formerly Zaïre), Diop argued that the emphasis for the development of technological capabilities should be oriented towards the pressing basic needs that were being faced at the time, namely self-sufficiency in food production and health.[58] As such, he prioritized the training of engineers and technicians to construct and maintain decentralized

---

54   Cheikh Anta Diop, *Black Africa*.
55   Ibid.
56   Cheikh Anta Diop, *Notre Conception de l'Assistance Technique*.
57   Cheikh Anta Diop, *Black Africa*.
58   Cheikh Anta Diop, *Le problème énergétique africain*.

energy technologies, such as biogas generators, micro-hydroelectric generators, solar photovoltaic panels and wind mills that would be critical, particularly for rural industrialization.[59]

3.) In the last stage, Africans could then go on to the phase of "autonomous" or indigenous development of technologies.[60] It should be noted here, that this is remarkably identical to China's current policy (2005-2020) of indigenous innovation.[61] To this end, Diop advanced a model of science policy that would firstly require much more coherent coordination within various regions, in an attempt to pool together both information and financial resourcesand secondly, to have a certain degree of secrecy, such that scientific teams, and ultimately nations, could benefit from a sort of first mover advantage when the timing was appropriate for diffusion.[62]

One additional consideration that would make it more effective to embed science, technology and industrialization policies into a national framework rather than a merely civic one, is the "bureaucratic mentality" with which most of the states typically deal with the challenges of its people – an approach that is devoid of substantive cultural policies and few systematic efforts to elevate any indigenous languages to the status of official languages (Kenya and Tanzania, being among few exceptions).[63] Furthermore, Kwesi Kwaa Prah has argued that scientific concepts and abstract notions are most accessible if they are based on the mother tongue, which provides a systemic framework for interpreting reality, and which enables people's creativity and ingenuity to be expressed most naturally.[64] In fact, he has more forcefully argued elsewhere that African languages are the only means by which Africans can gain confidence in themselves and in

---

59 Ibid.
60 Cheikh Anta Diop, *Black Africa.*
61 Xielin Liu and Jianbing Liu, *Science and Technology and Innovation Policy in China.*
62 Cheikh Anta Diop, *Perspectives de la Recherche Scientifique en Afrique.*
63 Cheikh Anta Diop, *Black Africa.*
64 Kwesi Kwaa Prah, *Mother Tongue for Scientific and Technological Development in Africa.*

their cultures, and is the only viable vehicle for their economic and social development.[65]

Technological Upgrading and Economic Catch-up in China:
Lessons for Africa

An enlightening synopsis of Afro-Chinese economic and trade relations in the past and their implications for the future has been articulated in several contributions in the edited book by Kwesi Kwaa Prah.[66] However, the analysis of the cases presented reveals that the opportunities for technological upgrading have been marginal considerations in those relations, and as such, it is useful to provide a brief overview of how China itself was able to emerge as a technological power. This section therefore seeks to draw retrospective lessons from this Chinese experience, and offer prospective recommendations for African societies, bearing in mind that despite the articulation of the continuity of the its civilization over time, China has faced many tumultuous changes in its history. Indeed, the country's transition toward rapid modernization (known as the four modernizations: agriculture, industry, defense, and science and technology), the implementation of which is generally attributed to its leader Deng Xiaoping in 1978, was carried out based on cautious experimentation that he characterized as the "path of gradual reform with Chinese characteristics" or as "feeling for the stones with your feet as you cross the river" in it more proverbial formulation.[67] As explained earlier, such a *longue durée* perspective of African history, which would inform the present, has also been articulated by a number of African scholars, but the extent to which it influences current state management remains peripheral.

Until about 2011, China had achieved rapid economic growth over a period of three decades, including double-digit economic growth over a period of more than a decade, according to World Bank Statistics. Some scholars have attributed this to its STI policies since the major reforms in 1978 that shifted it from a centrally planned

65 Kwesi Kwaa Prah, *Les Langues Africaines Pour L'éducation des Masses en Afrique*.

66 Kwesi Kwaa Prah, *Afro-Chinese Relations: Past Present and Future*.

67 Wu Xiao-bo, *China Emerging*, 17

economy to a more decentralized and market-oriented one.[68] However, others have emphasized that this shift was actually based on the so-called Beijing Consensus, which can be defined as an unconventional approach to economic planning that combines basic property rights with public-private ownership and substantial government intervention.[69] This approach is opposed to the Washington Consensus, which emphasizes trade liberalization, state enterprise privatization for poor countries, in a manner that critics consider to be extremely premature, and the dis-incentivization of tertiary education and scientific research, which they view as being erroneous advice.[70] Since its emergence as a state, China's National System of Innovation can be characterized by three main periods. The first period was the "Big Push" under the centrally planned economy from 1949 to1978, the second period was one of reform and opening up of the economy from 1978 to 2005, and the third period has been one of indigenous innovation since 2005.[71] Under the centrally planned economy, China's functionally specialized organizations were managed by the central government, which was the Soviet Union's model of industrial organizational structure, and was based on high centralization and complete state ownership.[72] During this period, they relied heavily on subsidized imports from the USSR., established more than 400 research units for the purpose of reverse engineering, and created a range of broader actors in the economy, such as the State Planning Commission to facilitate the work of primary researchers and core STI workers in various ways.[73]

However, due to the inefficiencies and lower effectiveness of the centralized economy, the reform period was defined by two main institutional changes namely, the use of economic measures as the dominant criteria for evaluating performance, and the decentralization

---

68 Xielin Liu and Jianbing Liu, *Science and Technology and Innovation Policy in China.*

69 Yang Yao, *The End of the Beijing Consensus.*

70 Keun Lee and John A. Mathews, *From Washington Consensus to BeST Consensus for World Development.*

71 Xielin Liu and Jianbing Liu, *Science and Technology and Innovation Policy in China.*

72 Xielin Liu and Steven White *Comparing innovation systems: a framework and application to China's transitional context.*

73 Ibid.

of decision-making over operational decisions among the primary actors in STI.[74] Overall performance improved as a result, and the government allowed new primary actors to emerge, including multinationals. However, China's national STI policy not only leveraged the country's large market to require foreign companies to license a sector-specific technology to domestic firms as a precondition for their investment, but this policy also required the multinationals to sell most of their products internationally in order to protect infant Chinese industry.[75]

The third period, which is still underway, is being marked by firms having to invest more revenue in intangible assets (intellectual property, brand reputation, etc.) to meet the requirements of intensified competition and more demanding customers.[76] Furthermore, due to the direct participation of local and central governments, officials have developed vested interests and amassed enormous personal wealth, and so China has been trying since then to move toward reforms of the interest-redistribution kind.[77] These three periods reflect an adaptive and flexible approach to China's industrial development, with respect to the global political and economic changes during the period of its modern rise. It is difficult not to observe the corollary with Cheikh Anta Diop's three-stage approach to industrialization described above, which he first made in 1960, and one can only wonder what might have been today, if his call had been heeded by the then-nascent African countries.

The award-winning book by Keun Lee, which looked at the processes of economic catch-up (including technological catch-up) in upper-middle income countries, provided a positive assessment of China's innovation capability and sequence of technological upgrading, and predicted its ability to break free from the proverbial "middle income trap" in contrast to India's trajectory, which it deemed to be inconclusive.[78] A review of this work and its implications for Africa has pointed out that while Lee's theory of economic catch-up and the techno-economic models he deployed to that end were

---

74 Ibid.
75 Xielin Liu and Jianbing Liu, *Science and Technology and Innovation Policy in China.*
76 Shulin Gu and Bengt-Åke Lundvall, *China's innovation system and the move towards harmonious growth and endogenous innovation.*
77 Ibid.
78 Keun Lee, *Schumpeterian Analysis of Economic Catch-up.*

convincing, the process of catching up is nevertheless, not a deterministic one, but rather a potential road map for those countries that deliberately choose a more liberated path to their own development.[79] Xiaolan Fu has recently offered a model of China's Open National Innovation System (ONIS) in which she proposes that China's path to innovation is not necessarily the "state-led" model that it is often presented to be, but that it is rather a multi-driver model that is simultaneously led by the state, industry and multi-national companies in different sectors of the economy.[80] However, a more pessimistic assessment of the Chinese innovation system by Wei Zhao and Rigas Arvantis suggested earlier that there is actually a dual system, with one driven by state-owned enterprises heavily favoured by government agencies, and another that is led by smaller private firms, and that finds it more difficult to access incentives from the government – a situation, which according to them, explains China's inability to follow the same trajectory as South Korea and Japan in terms of innovation capability.[81]

One example of China's innovation and catch-up that could represent a practical example for African nations is in the area of rural electrification and leapfrogging in renewable energy. The country's rural electrification challenge was resolved when its government changed the ownership structure from being centralized and fully state-owned with poor profitability, to a diverse structure including shareholders, cooperatives and others.[82] With respect to its small hydroelectric power (SHP) program, which was subsidized by the government, the devolution of governance and management responsibilities from the central government was guided by three principles: 1.) Self-construction: Local governments and populations were encouraged to use local materials, technology and water resources to build the systems; 2.) Self-management: Under this principle, local investors managed and owned the stations, avoiding administrative interference and preserving the enthusiasm of the local communities to develop SHP; 3.) Self-use: This principle required the electricity

---

79 Ogundiran Soumonni, *Review of Schumpeterian Analysis of Economic Catch-up.*
80 Xiaolan Fu, *China's Path to Innovation.*
81 Wei Zhao and Rigas Arvantis, *The Innovation and Learning Capabilities of Chinese Firms.*
82 Xiangjun Yao and Douglas F. Barnes, *National Support for Decentralized Electricity Growth in Rural China.*

produced by the stations to be used locally, and the conventional grid was not allowed to compete in the locally integrated markets.[83]

An enlightening corollary to this experience on the African continent was the Self-Help Electrification Project (SHEP) instituted by the government of Ghana, as part of its thirty-year National Electrification Scheme (NES) initiated in 1990 and with the intention of achieving universal access by 2020. The government initially selected 110 communities in the Ashanti and Brong Ahafo regions through the SHEP programme that was designed to provide grid-based electricity to communities of more than 500 people within twenty kilometres of an electrified town, but it required them to wire at least 30 percent of their own homes and purchase their own low-voltage electric poles in order to qualify for state support for the remainder.[84] Such a programme likely led to an access rate of about 72 percent in Ghana in 2014, which is among the highest in Sub-Saharan Africa.[85] This approach, if extended to a diversity of decentralized energy solutions as in the Chinese case, strongly suggests that the ability to consistently provide a basic, affordable service to residents of a given community, largely depends on their ability to manage, repair and even build the required amenities, while simultaneously building an industry around the particular technology.

The development of the solar photovoltaic industry in China was similarly spearheaded by a national government drive to support the diffusion of solar home systems (SHSs), which subsequently became the basis for its dominant solar PV industry. According to Xiaolan Fu, China employed a "two-leg forward" strategy that involved technology transfer, which in the first step included inward FDI, but was critically accompanied by joint ventures with multinational companies that imported machinery and trained local labour. This then led to horizontal technology spillovers to other firms in the industry through industry mobility, vertical technology spillovers across the value chain, and the competitive effect that forced domestic firms to innovate or exit.[86] Other approaches to technology transfer included the licensing of patents from foreign firms for local production, and the importation

---

83   Ibid.
84   Phyllis D. Osabutey, *Ecowas Bank Supports Self-Help Electrification Project.*
85   International Energy Agency (IEA), *World Energy Outlook 2016 Electricity Database.*
86   Xiaolan Fu, *China's Path to Innovation.*

of foreign machinery to produce the technologies and outward FDI, which included joint ventures and research collaborations with foreign firms on their territory. The second leg of this approach involves indigenous innovation for the purpose of catching up, which is very important because multinational companies are often unwilling to share their technological capabilities as this is the source of their competitive advantage. It is therefore important for domestic firms to invest in in-house Research and Development because this will enable them to acquire the tacit know-how that comes only through practice, and it allows them to adapt both the original manufacturing equipment acquired abroad, and the products that are developed, to the local context.[87]

Conclusion

In this chapter, I have argued that Africa's industrial development and technological advancement can only fundamentally come through the type of impetus, trust, and collective vision that are associated with nationhood, rather than a civic notion of citizenship. Following Peter Ekeh's formulation, I maintain that this bifurcation between the civic public and the primordial public is still dominant in Africa. Furthermore, I argue that one of the more important challenges is the development of modern polities that are based on the moral relationship that was, and is historically characteristic of the primordial public. China, for example, has cemented its place as a modern nation-state that has to be reckoned with by other powers, and even views itself as a civilizational state; that is, as the current embodiment of its ancient history and culture. While this is an important part of the world's heritage that African peoples can learn and draw from, they nevertheless have their own intellectual, spiritual and scientific inheritance to draw from in fashioning their own modernity and progress. However, given its national coherence, many of the general approaches and more specific strategies that China has employed to transform itself from a peasant agrarian country to a modern, technologically competitive one, are highly instructive for African societies in their relations with the Chinese, as well as with other nations. These strategies, which have been reversible, interactive and adaptive in the face of various global events, represent an evolutionary

---

87   Ibid.

path, but with a clear telos or purpose; being at all times, the self-determination and sovereignty of the Chinese nation-state.

The examples that were provided with respect to the development of a renewable energy industry in China demonstrate that the enthusiasm shown by communities, when provided with the capabilities and support needed for them to address their own problems, goes a long way towards resolving national challenges, rather than depending on the central government to solve them directly. In African contexts, it may still be the primordial communities that are more likely to have this level of cohesion and trust, and if so, the majority of socio-economic initiatives should be directed towards them. While the amoral civic realm as it is currently constituted is unlikely to reform itself autonomously, at least some of the actors who are dominant in that realm can be challenged to spearhead development initiatives in their locales of origin, where presumably they would demonstrate a greater sense of loyalty. However, other actors in different walks of life could begin to self-organize around developmental initiatives for mass empowerment (e.g. renewable energy, clean water, sanitation, food security and healthcare) and demand assistance from those who seek elected office as a precondition for further support. Similarly, these organizations can offer their communities the needed transformative education, that is, cognitive, cultural, political and linguistic training that will develop the people we need to build the nations we want. Such communities, many of which are multi-ethnic and trans-border, could ultimately become the building blocks for organic nation-building, while the various administrative structures would serve as instruments to facilitate and promote that end.

Finally, I have argued in this chapter that no system that is merely operational or mimetic, even if functional at a threshold level, could have accomplished as much as China did in such a short span of time. Therefore, the rise of modern China ought to be studied much more closely by African scholars and laypersons alike, and should serve, both as an inspiration and as a positive challenge to African societies, that a brighter future is indeed possible as long as we choose to make it so. Indeed, this is probably one of the most reliable bases for the continuation of mutually respectful and friendly ties between our two peoples.

Bibliography

Akanle, Olayinka. "The Development Exceptionality of Nigeria: The Context of Political and Social Currents." *Africa Today*, no. 59, 3 (2013):31–48.

Akinjogbin, I.A. *Dahomey and Its Neighbours*, Cambridge University Press, 1967,1708–1818.

Asante, S.K.B. *Regionalism and Africa's Development: Expectations, Reality and Challenges*: Macmillan Press Ltd., 1997.

African Union. "Science, Technology and Innovation Strategy for Africa 2024", ed. African Union. Addis Ababa, Ethiopia, 2014.

Bello, Bayyinah. *Jean-Jacques Dessalines: 21 Pwenkonnen Sou Lavi Li*. Port-au-Prince: Bibliothèque Nationale d'Haïti, 2015.

Diop, Cheikh Anta. "Perspectives de la Recherche Scientifique en Afrique." *Notes africaines* 144, (1974):85–88.

Diop, Cheikh Anta. "Notre Conception de l'Assistance Technique," *Taxaw*, 2 (1977):1–2.

Diop, Cheikh Anta. "Le problème énergétique africain," *ANKH* 14/15 (1985):163–167.

Diop, Cheikh Anta. *Black Africa – The Economic and Cultural Basis for a Federated State*. Chicago & Trenton: Lawrence Hill Books. Original edition, Les fondements économiques et culturels d'un état fédéral d'Afrique noire, 1987.

Diop, Cheikh Anta. *The Cultural Unity of Black Africa: The Domains of Patriarchy and Matriarchy in Classical Antiquity*. London: Karnak House, 1989.

DST. Final Report of the Ministerial Review Committee on the Science, Technology and Innovation Landscape in South Africa, edited by Department of Science and Technology. Pretoria, South Africa, 2012.

Dupont, Bethony. *Jean-Jacques Dessalines: itinéraire d'un révolutionnaire*. Paris: L'Harmattan, 2006.

Ekeh, Peter P. "Colonialism and the Two Publics in Africa: A Theoretical Statement." *Comparative Studies in Society and History* no. 17, 1 (1975):91–112.

Freeman, Chris. "The 'National System of Innovation' in historical perspective." *Cambridge Journal of Economics* 19 (1995):5–24.

Freeman, Chris. "Continental, national and sub-national innovation systems - complementarity and economic growth." *Research Policy* 31 (2002):191–211.

Fu, Xiaolan. *China's Path to Innovation*. Cambridge: Cambridge University Press, 2015.

Garvey, Amy Jacques, *Garvey and Garveyism*. New York: Collier Books, 1974.

Gu, Shulin and Bengt-Åke Lundvall. "China's innovation system and the move towards harmonious growth and endogenous innovation." *Innovation: management, policy and practice* no. 18 (2011): 413–440.

IEA. World Energy Outlook 2016 Electricity Database – Electricity Access in Africa in 2014, 2016.

Inikori, Joseph E. "Slavery and the Development of Industrial Capitalism in England." *Journal of Interdisciplinary History* no. XVII, 4 (1987):771–793.

Kavalski, Emilian. "Review of 1.) *The China Wave: Rise of a Civilizational State*; and 2.) *The Politics of Imagining Asia*." *Europe-Asia Studies* no. 65, 8 (2013):1667–1685.

Lee, Keun. *Schumpeterian Analysis of Economic Catch-up: Knowledge, Path-creation, and the Middle-income Trap*: Cambridge University Press, 2013.

Lee, Keun, and John A. Mathews. "From Washington Consensus to BeST Consensus for World Development." *Asian-Pacific Economic Literature* no. 24, 1 (2010):86–103.

Legesse, Asmarom. *Oromo Democracy: An Indigenous African Political System*. Trenton, NJ: The Red Sea Press, Inc., 2006.

Liu, Xielin, and Jianbing Liu. "Science and Technology and Innovation Policy in China." In *BRICS and Development Alternatives: Innovation Systems and Policies*, edited by José Eduardo Cassiolato and Virgínia Vitorino, 133–161. Anthem Press, 2011.

Liu, Xielin, and Steven White. "Comparing innovation systems: a framework and application to China's transitional context." *Research Policy* no. 30, 7 (2001):1091–1114.

Marable, Manning. "Booker T. Washington and African Nationalism." *Phylon (1960-)* no. 35, 4 (1974):398–406.

Martin, Tony. *Race First: The Ideological and Organizational Struggles of Marcus Garvey and the United Negro Improvement Association, The New Marcus Garvey Library. No. 8*. Dover, Massachusetts: The Majority Press., 1976.

Muchie, Mammo. "Re-thinking Africa's Development through the National Innovation System." In *Putting Africa First: The Making of African Innovation Systems*, 43–62. Aalborg, Denmark: Aalborg University Press, 2003.

Muchie, Mammo. "Towards a Unified Theory of Pan-African Innovation Systems and Integrated Development." In *Innovation Africa: Emerging Hubs of Excellence*, edited by Olugbenga Adesida, Geci Karuri-Sebina and João Resende-Santos, 13–35. UK: Emerald Group Publishing Limited, 2016.

Nkrumah, Kwame. *Class Struggle in Africa*: Panaf Books Ltd, 1970.

Osabutey, Phyllis D. "Ecowas Bank Supports Self-Help Electrification Project." *The Chronicle*, December 8, 2011.

Oyelaran-Oyeyinka, Banji. "The state and innovation policy in Africa." *African Journal of Science, Technology, Innovation and Development* no. 6, 5 (2014):481–496.

Oyewumi, Oyeronke. *What Gender is Motherhood? Changing Yoruba Ideals of Power, Procreation, and Identity in the Age of Modernity*: Palgrave McMillan, 2016.

Prah, Kwesi Kwaa. *Les Langues Africaines Pour L'éducation des Masses en Afrique, CASAS Book Series No. 29*. Cape Town: CASAS, 2002.

Prah, Kwesi Kwaa. *The African Nation: The State of the Nation, CASAS Book Series No. 44*. Cape Town: CASAS, 2006.

Prah, Kwesi Kwaa. *Afro-Chinese Relations: Past Present and Future*. Vol. No. 25. Cape Town: CASAS, 2007a.

Prah, Kwesi Kwaa. "Introduction: Defining a Relationship." In *Afro-Chinese Relations: Past Present and Future*, edited by Kwesi Kwaa Prah, 392. Cape Town: CASAS, 2007b.

Prah, Kwesi Kwaa. *Mother Tongue for Scientific and Technological Development in Africa*. 3rd ed, *CASAS Book Series No. 8*. Cape Town: CASAS, 2008.

Robinson, Cedric. *Black Marxism: The Making of the Black Radical Tradition*. Chapel Hill & London: The University of North Carolina Press, 2000.

Rodney, Walter. *How Europe Underdeveloped Africa*. Washington D.C.: Howard University Press, 1972.

SADC. Protocol on Science, Technology and Innovation. Johannesburg, South Africa: Southern African Development Community (SADC), 2008.

Senghor, Léopold Sédar. *Les Fondement de L'Africanité ou Négritude et Arabité*. Alençon (Orne): Présence Africaine, 1967.

Soumonni, Élisée. "L'Héritage Colonial et l'Unité Africaine." *Peuples Noirs Peuples Africains* 21 (1981):66–78.

Soumonni, Élisée. "Some Reflections on the Brazilian Legacy in Dahomey." *Slavery & Abolition* no. 22,1 (2001):42–60.

Soumonni, Élisée. "L'impact de la traite négrière transatlantique sur l'évolution de l'Afrique." In *Mémoire de Révolution d'Esclaves à Saint-Domingue*, edited by Franklin Midy. Montréal, Québec: Les Éditions du CIDIHCA, 2006.

Soumonni, Ogundiran. "Review of Schumpeterian Analysis of Economic Catch-up: Knowledge, Path-creation, and the Middle-income Trap." *African Journal of Science, Technology, Innovation and Development* no. 6, 2 (2014):159–161.

Stinchcombe, Arthur L. "Turning Inventions into Innovations: Schumpeter's Organizational Sociology Modernized." In *Information and Organizations*, edited by Arthur L. Stinchcombe, 152–191, University of California Press, 1990.

UNCTAD. Science, Technology and Innovation Policy Review: Ghana. edited by United Nations Conference on Trade and Development (UNCTAD). Geneva, Switzerland, 2011.

Walker, Robin. *Blacks and Science Volume Three: African American Contributions to Science and Technology*. London: Reklaw Education, 2012.

Weiss, Ellen. *Robert R. Taylor and Tuskegee: An African American Architect Designs for Booker T. Washington*. Montgomery: New South Books, 2011.

Weiwei, Zhang. *The China Wave: Rise of a Civilizational State*. Singapore: World Century Publishing Corporation, 2012.

Xiao-bo, Wu.. *China Emerging: 1978–2008*. Singapore: Cengage Learning Asia Pte Ltd, 2009.

Yaï, Olabiyi. "African Diasporan Concepts and Practice of the Nation and their Implications in the Modern World." In *African Roots/American Cultures: Africa in the Creation of the Americas*, edited by Sheila S. Walker. Rowman and Littlefield, 2001.

Yaï, Olabiyi. Africa, African Diaspora and the Prospect of Global Cultural Dialogue. *India International Centre (IIC) Occasional Publication; 2*, 2008.

Yao, Xiangjun, and Douglas F. Barnes. "National Support for Decentralized Electricity Growth in Rural China." In *TheChallenge of Rural Electrification: Strategies for Developing Countries*, edited by Douglas F. Barnes, 225–258. Washington, DC: RFF Press, 2007.

Yao, Yang. The End of the Beijing Consensus: Can China's Model Authoritarian Growth Survive? *Foreign Affairs* (February 2), 2010.

Zhao, Wei, and Rigas Arvantis. "The Innovation and Learning Capabilities of Chinese Firms: Technological Development in the

Automobile and Electronics Industries." *Chinese Sociology and Anthropology* no. 42, 3, (2010): 62–7.

PART II

Chapter Seven. Opportunism or Partnership for Development: Trends and Patterns in Sino-Nigerian Relations

=============❖=============

Samuel O. Oloruntoba

Introduction

The relationship between Africa and China has become a matter of significant interest for scholars, policy makers and the global development community in general. While the relationship has witnessed some resurgence since the 1990s, scholars have contended that it was not altogether new, as a previous relationship existed between the two economic blocs as far back as the establishment of the modern state of the Peoples' Republic of China in 1949.[1] The interest that this relationship has generated has also been critically analyzed from the perspectives of the negative reaction from the West, especially among scholars, journalists and politicians.[2]

The West has expressed various concerns about China's lack of respect for human rights, (as evidenced, for example, by China's involvement with Omar Bashir's government in Sudan), the country's lack of observance of the basic principles of lending as defined by the West, and that self-indicting allegation that China is planning to

---

1. Brautigam, *The Danger Gift;* and Brautigam and Gay, *Chinese Investment Good?*
2. Oloo, *China's Threat;* and Tull, "China's Engagement in Africa".

recolonize Africa.[3] However, whatever the charges of impropriety, evidence in terms of increased volume of trade, investment, aid and strategic diplomacy shows that China has made significant inroads into Africa. As Deborah Brautigam,[4] the increasing influence of China in Africa has to do with the methods that the country adopts and the beliefs it has about the continent in terms of giving Africa what it needs regarding infrastructure, aid and investments.

What are the key variables in Sino-African relations, especially in the post-Mao era? How is this relationship transforming or undermining economic development in Africa? What are the implications of Sino-African relations for the reconfiguration of global politics? How can Africa maximize the benefits of increasing Chinese presence on the continent, while minimizing the negative effects? Using Nigeria as the entry point of analysis, this paper engages with these questions. The rest of this paper proceeds as follows: section two examines the key economic variables that define Sino-African relations in the twenty-first century in terms of infrastructure, inflow of investment, trade and aids. Section three examines the effects of Chinese presence on the economic and political development of Africa, while section four analyses the Sino-Africa relations within the context of the changes in the economic order. Section five concludes with recommendations on how Africa can maximize the benefits that China's increased involvement on the continent can bring, while minimizing the downsides of the relationship.

Chinese-African Economic Relations in Historical and Contemporary Perspectives

Although relations between China and Africa can be viewed from various perspectives, which include political, cultural, strategic and economic, this section deals essentially with the latter, as it is the major issue driving other aspects of the relationship today. The tempo of China's economic involvement with Africa has largely been defined by the prevailing ideological orientation of the country's leaders. In this connection, while Sino-African economic relations were at a low ebb in the period 1949–1976 (the Mao years) and during1978–1989 (the Deng Xiaoping years), this tempo changed after the Tiananmen Square

---

3.   Wenping, "The Balancing Act."
4.   Brautigam, *The Dragon Gift.*

protest of 1989.[5] As Emma Mawdsley[6] argues, the change in the foreign economic policy of China towards Africa after this period was essentially on account of the shock that the Chinese authorities received from the reactions of the West to the protests. The support which the protesters received from the West, and the condemnation that followed the repression, more or less forced the Chinese authorizes to seek new alliances, especially from Africa and other Asian countries.[7]

As testimony to the growing relations between China and African countries, many diplomatic exchanges and visits at the highest level have taken place between the two blocs over the past two decades. For instance, between 1997 and 2004, thirty heads of state or government from Africa visited China while successive premiers and presidents from China have also visited many African countries.[8] The Forum on Africa-China Cooperation (FOCAC), which was established in 2000, has as one of its major objectives the economic cooperation between China and Africa.[9] It is important to state upfront that one of the major factors driving Sino-African relations is the abundant natural resources that are available in Africa. The massive expansion of the Chinese economy necessitates demands for raw materials, which are amply available in Africa. Besides, the growing African market also provides a veritable avenue for sales of manufactured products from China.

A theoretical justification for Chinese engagement with Africa is the dependency theory. In the opinion of the proponents of this theory such as Raul Presbrich, Paul Baran, Andre Gunder Frank, the relationship between the North and South has, through the historical trajectory of their existence, been driven by unequal exchange and exploitation of the latter by the former. One of the solutions to these problems, they argue, is delinking their economies from the North, while building regional integration and fostering South-South cooperation.[10]

The idea of a South-South cooperation has gained currency in the last five years, most especially with the coinage of the word BRICS

5. Mawdsley, "China and Africa."
6. Ibid.
7. Taylor, *China and Africa.*
8. Muekalia, 2004 cited in Mawdsley, "China and Africa."
9. Anshan, "China and Africa: Policy and Challenges."
10. Baran, *Political Economy of Growth;* Frank, *Capitalism and Underdevelopmen.t"*

which is the umbrella body for emerging countries of Brazil, Russia, India, China and now South Africa.[11] It is essentially in the context of this categorization and opportunity for cooperation that China sees itself in Africa, not as a new imperialist, but as a genuine partner in development.[12] Economic relations between China and Africa manifest in areas of trade flows, foreign direct investment, infrastructure and foreign aid. These are now examined.

Trade Relations between China and Africa

Trade flow between China and Africa has continued to grow exponentially from 2000 to the present. This, as noted already, was due essentially to the expansion in Chinese economy, which has necessitated demands for raw materials. From 2000 to 2009, trade and economic cooperation between China and Africa grew rapidly. Yearly statistics show that bilateral trade rose from $10.6 billion to $91.07 billion.[13] By 2014, the trade volume between Africa and China had reached the $200 billion mark, thereby making China the second-largest trade partner with Africa just behind the United States of America (USA), but well ahead of traditional partners such as France and Britain. As Sautman and Hairong[14] argue, in 1995, Africa-China trade was $3 billion; $55 billion in 2006; and in 2010 it was over $100 billion. Cotton was the traditional export product from Africa to China. In 2008, China's exports to Africa reached $50.8 billion while imports from Africa stood at $56 billion, creating a $5.2 billion deficit on the Chinese side.[15]

Further details of the trade relations between Africa and China include: From 2000 to 2012, the proportion of Africa-China trade volume as part of China's total foreign trade volume increased from 2.23 percent to 5.13 percent, with the proportion consisting of China's imports from Africa up from 2.47 percent to 6.23 percent, and that of China's exports to Africa increasing from 2.02 percent to 4.16 percent. On the African side, the changes are even more remarkable. From 2000 to 2012, the proportion of Africa-China trade volume as part of Africa's total foreign trade volume increased from 3.82percent to 16.13

11. Akinboye and Oloruntoba, "Global Trade Governance."
12. Melville and Owen, "A New Era in South-South Cooperation."
13. FOCAC, "Annual Report."
14. Sautman and Hairong, "The Forest for the Trees."
15. FOCAC, "Annual Report."

percent, with the proportion contributed by Africa's exports to China up from 3.76 percent to 18.07 percent, and that contributed by Africa's imports from China increasing from 3.88 percent to 14.11 percent.[16] Over the same period, there has been a massive diversification in the portfolio of products from Africa to China: "In 2004, oil and gas accounted for 62 percent of Africa's export to China; ores and metals, 17 percent; agricultural raw materials, 7 percent."[17] The increase in the volume of exports to China was also partly made possible by the trade policy of China, which charges zero tariffs for most goods coming from Least Developed Countries in Africa to China. China also organizes commodity exhibitions and trade fairs for African and Chinese businessmen through which awareness about available products is created. In a somewhat unusual experience of African countries, in recent years Africa has recorded a trade surplus in relation to China.

Foreign Direct Investment

Another area in which Chinese presence in Africa has made much impact is that of foreign direct investment (FDI). Although there are concerns that the inflow of FDI from China is essentially concentrated in the extractive sector such as oil and minerals,[18] the benefits of investments from China, especially as these have to do with development of infrastructure, have also been highlighted.[19] Table 1 shows recipients of Chinese foreign direct investment (CFDI) in Africa from 2003–2008:[20]

Rank	Individual countries	Average CFDI received	Rank	Country groupings	Average CFDI received
				Regional concentration	

16. Xinhua, "China Africa-Economic Relations."
17. Sautman and Hairong, "The Forest for the Trees."
18. Asiedu, "Policy Reform and Foreign Direct Investment in Africa: Absolute Progress but Relative Decline"
19. Brautigam, *The Dragon Gift to Africa.*
20. Source: Ministry of Commerce of the People's Republic of China (MOFCOM) 2008: World Bank 2010

1	South Africa	896.2million	1		
2	Nigeria	124.0 million	2		
3	Zambia	73million	3		
4	Algeria	64.3million	4		
5	Sudan	58.2million	5		
6	Niger	23.2million		Based on diversification	
7	Democratic Republic of Congo	22.5million	1	Diversified economies	203million
8	Madagascar	15million	2	Oil exporters	30.8million
9	Mauritius	13.2million	3	Transition economies	12.9million
10	Egypt	11.6million	4	Pre-transition economies	10.8million
11	Gabon	9.7million	5	Other	8.4million
12	Angola	9.1million		Based on historic economic growth	
13	Guinea	9million	1	Medium growth economies	63million
14	Ethiopia	8.9million	2	High growth economies	8million
15	Libya	7.5million	3	Low growth economies	6million
16	Congo	6.8million			
17	Benin	6.3million			
18	Kenya	6.3million			
19	Tanzania	5.9million			
20	Sierra Leone	4.9million			

Table 1: Chinese foreign direct investment (CFDI) in Africa from 2003–2008

178

Note: The values representing the regional concentration levels of diversification and historical growth performers are obtained by averaging the amounts of CFDI inflow received by individual countries within the regions or groups over the period 2003 to 2008.

The table shows that CFDI to Africa has been diversified across different parts of Africa. It also shows that countries that are rich in oil and gas attract more FDI flow than countries that are not. The only exception to this is South Africa. Nigeria, Sudan and Algeria are countries with high concentrations in oil and gas. Elsewhere Brautigam[21] shows that FDI in 2008 was $7.8 billion with $5.5 billion of direct investment, which was related to the pledge made by the Chinese Government that year. She also shows that there is a form of diversification in the portfolio of FDI from China to Africa. For instance, "in 1979 – 2000, 46 percent of PRC FDI in Africa went to manufacturing, (15 percent to textiles alone), 28 percent to resource extraction, 18 percent to services, mostly construction and 7 percent to agriculture."[22]

Development Aid

Another area of Chinese involvement in Africa is the granting of aid. This has taken the form of helping African countries construct roads, dams, railway lines, palaces, and goes as far as building the secretariat of African Union at Addis Ababa in 2012. As Brautigam[23] contends, the Chinese approach to aid in Africa is markedly different from that of the West. This is because China makes a deliberate effort to bring in the development needs of people, as well as its own strategic interest in designing aid programmes. Over the past half century, Chinese aid in Africa has taken the form of infrastructure development; education assistance, including the granting of scholarships to African students to study in China; and sending health workers to Africa and production. Critics of China's aid policy in Africa argue that some of its aid programmes are linked to Chinese firms and that China worsens the standards of governance in Africa by patronizing rogue regimes such as Al Bashir in Sudan and Robert Mugabe in Zimbabwe.[24]

---

21. Brautigam, *The Dragon Gift to Africa*.
22. Ibid.
23. Ibid.
24. See Collier, 2007 cited in Brautigam, *"The Dragon Gift to Africa."*

In furtherance of its aid programme in Africa, China also grants loans and credits, writes off debts which run into billions of dollars for Least Developed Countries, and has instituted a development fund for Africa.[25] As is noted,[26] in the third forum on Africa-China Cooperation, the Chinese government provided a preferential loan of $3 billion and a preferential buyer's credit of $2 billion. It also instituted the Africa-China development fund. In addition, debts were cancelled both in the third and fourth forums. Despite concerns that Chinese involvement in Africa smacks of a repeat of Europe's Scramble for Africa in the wake of the Industrial Revolution of the seventeenth century,[27] this emerging phenomenon, in our view, provides Africa with leverage and a unique opportunity for having alternative partners in its search for development. The need for such diversification of development partners is underscored by the failure of the West to work genuinely with Africa in facilitating development over the past five decades. On this score, Sally Mathews' submission on the contradictions between the West and development in Africa is apposite. Mathews contends:

> There has been considerable variation in the relations between Africa and the West over the last few centuries. Different eras have seen different relations, and different countries and institutions of the West have varied in the nature of their relations with Africa, with relations between the two regions more often than not being characterized by exploitation of Africa by the West. While it may be unfair to assume, on the basis of past experiences, that the West is necessarily a bad partner for Africa's development, it certainly cannot be assumed that all western countries and institutions are helpful, well-intentioned partners eager to further Africa's development.[28]

It thus behooves Africa to seize this moment and to engage proactively with the new partners while restructuring the pattern of its relationship with the West to its own advantage.

---

25. Cheung et al., *"China's Outward Direct Investment in Africa."*
26. Ibid.$
27. See *Economist* 2006. *"Africa and China."*
28. Matthews, "Investigating NEPAD's Assumptions," 504.

African-Chinese Relations and Economic Development in Africa

There is a current euphoria about economic growth in Africa. From a continent described by the *Economist* of London as "hopeless" less than two decades ago, Africa today has become the toast of investors as high population figures and a booming middle class are fueling mass consumption. As the World Bank has observed, "Africa provides the highest returns on foreign direct investment of any regions in the world."[29] There is no doubt that the current rate of growth in Africa is coterminous with the increasing engagement of China in the continent. The growth in the economies of Africa is directly related to the boom in commodities, which reached its peak in 2007. The boom in commodities itself is a direct response to the expansion in the Chinese economy. Many of the countries that have witnessed an above 6 percent annual growth-rate over the past ten years such as Mauritius, Nigeria, Algeria and so on, are countries with a large Chinese investment presence. Despite the hitches in Zambia, Chinese investment in that country has led to the creation of over one thousand jobs. The establishment of Chinese Economic Zones in different parts of Africa has also led to the creation of jobs in the construction, retail and manufacturing sectors of the economies. With the cancelation of billions of debts for poor African countries, substantial resources have been freed up for productive investment and social services.[30]

Despite these seemingly innocuous success stories, there are concerns that Chinese companies in Africa have formed the habit of bringing in Chinese workers and technology. This practice, critics argue, deprives Africans of space for the acquisition of jobs and technology. At the political level, China has been accused of undermining democratic processes by supporting rogue regimes and blocking sanctions against terrorist governments such as that of Sudan. Others have also charged that China fuels conflict in Africa by supplying arms to insurgent groups. However, most of these allegations have been disproved by Chinese scholars who argue that Chinese policy in Africa is essentially defined by the principle of respect for the sovereignty of the countries to which they relate, without interfering in their internal affairs.

---

29. World Bank, *Global Development Finance.*
30. Brautigam, *The Dragon Gift.*

Notwithstanding these polemics, the activities of some Chinese companies in a country like Nigeria leave much to be desired. For instance, in the mineral sector in Nigeria, many Chinese companies operate without a valid license from the authorities concerned and they could not care less for the environment. The activities of the Chinese miners also pose serious threats to artisanal miners, who are more or less displaced by the Chinese with their more sophisticated technologies and cheap capital. As of today, there are many Chinese in different parts of Nigeria, particularly in remote areas such as Jos, Plateau State, Abakaliki in Ebonyi State and Nassarawa State where they carry out massive mining activities. Labour standards are almost zero as the miners are engaged on the basis of daily pay.

Similar to what happened in Zambia where many workers are killed and injured due to protests over poor environmental standards and safety for workers, Chinese workers in the mineral sector in Nigeria do not pay much concern for the safety of the workers. However, most of the blame for this laxity should be on the Federal Government who fail to establish and enforce standard regulatory regimes for mining activities in the country. The immigration service also shares the blame by not enforcing the expatriate quota system for aliens.

Africa and China Relations in a Changing Global Order

The international economic environment is witnessing some dramatic changes with regard to the rate of economic growth, profitability and return on investment, as well as the volume of outbound investments. The global economic crisis that started in 2007 has had severe consequences on the economies of developed countries, from which many are yet to recover. The Eurozone has been particularly badly affected as many of the countries such as Portugal, Ireland, Italy, Greece and Spain have resorted to austerity measures as a strategy to survive the crisis. The economy of the USA is also undergoing some strains and stress as deficit is well over a trillion dollars, with unemployment still above 8 percent. These domestic problems are having serious effects on the global reach and influence of the global hegemons. While the lags in these economies continue, emerging economies in Asia, Latin America and Africa have witnessed growth and have largely been insulated against the debilitating effects of the crisis.

Consequently, there is a shift in the global geography of power. This shift is expected to affect the geo-political strategy of countries in terms of alliances, cooperation and contestation over the control of international institutions such as the International Monetary Fund (IMF), the World Bank and the World Trade Organization (WTO). Membership of sensitive organs of the United Nations such as the Security Council is also expected to reflect this shift in the global geography of power.

It is in the context of these changes that Chinese and Africa relations are examined here. Although reactions to Chinese presence in Africa have triggered some negative reactions from the West, it is incontrovertible that China has penetrated deeply into the continent. The country also has political leverage as leaders in virtually all countries in Africa welcome China as a new development partner. Africa now has the choice, in the model of development, to adapt according to its own development and sources of financial and technical assistance. The alteration in the balance of relations, which China's presence in Africa has triggered, has many implications for the continent in the changing global order. Firstly, Africa now possesses leverage which can be used to extract more concessions on issues of trade, investment, migration and technology transfer from traditional partners like Europe and the USA.

On issues of trade, the overbearing influence of the West and their rigid stand with regard to the subsidization of agricultural products, which has adversely affected the prospects of agricultural exports from Africa, can now be more forcefully challenged at the WTO. Given the appellation of China as a developing country and the solidarity that exists under the auspices of South-South cooperation, Africa will expect to have support from China on issues that affect the continent at the multilateral-trade level, especially under the Doha Development Round. Relatedly, Africa and other countries in the Caribbean and Pacific region have been locked in a trade and development negotiation with the European Community under the Economic Partnership Agreements for the past ten years. It can be argued that the inability of the European Community to force the hands of the African, Caribbean and Pacific Group of States (ACP) to sign this proposed agreement, is borne out of the cold realization that Africa now has a choice of whom to partner with. The same can be said of the renewal or elongation of the African Growth and Opportunities Act of the USA, which ordinarily would have expired in 2004. Thus, China's presence in Africa provides the continent with a unique opportunity to extract more favourable concessions from the West on issues of investment, trade and finance.

Secondly, the window of opportunity, which the changes in the global geography of power provide with the increasing presence of China in Africa, further creates an avenue to renegotiate the global governance architecture of trade, finance and investment. Reform of the IMF and the World Bank is well overdue. Also, against the backdrop of the uniqueness of the Chinese model of development, which is different from the market-oriented capitalism the West has been promoting in Africa (with its disastrous consequences), there is need for broader engagement on what works in Africa. There is no doubt that Western-oriented global capitalism in itself contains some contradictions that now call into question its utility in human society.[31]

Increasing levels of inequality and poverty, violence and conflict, as well as exclusion at the core of global capitalism, necessitates a new form of economic principle that can serve the interest of the majority of people on the planet. Although the Chinese model of development is not perfect as inequality is high, studies by Martin Ravallion clearly show that over the past three decades, China has successfully lifted millions out of poverty. Inequality has also been drastically reduced.[32] Notwithstanding its ongoing global policy, the state in China has been active in propelling the fast rate of development that has attracted many interests today. The salience of the role of the state in development, which China has so forcefully demonstrated, should form part of the issues for debate in constructing a new global order.

Recommendations and Conclusions

This paper has looked at the increasing penetration of China in Africa and the effects this is having on the continent. We have argued that even though China's engagement with Africa dated back to the establishment of the Republic in 1949, the current high tempo in the relationship with Africa resumed in the 1990s. From the early 2000s to the present, the volume of trade and investment between China and Africa has grown in leaps and bounds. Rather than limiting the relationship to just the issue of trade, it has assumed a form of summit diplomacy, in which Chinese leaders visit African countries and

---

31. Robinson, *Theory of Global Capitalism.*
32. Ravallion, "*A Comparative Perspective on Poverty Reduction in Brazil, China and India.*"

African leaders visit China. The formation of FOCAC constituted the watershed in the economic and political relationship between the two blocs. While the West is nervous about the increasing influence of China in Africa, evidence abounds that Africa has benefited in terms of trade, investment and aid from China.

However, there are justifiable fears that unless Africa positions itself well in terms of building institutions and having a clear agenda of political economy in engaging China, the continent may end up missing the benefits that are inherent in this new relationship. It therefore becomes imperative for Africa to engage with China, not just at a political level, but on an intellectual level. In this regard, Africa must be guided by a sense of history and a concern for the future. Historically, this is not the first time that Africa is engaging with a more developed country. Africa's experience with the West over almost half of a millennium has left nothing but underdevelopment, chaos and conflict. The future of the continent will be imperiled if the present experience with China is not well mediated by political elites, the intelligentsia and civil society.

In order to derive maximum advantage from China, Africa must do the following: firstly, the continent must clearly define its national interest both at the continental and national levels. Such interests must be based on reciprocal profitability rather than on seeking mere gestures such as the building of a secretariat for the African Union (AU) as China did in 2012, or the building of palaces for some chiefs. This must be contained in the AU's foreign economic policy. While Africa and China may not be partners in the real sense of equality, the fact that China derives raw materials from the continent, and that it also has a market for its products, is enough reason for Africa to seek its own benefits in the relationship.

Secondly, it has been reported that most of the Chinese businesses in Africa, outside mineral extraction, are contract-based.[33] This has implications for job creation and economic multiplier effects. This is because Chinese companies that win contracts do come with their own workers or so-called technical experts. It is therefore important for Africa's leaders to emphasize that China brings in more investment to the continent. Such investment could be in the form of establishing manufacturing outfits where the production of machinery, electronic

---

33. Atuanya, "Assessing Nigeria".

materials and other materials can take place. That way, jobs will be created and new technologies can be learned.

Thirdly, there is a need for regulation by African countries regarding the activities of Chinese companies and nationals, especially those in the mining sector. Issues of standards relating to labour, care for the environment and payment of taxes should be well spelt-out. Migration issues such as monitoring the expatriate quotas should also be enforced.

Lastly, beyond concern for economic development, Africa must work with China and other countries in the global South to restructure the global architecture of development. As the biggest economy in Africa, Nigeria has a role to play in the way Africa can use its leverage in the current tempo of its relationship with China both at the diplomatic and economic levels. Although the current challenges that Nigeria is faced with appear to have affected its clout in the international environment, the potentials remain high for a strategic engagement with China both in the pursuit of national interest and continental advantage. As Srinivassan argues, "Nigeria has considerable opportunities to shape a more sophisticated Chinese role in its own development programme, which can both augment and counter-balance ongoing Western engagements on the continent. Africa's most populous country has unique economic and political leverage in this regard and it cannot afford to squander this."[34] Beyond the rhetoric of South-South cooperation, Nigeria should work with other African countries in defining the relationship with China in ways that can benefit the continent economically, technically and diplomatically.

Bibliography

Akinboye, Solomon, and Samuel Oloruntoba. "Global Trade Governance and Economic Development Africa: Exploring Opportunities in South-South Cooperation." *Nigeria Journal of International Relations*, Vol. 39, No.2 (May–August, 2013): 93–113.

Alden, Chris. *China in Africa*. London: Zed Publishers, 2007.

Anshan, L. "China and Africa: Policy and Challenges." *Chinese Security* Vol.3. No. 3 (2007): 69–93.

Atuanya, Patrick. "Assessing Nigeria, Chinese Global Investments." *Economic Watch. Business Day*, April 10, 2013.

---

34. Srinivassan, "Rising Great Power," 355.

Asiedu, Elizabeth. *"Policy Reform and Foreign Direct Investment to Africa: Absolute Progress but relative decline"*, Development Policy Review, 2004, 22 (1), 41-48.

Baran, Paul. *The Political Economy of Growth.* New York: Monthly Review Press 1968.

Brautigam, Deborah. *The Dragon Gift to Africa. The Real Story of China in Africa.* Oxford: Oxford University Press, 2009.

Brautigam Deborah and Adama Gaye. *Is Chinese Investment Good for Africa?* Washington, DC: Council on Foreign Relations, 2007.

Cardoso, Fernando and Enzo Faletto. *Dependency and Development in Latin America.* Translated by Marjory Mattingly Urquidi. Berkeley and Los Angeles: University of California Press, 1979.

Cheung, Yin-Wong, Jakob de Haan, Xingwang Qian, Shu Yu. *"China's Outward Direct Investment in Africa."* Working Paper No. 13. Hong Kong Institute of Monetary Research, 2011.

Forum on Africa-China Cooperation (FOCAC), *"Africa-China Trade and Economic Relationship Annual Report"*, 2010. http://www.focac.org/eng/zxxx/t832788.htm.

Frank, Andre. *Capitalism and Underdevelopment in Latin America.* New York: Monthly Review Press, 1969.

Looy, J. van de. "Africa and China: A Strategic Partnership?" Working Paper 67/2006. Leiden, Netherlands: African Studies Centre, 2006.

Mathews, Sally. "Investigating NEPAD's Development Assumptions." *Review of African Political Economy.* Vol 31, No. 101 (2004): 497–511.

Mawdsley, Emma. "China and Africa: Emerging Challenges to the Geographies of Power" *Geography Compass.* 1/3 (2007): 405–421.

Melville C and Owen, O, China and Africa: A New Era in South-South Cooperation, Open Democracy, 2005, 8, July.

Muekaila, D, J Africa and China Strategic Partnership, African Security Review, 2004, 13 (1), 5 – 11.

O'Brien, R. "The Implications of China's Increased Investment in Africa: An Economic, Political and Cultural Analysis." *Journal of Washington Institute of China Studies.* Vol 13. No.1 (2008): 75–86

Oloo, Adams. *China's Threat to America in Africa.* Al Jazeera Centre for Studies of Africa, 2011.

Collier, Paul and Anthony J. Venables, "Rethinking Trade Preferences: How Africa Can Diversify its Exports," World Economy, 30(8), 1331, August 2007.

Ravallion, Martin. *A Comparative Perspective on Poverty Reduction in Brazil, China and India.* Policy Research Working Paper. 5080, 2009a

Robinson, William. *A Theory of Global Capitalism. Production, Class and State in a Transnational World.* Baltimore: John Hopkins University Press, 2004.

Sautman, Barry and Yan Hairong. "The Forest for the Trees: Trade, Investment and the China-in-Africa Discourse." *Pacific Affairs*. Vol. 81, No.1 (2008): 9–29.

Srinivassan, Sharath. "A 'rising Great Power' embraces Africa: Nigeria-China relations." In *Gulliver's Troubles: Nigeria's Foreign Policy after the Cold War*, edited by Adekeye Adebajo and Abdul Raufu Mustapha. South Africa: University of Kwazulu-Natal Press, 2008.

Taylor, Ian. *China and Africa: Engagement and Compromise*. Abingdon: Routledge, 2006.

The Economist, *Africa and China*, November 3, 2006.

The Economist, *Africa: A hopeless Continent*, May 13th, 2000.

Tull, Denis. "China's Engagement in Africa: Scope, Significance, and Consequences. *Journal of Modern African Studies*, 2006.

Wenping, He. "The Balancing Act of China's Africa Policy." *China Security*. Vol. 3, No. 3 (2006): 1–40.

World Bank *Global Development Finance*. Washington DC: World Bank, 2003.

Xinhua, "China Africa-Economic Relations," 2013.

Chapter Eight. Fifty Years of Sino-Tanzanian Relations–Change or Continuity?

============= ❖ =============

Ng'wanza Kamata

Introduction

In October 2014, Jakaya Kikwete, the president of the United Republic of Tanzania, paid a state visit to China. The visit was part of the culmination of a year-long celebration to mark the golden jubilee of Sino-Tanzania diplomatic relations. During the course of the year, there were many activities and displays of what this relationship had involved over time. It was also an occasion to cement what had been built over the period. In this relationship, China is positively portrayed by the Tanzanian political leadership, as the country is seen as a real friend who, according to President Kikwete, "... has been giving support to Tanzania even during the economic hardness in China, and today as a second biggest economy... China gives without conditions. It is a support from the heart, for the heart."[1] When he visited Tanzania in March 2013 the Chinese President, Xi Jinping, assured not only Tanzania but also other African countries of continued cooperation, despite the growing strength of China and her growing international status. President Jinping underscored that "China and Africa will continue to support each other on issues involving their core and major concerns, and China will remain committed to seek

---

1. Kikwete, Toast remarks.

strength through unity and make greater contribution to peace and development in Africa."[2]

The assuring statements from the two leaders and the numerous gestures expressing mutual cooperation and friendship, which range from high-level state visits by leaders of both countries to generous aid and assistance, widening of areas of cooperation, and an increase in forms and frequency of interactions, signal a desire to continue towards a future built on the foundations of the past, and nourished by the reality and circumstances of the present world. This means that although China and Tanzania have maintained their relations for the past fifty years, the relationship between the two countries has not remained the same. Changes have taken place that have partly been informed and necessitated by internal and external circumstances prevalent to both countries. For example, Tanzania remains a dependent and underdeveloped country and hence porous to external influence and manipulation. Because of this Tanzania as a nation is perhaps less confident and self-reliant today than it was three decades after independence.

China, on the other extreme, has grown into a more independent, self-reliant and more confident nation than it was in the late 1970s, a reality recognized by both the old and emerging powers. Because of the China factor, the power structure in the world is no longer the same as an incipient global power configuration is in the offing. Whereas Tanzania's major decisions over her economy are highly influenced and probably dictated from without, China's economy and society are relatively highly independent and autonomous. Briefly, it is argued that relations between Tanzania and China today are based on a changed political economic context. This would also mean the relationship itself has not remained the same.

This chapter looks very closely at what has characterized Sino-Tanzania relations over the fifty years of its existence. It also examines the foundation upon which the relations were built. To be able to do that, the chapter maps out some of the changes and the continuity in the relationship between the two countries, and tries to understand the conditions that have led to either changes or continuity in certain pattern of their relations. At any rate, we are of the view that China, both in the past and the present, has provided possibilities to countries like Tanzania. Such possibilities have never been made available by the

---

2. Jinping, Speech.

West. In the present context, however, it is up to Tanzania and Africa as a whole to exploit the possibilities created and to define and chart a new path of autonomous development. While this is desirable, we are of the view that it cannot be realized outside a Pan-African framework.

The Pillars of the Sino-Tanzania Relations

Sino-Tanzania relations rest on the foundations created in the first two decades of the relationship and cooperation between the two countries. Three major historical pillars guide their relations today as happened in the past. This is despite the changes in some situations. These pillars include: a shared anti-colonial and ant-imperialist stance; a shared ideological vision on what kind of society both countries wanted to build; and a shared view of the world where there is equality, justice, and peace. In addition, through years of closely working together and constantly consulting on many issues of mutual concern and interests pertaining to their countries, a mutual confidence and trust between generations of political leadership from both countries was built and maintained. It is this foundation which, to a large extent, continues to guide relations between the two countries even in the circumstances of a changed world.

Some of these pillars have survived the test of time and some are deemed to have lost relevance as both countries gave in to a new political-economic dispensation. For example, anti-colonialism is no longer an important agenda, as decolonization ended after all countries in Africa under European colonialism won their independence in the 1980s; and apartheid formally ended after the release of Nelson Mandela and the election of majority rule in South Africa in 1994. However, this does not mean that Africa has achieved total liberation. This is because liberation, if is based on a broad and profound notion of a victory against imperialism; and that direct colonialism was just one form of imperialism as manifested in Africa; and that decolonization was one stage of liberation from imperialism, the struggle to defeat neo-colonialism – a new form of imperialist domination in Africa after political independence – remains an unfinished agenda.[3] The major difference between now and the past is that imperialism in both countries is no longer seen as an important and immediate question. In Tanzania, for example, imperialism is no longer perceived as an enemy in the same way it was in the past. Neo-

3. Cabral, "The Weapon." 81 – 82.

liberalism seems to have normalized many of the forces and leadership in the anti-imperialist struggles.

The normalization of many African states during the neo-liberal era have either diluted or sidelined any ideological tenets in the ruling political parties. In Tanzania, for example, the ruling party, Chama cha Mapinduzi (CCM), remains socialist officially although its government implements neo-liberal policies. The CCM Constitution[4], Article 4(3), states that CCM believes that: "Socialism and self-reliance is the only way to build a society of equal and free individual." And Article 5(3) and (4) states that the objectives and goals of CCM are: "To promote the building of socialism and self-reliance on the basis of the Arusha Declaration"; and subsequently it further states: the aim of the party is "to supervise implementation of CCM's policies and maintain and carry forward the ideological line of the founding fathers[5] of TANU and ASP as enunciated in various writings of the two parties."

On the contrary, the government of Tanzania, under CCM leadership has, since the mid-1980s, been implementing neo-liberal policies. Consequently, its leaders, with the exception of Nyerere, started to distance themselves from the official party ideology. In a few incidences when leaders were pressurized to state what the party stands for ideologically they would stumble, shy away, or dismiss it as an ideology with no relevance in the twenty-first century. This is how President Kikwete, who is also the CCM chairman, behaved in December 2014 when addressing elders of Dar es Salaam. The president categorically stated, in reaction to a parliamentary committee proposal to nationalize the Independent Power Tanzania Limited (IPTL), that nationalization was an old-fashioned *Ujamaa* idea which had no place in today's Tanzania.[6]

China, like Tanzania, is still under the leadership of the Communist Party of China (CPC). Its official ideology remains socialism, but Chinese leaders today claim they are building socialism with Chinese characteristics. Addressing the press on November 15, 2012, President Xi Jinping stated:

---

4. CCM 2010.
5. "Founding fathers" means Julius K. Nyerere, the first president of Tanzania, and Abeid A. Karume, president of Zanzibar and first vice-president of the United Republic of Tanzania.
6. President Jakaya Kikwete on a live TV broadcast through ITV and TBC, on December 22, 2014.

Our responsibility is to work with all comrades in the party to be resolute in ensuring that the party supervises its own conduct; enforces strict discipline; effectively deals with the prominent issues within the party; earnestly improves the party's work style and maintains close ties with the people. So that our party will always be *the firm leadership core for advancing the cause of socialism with Chinese characteristics.*[7]

But socialism with Chinese characteristics is nothing but the adoption of market fundamentals. The major difference, however, is that in this market economy, the state plays a key and important role.

Besides the changes alluded to above, relations between China and Tanzania are also built on mutual respect and trust. This has been the result of many years of interactions and exchange. There are many ways in which this is demonstrated but we will discuss only three of these. First is the question of how the Tanzanian leadership continues to be inspired by the levels of development of China; second – the high-level state and government diplomatic exchanges and visits between the leadership and officials from the two countries; and the third aspect is the constant consultation between the leaders of the two countries at both the party and governmental levels.

China and its people and leadership have inspired and continue to inspire generations of political leadership in Tanzania. Many leaders of Tanzania who have visited China before have come back home amazed and inspired. They have been amazed and inspired by how Chinese people have been able to transform their country within a short period. When Julius Nyerere first visited China in 1965, he came back home stirred up with a new outlook on how development goals could be achieved. Nyerere drew a number of lessons from China that influenced his later approach to development issues. These included the qualities of self-reliance, being hardworking, frugality, and setting national priorities right. In his remarks to the Tanganyika Nation Union (TANU) Congress in March 1965, Nyerere could not conceal his admiration and respect for the Chinese people and their leaders. One of the things that struck him was the ability of the Chinese to resolve the agrarian question and thus their ability to feed themselves. He was equally pleased with their priorities, which were people-centered and included the provision of shelter, food and clothing for

---

7. Jinping, "Full text: speech."

all. Much more important was that all these developments entailed China using its own resources and involved the principle of self-reliance. To Nyerere, China was a good example of a country encouraging other underdeveloped countries that it was possible to transform their societies using their own resources, and to take full control of their destiny. China both encouraged and gave Nyerere more confidence to go ahead with his idea of transforming Tanzania into an *Ujamaa* society based on the principal of self-reliance (TANU 1965). Fifty years later, Kikwete was mesmerized by the Chinese people. A few days after he concluded his visit to China, President Jakaya Kikwete addressed the elders in the country's capital city Dodoma. In his address, Kikwete could not hide his admiration of the Chinese people when he stated, "If a country of 1.3 billion people can feed itself with no one going hungry what else does one describe as development."[8] President Kikwete admitted that China was motivating countries like Tanzania to believe in themselves and their ability to transform their societies.

The level of confidence between the leadership of the two countries is high. This has been maintained through constant exchanges of official visits involving the countries' top leadership and officials. After Tanganyika's independence, for example, Nyerere paid several visits to China. In these visits, he would hold talks and discussions with his counterparts in China. The visits were reciprocated by Chinese leaders. In the 1960s, for instance, the most influential prime minister of China, Zhou Enlai, visited Tanzania. Such visits have been maintained so that to date, in the most recent years, Tanzania has welcomed two Chinese presidents in a span of five years. In February 2009, President Hu Jintao visited Tanzania, and in 2014, President Xi Jinping did likewise. Jinping's visit to Tanzania was his second foreign trip, after Russia, since he had been appointed president of the People's Republic of China in February 2014. This was evidence that the Chinese leadership accords great respect and confidence in, and attaches importance to, Tanzania. Since the beginning of the twenty-first century, there have been numerous visits from China to Tanzania and from Tanzania to China.[9]

Through these diplomatic gestures and exchange, constant consultation has been maintained between the leaderships of the two

---

8. Kuhenga, "Welcome Partner."

9. Shi and Hoebink, "Continuity and Change."

countries. They consult and iron out differences, and clarify any misunderstandings between them. In the mid-1980s, for example, a Chinese party delegation paid a visit to Tanzania on a mission to explain to their Tanzanian counterparts the nature of reforms taking place in China and why such reforms were necessary.[10] The Chinese delegation met Nyerere, among other leaders in Tanzania, who was then serving as chairman of the ruling party after he had stepped down from the presidency in 1985. These kinds of consultations have contributed in maintaining trust and confidence between the leaderships of the two countries for many years. It is important in this respect to note that China of late has sought to consolidate the historical ties with Tanzania and the Southern African region through the surviving former national liberation movements still in power in their respective countries, of which CCM is one. The others include the African National Congress (ANC) of South Africa, the Popular Movement for the Liberation of Angola (MPLA), the Mozambique Liberation Front (FRELIMO); the South West African People's Organization (SWAPO) of Namibia, Zimbabwe African National Union Patriotic Front; and the Chinese Communist Party (CPC). These groups of parties call themselves the Front Line Parties. Through this new arrangement, the parties consult and share experiences about various political problems and challenges facing their countries.

The Socio-economic Basis of the Relations

Over the years, many changes have taken place so that the socio-economic context within which relations between Tanzania and China take place today is different from what it was in the early two decades of its foundation. From the mid-1980s, Tanzania, like other African countries, was coerced into adopting neo-liberal economic fundamentals. This has had many implications, which include retrenchment of the developmental state, de-industrialization;[11] and a new wave of plunder of African resources described by some Africa scholars as the new scramble. The essence of the new scramble is to continue a form of primitive accumulation, otherwise called accumulation by dispossession, through dispossessing the African masses of their resources – especially natural resources such as land,

---

10. Some notes with the author.
11. Mkandawire and Soludo. *Our Continent*.

water, and minerals.[12] But market liberalization in Africa opened up trade opportunities for Chinese manufacturers at the expense of the small and shaky industrial base in the continent.

Both in Tanzania and China, a change in the social structure of society has taken place. Although Tanzania remains predominantly a peasant society as more than 75percentof its population is rural and dependent on agriculture, its urban population has bourgeoned over time and the rate of urbanization in the country has been on the increase since neo-liberal reforms were adopted in the late 1980s. Most of this urban population though is made up of unemployed youth. Tanzania has a general unemployment rate of over 12 percent. In the midst of this, an emergent *petit-bourgeois* class is growing and claiming space, special attention and privileges. This class has arisen largely as a result of various connections created by emerging new forms of accumulation in the various sectors of the neoliberal economic setting on one hand, and their connection to the state and politics on the other. These socio-economic conditions and the class positions and interests that different classes hold determine their reactions to the Sino-Tanzania relations.

A few examples will shed some light on how this is reflected within the Tanzania polity. It is clear that although some people in Tanzania ridicule the quality of Chinese goods, many others survive and eke a living from the usage of Chinese gadgets and machinery. For instance, the thousands of youths who have found employment by riding on Chinese-made motorcycles, which serve as taxis, would proudly talk about their new-found job opportunities, thanks to the Chinese motorcycle. This is despite the fact that majority of these youths do not own the motorcycles as they are owned by those with better and extra incomes. But for them, these simple motorcycles have given them some means of earning an income. It also applies to other made-in-China goods that are easily and affordably found in many stores in both the rural and urban areas. However, these same people would complain about Chinese people taking up their jobs, or Chinese employers mistreating them. Both reactions are understandable and expected because in the first place, Tanzania has a very big army of unemployed youth, and secondly, with the high rate of unemployment, employers have a free hand regarding whom to employ, how much to pay, and how to treat their employees. This however applies to all

---

12. Moyo and Patnaik, 11.

employers in Tanzania regardless of their nationalities.[13] But Chinese employers are singled out regarding their origin, hence somehow replacing the Asian employers who were detested by their employees. The *petit bourgeoisie* have other concerns. Some seethe Chinese companies and businessmen coming to Tanzania as an opportunity and some perceive them as a threat. In most cases their loyalty and opportunism is divided and fluid. They swing between Western (European) potential "investors" to the Chinese. There have been reports in the papers and in the "grape vine" of divisions within the political class regarding who should be given a deal – whether this should be a Chinese or a European company. The division is based on the "political rent" paid to the officers individually or as a group of a political class. Because of these divisions and concerns, contracts have been cancelled, and/or projects have been delayed. A case of this nature was reported in 2011 involving the expansion of the Dar es Salaam port. The Chinese government, through the Exim Bank, had agreed to extend a loan to Tanzania for the project, and a company had already been appointed. But it was alleged that the minister responsible for the sector was looking for a different company that would meet his personal interests.[14] In a related incident, the Tanzania Port Authority (PTA) director-general, Mr. Ephraim Mgawe, appeared in court on charges relating to the misuse of his authority after allegedly granting a contract to a Chinese Company, China Communications Company Ltd (CCCCL), without following tendering procedures.[15] And since Tanzania has in recent years discovered huge gas deposits, and the potential for discovery of oil is high, it has become a theatre of power struggles among the old and emerging powers.

In China, the social structure has not remained the same during the past fifty years. Different studies show that social stratification in Chinese society has taken place since the beginning of reforms in 1979.[16] According to Yi,[17] Chinese society is divided into five classes: the upper class who are between 0.6 percent to 1percentof the population; the upper middle class constituting between 6 to 8 percent of the population; the middle class who are between 36 to 44 percent;

---

13. Kamata, "Perspectives."
14. Reporter, "The good, bad side" in *The Citizen*.
15. Michuzi, "Mgawe Akiri."
16. Lu, "A Guide to Social Class."
17. Yi, "New Changes."

the lower middle class who are between 34 and 28 percent; and the lower class who are between 24 and 20 percent of the Chinese population. Using a report widely covered in the media in China in 2005, Qu[18] presents ten categories of the social classes in China. The classification is based on occupation rather than the position one holds in a socially determined process of production. The ten categories however are indicative of what has been taking place in China that, as Qu observes, the Chinese society can no longer be referred to as a society of predominantly peasants and workers. However, even in this crude occupational-based classification, the peasantry in China form the majority (42.9 percent), and most of those who fall between mid and lower categories (between categories seven–nine) are in the lower income brackets; and the rest (especially under three–six) constitute a small but bourgeoning section of the society which is prospectively rich – the new and emerging *petit-bourgeois* class. Compared to Tanzania, China's rural and peasantry population has decreased over time.

What we cannot tell and explain from these studies are the social relations between these classes. But what is obvious from someone looking at them from the Tanzanian vantage point, is that all the classes seem to have taken advantage of the present relations between Tanzania and China. Perhaps one of the major features of the present relations between Tanzania and China is a big influx of Chinese people. There is a category of Chinese professionals – project managers and engineers in various Chinese construction companies and projects, and doctors, among others. There are also those who come to do business as merchants or retailers. There are those too who open small factories, garages for maintenance and repair of motor vehicles, and restaurants. And there is a category of Chinese workers employed by these garages, construction companies, and restaurants, among others. Some of these have the potential inclination of settling in the country. There is also a category of academics who come to Tanzania through various exchange programs between Tanzania and Chinese universities. So far Tanzania has been receiving some students in its various public universities, including the University of Dar es Salaam, the oldest university in the country. They enrol in different university programmes for short-term (about six months) and long-term periods, which range from one to three years. There is also a significant presence of Chinese teachers affiliated to the Confucius Institutes

---

18. Qu, "Understandings."

established in various public universities of Tanzania. The increased presence of Chinese people in Tanzania has been a cause, in some cases, of tensions and concern – especially among unemployed youth and petty traders. Although Tanzania has been sending students to study in Chinese universities, their numbers, plus those doing business and other activities in China, are still minimal.

The Actors, the Forms and Areas of Interactions

After fifty years of relations between China and Tanzania, the state remains the main actor. The state is hereby understood only in its limited sense of an "abstract legal entity, representing the conceived unity of the population of a defined territory, legally sovereign, having a government to act on its behalf, and existing to serve the general purpose of its population."[19] States of both countries have, directly or through their various institutions, cooperated and entered into and implemented various agents. Some of the major areas of cooperation have been in the form of projects that have been financed, implemented, and managed by the states themselves. This is exemplified by three projects: one is old; two are new and most recent. The oldest of all is the Tanzania Zambia Railway (TAZARA) which has continued to enjoy generous financial, material and technical assistance from China since the completion of its construction in the 1970s. The most recent new projects include the gas pipeline from Mtwara to Dar es Salam, and the Iron and coal project at Liganga and Mchuchuma. The gas-pipeline from Mtwara, in the Southern part of Tanzania, to Dar es Salaam received a generous loan of more than $1 billion from the government of China. The project was completed in July 2015. Similarly, the Iron and coal project at Liganga and Mchuchuma is financed by the Chinese government and is jointly owned by the National Development Corporation (NDC), a state-owned company in Tanzania, and the Sichuan Hong da Group Corporation from the Sichuan Province of China.[20] In another move, China and Tanzania signed an agreement in November 2014 in which the Chinese government and a Dubai-based company and the Tanzania government will jointly finance the construction of a new port at Bagamoyo.

---

19. Reynolds, *An Introduction to International Relations*, 18.
20. Kabwe, "Taarifaya Zitto."

However, there are many other actors and non-state actors especially since reforms took place in both countries. These include private companies and merchants from China and Tanzania. Because of the myriad of actors and the nature of activities they conduct, relations have become more complex than they were in the 1960s and towards the end of the 1980s. During this period, all forms of interactions were regulated by and mediated through the state. This survived up to the end of the 1980s as Tanzania reformed its economy thereafter. The reforms led to the liberalization of the economy and hence privatization of parastatal organizations. By 1979, China had already reformed its economy and a myriad of private, public, and joint venture business enterprises had already been introduced. Mobius,[21] for example, reported that China today has 112 central government-owned companies which the state wants to reform. But there is an array of companies owned by lower state administrative units such as municipalities. Their operations abroad are encouraged and supported by the Chinese government.

The multiplication of actors, forms and frequency of interactions has made the relations between the two countries more complex than before. This has consequently resulted in an inability by the states to predict and fully monitor and guide the behaviour of some actors, especially the many non-state actors. Because of this, relations between China and Tanzania have sometimes been caught in some controversies. Although such debates have not strained their relations, they have necessitated collective and joint efforts and intervention to iron them out in order to maintain mutual trust and confidence. In most recent times, for example, Sino-Tanzania relations were plagued with allegations of the illicit export of elephant tusks from Tanzania to China. *The Guardian*[22] quoted a report produced by the US-based Environmental Investigation Agency (EIA), alleging that Chinese nationals were actively involved in the business which was "stripping Tanzania of its elephants". The report went further to allege that officials from both the Tanzanian and Chinese government were aware of the business. Both the Tanzanian and Chinese governments dismissed the report as baseless. Tanzania's Foreign Minister, Bernard Member, speaking before Tanzania's Parliament, dismissed the report and the allegation that some members in President Xi Jinping's

---

21. Mobius, "Reform is Happening."
22. Vaughn and Kaiman, "Chinese Demand" in *The Guardian*.

delegation, which included a businessmen and officials, had sent the ivory to China in diplomatic bags on the presidential plane.[23] As a response to these accusations, China and Tanzania have upped their cooperation in the fight against wildlife poaching and trade on elephant tusks. As a gesture of its commitment to anti-poaching efforts, the Chinese government in July 2015 granted the Tanzanian government equipment and cars to boost the anti-poaching campaign in the country.

Besides the illicit business in ivory, there are some other trans-sovereign activities which involve nationals from both countries. Reports suggest that some Tanzanians carried out drug business in China. According to such reports, the number of cases of Tanzanians arrested in China on drug trafficking has been on the increase.[24] There have been consultations between the two governments on how to curb the business. That aside, there are many Tanzanians and Chinese in both countries who are involved in legal businesses.

The multiplicity of actors also means an increase in the number of interactions, and a diversification of forms of interactions between the two countries. Although there are numerous ways of measuring interactions, the most common and visible ones include volumes of trade, foreign investment, tourism and travel, telephone calls and data transfers, international conferences, academic exchanges, and cultural and sports exchanges, and state and government diplomatic visits and exchanges.[25] In the subsequent discussion, we will focus on only a few areas of interactions to demonstrate what has changed and what has not. One area is trade and investment. The TAZARA railway line has always been cited as the most outstanding indicator of China's commitment to Tanzania. While this is true, recent developments suggest that there is more to showcase today than TAZARA. Trade between Tanzania and China, for example, has been on the increase since both countries reformed their economies. Data for 2005 –2013 is indicative of the tremendous growth in the volume of trade between the two countries. During the period, trade between China and Tanzania increased from $290 million in 2007[26] to $3.7 billion in 2013.

23. Membe, "Kauliya Waziri."
24. Majani, "Tanzania Destination of Drugs."
25. Holsti, *International Politics,* 64.
26. China Embassy 2007 and Trademark, 2014.

Chinese-made consumables dominate the market in Tanzania. They are available in all qualities and prices. Their consumers range from those in the upper echelons to the lowest stratum of the society. Because of this mix, Chinese goods have heightened a confused and sometimes conflictual debate in Tanzania on their quality and durability. The Chinese government and embassy in Tanzania however have not stood by and watched, but have made some interventions to clarify this and have at times assured the Tanzanian public on the measures the government was taking to curb this problem. This was the case when Liu Xinsheng, Chinese Ambassador to Tanzania, said that it was improper to judge everything made in China as forged. He further argued that at times, China is accused of producing substandard goods while some of them were not necessarily made in China.[27] While this is true, it is important to recognize the fact that China, in the daily discourse in Tanzania, has come to mean many things: one of these is that anything considered to be of lower quality or substandard is assigned the labelled *Mchina* (read: "that is Chinese"), meaning it is of low quality, substandard, not durable. This adage is sometimes used without necessarily meaning that it is made in China. Along these lines, a Chinese deputy director-general for the Department of West Asia and African Affairs in the Ministry of Commerce, Cao Jiachang, in his address to visiting Tanzanian journalists in China, echoed Ambassador's Xisheng's concerns but also admitted that there were "unscrupulous Chinese manufacturers who colluded with greedy business people from Tanzania . . . to flood their markets with substandard imports that are badly fashioned or are dangerous to health."[28]

Investment is another area of interaction between the two countries which has attracted important attention. However, this is one-way traffic for most investments flow from China to Tanzania. Investment takes at least two major forms. The first is official investment, where the Chinese government extends a grant or loan to the Tanzanian government, and the second is private, which involves Chinese people or companies directly investing in Tanzania. According to the official site of the Chinese embassy, there were slightly over 300 Chinese companies investing around $200 million in Tanzania by 2010. The number had risen to more than 500 by 2013, with over $2,490 million

---

27. *Daily News*, May 9, 2011.
28. *Daily News*, August 24, 2012.

being invested.[29] Of these investments, 80 percent were made by private Chinese companies.[30] This is a major departure from the types of investments characterising the 1960s through to the 1980s, which were mostly governmental.

But it is important to note that China's official support to state-owned and state-run projects form a major feature, in terms of the volume of investment, in Tanzania. Between 1995 and 2014, the Chinese government has supported and financed many governmental projects of different magnitudes. In the list, they include the construction of the Chalinze Water Project, the National Stadium,[31] and investment in the state-run Kiwira Coal Mine.[32] As stated before, there are two most recent major projects that have received support and funding from the Chinese Government. These include the Liganga iron-ore site and the Mchuchuma Coal mine. An agreement to carry out the Liganga and Mchuchuma project was reached by the Government of Tanzania and the Government of China in September 2011. Construction of the project was expected to commence in 2015. In the agreement, the Chinese company has 80 percent of the stakes while the National Development Corporation (NDC), a government development entity, has 20 percent, with an opportunity of increasing its stakes to 49 percent in the future after the Chinese company has recovered the costs of investment. The project will cost $3 billion which will be given as a soft loan to Tanzania by the Government of China.[33] Another project is an agreement between the Tanzanian Government and Exim Bank of China to finance a 532-km pipeline for transporting natural gas from Mnazi Bay in Mtwara to Dar es Salaam. In this agreement, Exim Bank of China granted Tanzania credit of $1.2 billion. The project was implemented by the Joint China Petroleum and Technology Development Company (CPTDC), a unit of the China National Petroleum Corporation (CNPC). Construction was completed in July 2015. These projects follow the pattern of state-to-state relations which characterized China and Tanzania relations in the first three decades of their diplomatic ties.

---

29. Kikwete, Keynote address.
30. Chinese Embassy 2011.
31. Moshi and Mtui, "Scoping studies."
32. *Daily News*, August 20, 2012.
33. *Daily News*, September 22, 2011.

Construction of a new port is another major project in the pipeline. When President Xi visited Tanzania in 2013, thirteen bilateral cooperation agreements were signed. The most outstanding was the building of a new port at Bagamoyo. The Bagamoyo port agreement was sealed when President Kikwete visited China in 2014. Kikwete mentioned the development of the Bagamoyo port and the construction of an economic special zone around the port as the major highlight of his visit to China. The Bagamoyo port and the economic special zone are estimated to cost over $10 billion, and involves the Government of Tanzania, which will provide more than 9,000 hectares of land; China Merchant Holding International, which will provide the expertise; and the Sultanate of Oman's General Reserve Fund, which will provide the finance.[34] The multilateral nature of this project provides a new model of cooperation involving China and Tanzania. It is important to note that even in the changed context, major development projects in Tanzania, with the support of China, are government or state based. The projects, as was the case in the 1960s and throughout 1980s, are constructed by Chinese companies.

Defense is another area which continues to be central in Sino-Tanzania state-state relations. China's support to the Tanzanian military started long after the army in Tanzania Mainland mutinied in January 1964. In the 1960s, China's support to Tanzania raised some eyebrows in the West. Writing about this, Hall and Peyman[35] suggested that although Nyerere admitted to some risk involved in bringing the Chinese into the army, he was of the view that the only risk, if any, would be a mutiny of the army. But "my army revolted in January", he remarked to those who questioned his decision to welcome the Chinese, and "it was not trained by the Chinese."[36] Such concerns in the West did not deter the two countries from continuing their cooperation. Recent records suggest that China has been key in Tanzania's efforts to modernize its military. In recent years, according to DefenceWeb,[37] China sold different types of military equipment to Tanzania in 2013, which included twenty-four Type 63A light amphibious tanks, twelve Type 07PA 120 mm self-propelled mortars, FB-6A mobile short-range air defense systems and A100 300 mm

---

34. *BBC News*, "Bagamoyo Port."
35. Hall and Peyman, *Great Uhuru Railway*.
36. Ibid., 72.
37. DefenceWeb, "Historic Naval Exercise."

multiple rocket launchers. Prior to this, China sold some military hardware delivered to Tanzania which included tanks, armoured personnel carriers and combat aircraft. In addition to military hardware, DefenceWeb[38] points out several other projects, which include the building of Tanzania Military Academy (TMA), and the construction of 12000 housing units on a $550 million loan from the Exim Bank of China. It is important to note that military information is not easy to obtain, but what DefenceWeb[39] is able to report is indicative of the level of cooperation between the two countries in the area of defense.

As noted earlier, the forms of interaction have diversified over time and efforts are made to expand into areas that have not achieved sound progress. These include tourism and international conferences, academic, sports and cultural exchanges. In the area of tourism, recent data suggests that Tanzania receives 5000 tourists[40] per annum. This is a significant increase and efforts are being made to tap into the growing number of Chinese travelling abroad for leisure. In the area of international conferences, a few such conferences, mainly business round tables and forums, have taken place. Some of these have been hosted in Tanzania. For example, two such events took place in June 2014 and April 2015. The forums were organized by the government of Tanzania and the Tanzania Private Sector Foundation. There are fewer conferences and forums bringing together scholars and intellectuals from China and Tanzania. The only major forum with some academic content was the "Joint Conference of the Confucius Institutes in Africa", held in June 2014. The conference was hosted by the University of Dar es Salaam.

While there are weak direct links and interaction between academics and intellectuals from the two countries, there are encouraging developments in the area of student exchange. There are many students from Tanzania studying in China and the number of Chinese students studying in Tanzanian public universities is on increase. Although numbers cannot be established, the presence of Chinese students on campuses and in the lecture rooms of Tanzania's universities is becoming a common feature. This was not the case a few decades ago. The streets and suburbs of major cities in Tanzania

---

38. Ibid.
39. Ibid.
40. Tairo, "Tanzania tries its luck."

are also dotted with Chinese people. They are either residents in these suburbs or they are workers involved in all sorts of activities. The same can be said of Tanzanians in China, especially in major commercial and industrial cities of China. According to Ambassador Shimbo, Tanzania's ambassador to China, the presence of a significant number of Tanzanians in different regions of China has resulted in the formation of associations of Tanzanians there. It is important to note that although there were people-to-people exchanges in the past, the difference today is that the number has increased and exchanges are on a private and not on an official basis. Travels to China from Tanzania have soared over time. In 2013 the Chinese embassy in Dar es Salaam estimated that the number of visa applications to China would rise to 10,000 per annum. While this is introducing a new avenue of interaction and relations, it is also creating the possibility for synergy between people and cultures.

Some Perceptions of China-Tanzania Relations

Many opinions are formed about relations between China and Tanzania. This was the case when such relations were predominantly state-to-state and now, when there are more actors and more forms and frequency of interactions. As such, views about China and Tanzania relations are many and more varied today than before. Some of the perceptions continue, although some are new and contentious. Opinions about relations between China and Tanzania can be grouped into two major categories: state/government perceptions of the relations on the one hand and popular views on the other.

At the state level, the general perception from Tanzania towards China remains the same as before: that of China as an all-weather friend. In the words of President Kikwete, China does not "have better friends in Africa than us."[41] This view on China has been maintained by a number of factors mentioned earlier: mutual cooperation and constant consultation between the top political leadership of the two countries, both at the party and government level; and China's continued support for Tanzania. This has also been strengthened by the belief among Tanzanian leaders that China is a real and trusted friend who understands "our" situation.[42] Evidence attesting to the notion that China is "our all-weather friend" could be seen in the way

---

41. *Financial Times,* 2007.
42. Kuhenga, "Welcome Partner."

in which China rescued some projects discouraged by the World Bank. In the 1960s for example, the Bretton Woods Institutions discouraged the construction of the TAZARA railway and China come in and rescued the project. Such a tendency was repeated when Tanzania approached the same institutions to construct the gas pipeline from Mtwara to Dar es Salaam. The Bank and the Fund dilly-dallied and China came in to rescue the project.[43]

In addition to this, there is a view among Tanzanian leaders that China "respects us." This perspective is shared by many African leaders who dislike the way other countries, especially the West, treats them. According to General Carter Ham, the Commander of the US Africom, African leaders feel that they are not treated as equals and they want to be treated with dignity and respect.[44] China does approach its relations with Africa along those lines, and unlike the West, China does not ask many questions when assisting an African country.[45]

Apart from this general perception of the state on China, there are a few dissenting views within the political class. However, these are not openly aired but could be said in private discussions, and in certain actions of government officials or members of parliament. On rare occasions, China is mentioned in parliamentary debates as was the case in July 2013 when Kabwe[46] implicated a Chinese Company for hammering the last nail into the Air Tanzania Corporation, a state-owned air company that was struggling to survive; and in June 2015 when Tundu Lissu, an opposition Member of Parliament, claimed that the reason the government was rushing the adoption of the Oil and Gas Bill was because both China and the US needed such a law in place before the government requested money from the two governments in September 2015.[47] There are also cases, as some informants shared with us, when cabinet ministers would differ on whether a Chinese or a Western company should be given a concession or project.

Opinions among various classes differ and depend on how one encounters and experiences China, and this is a new thing in China-Tanzania relations. Among the elite, an issue of concern is the fear that China is here to control and exploit the country's resources. This

---

43. Reporter, "The good, bad side" in *The Citizen*.
44. Campbell, "Dismantle AFricom!"
45. *Financial Times*, 2007.
46. Kabwe, "Taarifa."
47. Tibason, "Wabunge."

debate appears in print, social media, and electronic media. In one posting on China, Erick Kabendera[48] was critical of Chinese deals with Tanzanian officials, accusing them of corruption in such deals at the expense of the country's resources. He also accused Chinese companies of over-costing the projects they supported in Tanzania. His conclusion was that China and Europe should be compared to establish who Tanzania's truer friend was. Reactions to Kabendera's views are varied; however, the dominant one was that the problem was not China, but the leadership in Tanzania.

The most common and widely shared view however is about "Made in China." The general perception is that such goods are of low quality and do not last for a long time. But the same people who speak negatively about "Made-in-China" products would buy Chinese goods, and would appreciate their functionality and usefulness. With time however, people are starting to realize that not everything made in China is of low quality. In addition, people have started to appreciate China's development and what it has been able to achieve within a very short time. Their quest for development is drawn in ordinary and intellectual discussions to challenge the government for its inability to achieve rapid development. In a situation where corruption in government circles is rampant in Tanzania, China is often cited as a country with an uncompromising stance over corrupt officials. It is common to hear "if it were in China, this corrupt government official would have been hanged to death." The Chinese are also appreciated for their work organization, discipline, and diligence. This is based on the work in which Chinese people in Tanzania are involved – road construction, restaurants, garages, and building constructions.

It is important to emphasize at this juncture that most of the opinions are based on how one encounters and experiences China. It is not uncommon to find people criticizing and appreciating China at the same time.

Conclusion

Relations between China and Tanzania remain strong and signs suggest that this is going to be so for the foreseeable future. This is despite the conflicting views on the relations between the two countries. Here it is important to reiterate two factors that favour this position: firstly, the political leadership in both countries maintain

---

48. Kabendera, "In Tanzania we need to talk."

mutual trust and respect. This has been possible because, at a political level, relations have been built not only in the state but cemented through the ruling parties of both countries. The only uncertain factor lies in the event that the ruling party in Tanzania, CCM, is replaced by another party with no traits of national liberation history. Secondly, China has so far proven to be a reliable country that has speedily come in and has been ready to rescue a country in need. No country in Africa can ignore this fact. In this sense, maintaining good relations with China in the situation of the world today seems inevitable. Third, relations between China and Tanzania today have gone beyond the state. They involve many non-state actors in the form of people who travel between the two countries for business and education, and private companies seeking investment opportunities. These new actors define their interests in these relations beyond the confines of the state and would like the good relations to be maintained as long as they serve their interests which seem to involve the long term for now.

In its relations with Tanzania, China created some possibilities for Tanzania in the past and it continues to do so today. Such possibilities are two-fold: firstly, China invests in areas where the West has not ventured in Africa since independence. One example given in our discussion is the constructions of major infrastructure such as the TAZARA railway line. It is important to note here that most of the railway lines in Africa built after African independence have been built with Chinese money and technology. This trend continues today in Tanzania, and in some other African countries. We mentioned three major projects in Tanzania financed by China. These are the gas pipeline, the construction of the new port at Bagamoyo, and the development of the iron and coal mines at Liganga and Mchuchuma. They represent important developments for the country in infrastructure, provided that Tanzania takes advantage of their presence in the country. Otherwise it would be the same old story of serving as the source of raw materials for industries elsewhere. Secondly, most of the major projects in which China has been investing are state-owned and run. This creates a possibility of revisiting the developmental state as a vanguard in the development of African countries. This is inspired by the fact that China retains some leverage as a developmental state, and the projects it funds and supports in Tanzania defies the neoliberal dictum of retrenching the state as the agency of development.

Finally, China creates for Tanzania and Africa some breathing space. It creates what Shivji[49] calls a "great opportune moment for great social transformation in Africa." Vijay Prashad[50] argues that China has given and is giving Tanzania and Africa some oxygen – a period during which some serious thinking can take place as the pressure from the West can be contained. This makes sense in view of what has been happening in Africa after more than three decades of being pressurized and suffocated by the West and the Bretton Woods institutions to implement neo-liberal policy prescriptions as the only available alternative. This was the case in the 1960s throughout the 1980s when China, among other progressive countries, in the context of liberation struggles, offered an opportunity for Africa to wage a successful war against colonialism. China thus offers an opportunity for Africa to wage the second national liberation effort today. A final note on this line though is that as it was for the first liberation that happened within the framework of Pan-Africanism, this second phase of African liberation cannot be successful outside Pan-Africanism. As Nyerere said: "African nationalism is meaningless, is anachronistic, and is dangerous, if it is not at the same time Pan-Africanism."[51]

Bibliography

BBC. Bagamoyo Port: Tanzania Begins Construction on Mega Project. BBC News, 16 October 2015. Accessed 20 January 2017. http://www.bbc.com/news/world-africa-34554524.

Cabral, Amilcar. "The Weapon of Theory." *Revolution in Guinea: An African People's Struggle.* Stage 1: London, 1969.

Campbell, Horace G. "Dismantle AFRICOM!" *Pambazuka News* [Online]. December 13 2012. Accessed July 21, 2015. http://www.pambazuka.net/en/category.php/features/85780.

CCM. *Katibaya Chama cha Mapinduzi 1977,* CCM: Dodoma. 2010.

Daily News. Dar es Salaam, Tanzania: Tanzania Standard Newspapers. May 9, 2011.

Daily News. Dar es Salaam, Tanzania: Tanzania Standard Newspapers. November 25, 2011.

Daily News. Dar es Salaam, Tanzania: Tanzania Standard Newspapers. September 22, 2011.

---

49. Kamata, "Perspectives", 88.
50. Prashad, *"The Poorer Nations."*
51. Nyerere, *Freedom and Unity,* 194.

Daily News. Dar es Salaam, Tanzania: Tanzania Standard Newspapers. August 20, 2012.

Daily News. Dar es Salaam, Tanzania: Tanzania Standard Newspapers. August 24, 2012.

DefenceWeb. "China and Tanzania Conclude Historic Naval Exercise." November 18, 2014. Accessed July 20, 2015. http://www.defenceweb.co.za/index.php?option=com_content& view=article&id=37029:china-and-tanzania-conclude-historic-naval-exercise.

Embassy of China. "China and Tanzania on Economic and Trade Relations and Economic and Technical Cooperation." 2008. Accessed June 15, 2015. http://tz.china-embassy.org/eng/ ztgx/jj/t421433.htm.

Embassy of China. "China and Tanzania on Economic and Trade Relations and Economic and Technical Cooperation." April 13, 2011. Accessed June 15, 2015. http://tz.china-embassy.org/eng/ztgx/jj/t814946.htm

Financial Times. "FT: Interviews Jakaya Kikwete."www.ft.com/cms/s/0/d8a07e28-72a3-11dc-b7ff-0000779fd2ac.html#axzz25D4cJLSi.

Hall, Richard and Hugh Peyman. *The Great Uhuru Railway: China's Showpiece in Africa*. Littlehampton Book Services Ltd: West Sussex, 1976.

Holsti, Kalevi Jaakko. *International Politics: A Framework for Analysis*. Prentice-Hall International: New Jersey, 1992.

Jinping, Xi. "Full text: China's party chief Xi Jinping's speech." *BBC News* [Online], 2012. Accessed July 12, 2015. http://www.bbc.com/news/world-asia-china-20338586.

Jinping, Xi. Speech at the Julius Nyerere International Convention Center in Tanzania. Chinese Embassy in Tanzania [Online]. April 12, 2013. Accessed August 25, 2015. http://tz.china-embassy.org/eng/topics/xjpzxftzt/t1030626.htm.

Kabendera, Erick. "In Tanzania we need to talk about China," 2014. Accessed August 24, 2015. https://www.facebook.com/ zittokabwe/posts/704515409569159

Kabwe, Z. "Taarifaya Zitto Kabwe Kuhusu ATCL." *WAVUTI* [Online]. January 2015. Accessed July 21, 2015. http://www.wavuti.com/2015/01/bungeni-taarifa-ya-zitto-kabwe-kuhusu.html.

Kabwe, Z. "Mchuchuma – Liganga Project, A Milestone." [Online] September 24, 2011. Accessed July 20, 2015. https://zittokabwe.wordpress.com/2011/09/24/mchuchuma-liganga-project-a-milestone/

Kamata, Ng'wanza, ed. "Perspectives on Sino-Tanzania Relations, in Seifudein Adem." *China's Diplomacy in Eastern and Southern Africa.* Ashgate: Barlington (2013): 87-106.

Kikwete, Jakaya Mrisho. Toast Remarks by Jakaya Mrisho, president of the United Republic of Tanzania, at the state banquet hosted in his honour by Xi Jinping, President of the People's Republic of China, at the Great People's Hall, Beijing, China, October 24, 2014.

Kikwete, Jakaya Mrisho. Keynote Address by Jakaya Mrisho Kikwete, President of the United Republic of Tanzania, at the Third Tanzania-China Investment Forum, Beijing, China, October 23, 2014a.

Kuhenga, Makwaia wa. "Why China is a Welcome Partner in the Developing World." *Daily News.* Dar es Salaam Tanzania: Tanzania Standard Newspapers, November 16, 2010.

Lu, R. "A Guide to Social Class in Modern China" *Tea Leaf Nation* [Online]. April 28 2014. Accessed July 20, 2015. http://www.tealeafnation.com/2014/04/a-guide-to-social-class-in-modern-china/.

Majani, Florence. Tanzania: The Ideal Destination for Drug Gangs. *The Mail and Guardian.* April 30, 2013. Accessed January 20, 2017. http://mg.co.za/article/2013-08-30-00-tanzania-the-ideal-destination-for-drug-gangs.

Mkandawire, Thandika and Soludo, Charles C. *Our Continent Our Future: African Perspectives on Structural Adjustments.* Trenton: African World Press, Inc.

Mobius, Mark. "Reform is Happening in China's State-Owned Businesses." *Business Insider* [Online]. June 10, 2015. Accessed July 20, 2015. http://www.businessinsider.com/reform-is-happening-in-chinas-state-owned-enterprises-2015-6.

Membe, B. "Kauliya Waziri Membe Bungeni Kuhusu Biashara Haramuya Pembeza Ndovu." *Sonda Communications* [Online]. November 2014. Accessed August 30, 2015. http://www.sondacomblog.com/2014/11/kauli-ya-waziri-membe-bungeni-kuhusu.html

Michuzi, M. "Mgawe Akiri Kuusaini Mkatabawakibiashara Kati ya TPA naKampuniya China Communications Compnay."

Michuziblog. [Online]. September 11, 2014. Accessed July 20, 2015. http://issamichuzi.blogspot.com/2014/09/mgawe-akiri-kuusaini-mkataba-wa.html.

Moshi, H.P.B. and J.M. Mtui. "Scoping Studies on Africa-China Economic Relations: The Case of Tanzania." A report submitted to AERC, Nairobi, Kenya, 2008.

Nyerere, Julius. Kambarage. *Freedom and Unity.* Nairobi: Oxford University Press, 1974.

Patnaik, Utsa and Moyo, Sam. *The Agrarian Question in the Neoliberal Era: Primitive Accumulation and the Peasantry.* Pambazuka Press: Cape Town.

Prashad, Vijay. *The Poorer Nations: A Possible History of the Global South,* New York: Verso, 2013.

Qu, Lily. "Understandings About the Social Structure in Modern China." *ChinaScope*[Online]. February 5, 2008. Accessed July 20, 2015. http://chinascope.org/main/content/view/428/148/1/0/.

Raia Mwema. "Ufisadi Mpya Kuitikisa Dar." *Raia Mwema.* [Online]. December 14, 2014. Accessed June 5, 2015. http://www.raiamwema.co.tz/ufisadi-mpya-kuitikisa-dar.

Reporter. "The good, bad side of Beijing's billions in Tanzania." *The Citizen* [Online]. August 12, 2014. Accessed July 21, 2015. http://www.thecitizen.co.tz/News/national/The-good--bad-side-of-Beijing-s-billions-in-Tanzania/-/1840392/2416104/-/ufuiu2z/-/index.html.

Reynolds, Philip Alan. *An Introduction to International Relations.* London and New York: Longman, 1994.

Shi, Xuefei and Paul Hoebink. "Continuity and Change in Africa-China Relations: The Case of Tanzania." 8th Pan-European Conference on International Relations, Warsaw, Poland, September 18–21, 2013. Accessed August 29, 2015. http://www.eisa-net.org/be-bruga/eisa/files/events/warsaw2013/Shi_Continuity%20and%20Change%20in%20Africa-China%20Relations%20The%20Case%20of%20Tanzania.pdf.

Tairo, A. "Tanzania tries its luck, looking at lucrative Chinese Tourist Market." *Tanzania Gateway.* [Online] no date. Accessed July 20, 2015. http://www.defenceweb.co.za/index.php?option=com_content&view=article&id=37029:china-and-tanzania-conclude-historic-naval-exercise.

Tibason, D. "Wabungewa Ukawa Wakomaa, kuzuia Miswadanjeya Bunge." *Mwana Halisi* [Online]. July 5, 2015. Accessed August 13, 2015. http://mwanahalisionline.com/ukawa-wakomaa-wajipanga-kuzuia-miswada-nje-ya-bunge/.

Trade Mark. Accessed March 24, 2016. http://www.trademarksa.org/news/trade-volume-between-tanzania-and-china-rises-37bn.

Vaughan, Adam and Jonathan Kaiman. "Chinese Demand for Ivory is Devastating Tanzania's Elephants." *The Guardian* [Online]. June 6, 2014. Accessed July 21, 2015. http://www.theguardian.com/environment/2014/nov/06/chinese-demand-for-ivory-is-devastating-tanzanias-elephant-population.

Yi, Zhang. "New Changes in China's Social Class Structure." *Beijing Daily* [Online]. March 7, 2012. Accessed July 20, 2015. http://en.people.cn/102774/7750175.html.

Chapter Nine. Chinese "Soft Power" and Botswana's Higher Education: Confucius Institute and Chinese Studies Programme, University of Botswana

=================❖===============

Maitseo M.M. Bolaane

Introduction

Since the 1980s, China (People's Republic of China) has been noted as a country of great importance and political interest to the world. It has become one of the fastest-growing major economies and is the world's largest exporter. The research on Chinese politics, culture, environmental issues, and its rise to prominence has been covered in volumes of literature worldwide and among the emerging topics is the significance of the Confucius Institutes (CIs) in the world. Some of the academics interviewed at the University of Botswana (UB) have described China's soft power as some form of "cultural imperialism", in which China has been successful in promoting its culture and language through CIs, involving no direct monetary rewards, but being more of a subtle South-South relationship.[1] One of the leading debates on Africa-China relations has been developed by the Chinese in Africa/Africans in China International Research Working Group

---

1. Interview with Dr. B. Manatsha, a University of Botswana lecturer teaching Civilization in China and Japan, who provided his perspective on Africa-China relations, UB, 10 April 2016

established in 2007, formed by scholars who engaged in empirical research. The groups published a collection of papers in *African and Asian Studies*.[2] In their introduction, the guest editors of this collection cite events in southern Africa, indicating that Chinese people have become targets of anti-Chinese sentiments, often led by opposition political parties, civil society groups and media representatives who are confused and many times increasingly negative as "China and various African states' governments mutually agree to strengthen relations through economic deals in spite of Western critiques of neo-colonialism…". They argue that as engagement between African countries and China continues to deepen and broaden in different ways, most media coverage and scholarly work continue to focus primarily on the economic and political aspects of Chinese activities in Africa, and not much has been written about the people-to-people encounters that occur in different spaces.[3]

This paper concurs with the position that the presence of China in Africa has been the subject of many media reports, public debates, policy discussions, and academic publications and that there are contestations in the literature, with varied perspectives.[4] An additional contribution to the South-South relations and people-to-people relations will be an analysis of perspectives from students and staff at

2. See Yoon Jung Park and Tu T. Huynh, *Introduction: Chinese in Africa*, African and Asian Studies, 9 (2010): 207–212

3. Ibid., 208

4. Seifudein Adem, *The Paradox of China's Policy in Africa*, African and Asian Studies 9 (2010): 334–355; Antoine Kernen, *Small and Medium-sized Chinese Business in Mali and Senegal*, African and Asian Studies 9(2010): 252–268; Sarah Hanisch, *At the Margins of the Economy? Chinese Migrants in Lesotho's Wholesale and Retail Sector*, Africa Spectrum 3(2013): 85 – 97; Jean-Claude Maswana, *A Center-Periphery Perspectives on Africa-China's Emerging Economic Links*, African and Asian Studies 8 (2009): 67–88; Barry Sautman, and Yan Hairong, *Friends and Interests: China's Distinctive Links with Africa*, African Studies Review 50 (3), (2007): 75–114; Deborah Brautigam, *Chinese Aid and African Development: Exporting Green Revolution* (London: Macmillan Press Ltd, 2008); Deborah Brautigam, *Flying Geese' or 'Hidden Dragon'? Chinese Business and African Industrial Development*, Draft Chapter, prepared for Politics of Contemporary Africa-China Relations, 2007; Ching Kwan Lee, *Raw Encounters: Chinese Managers, African Workers and Politics of Casualization in Africa's Chinese Enclaves*, The China Quarterly (2009): 647–667; Yan Hairong, *Chinese Farms in Zambia: From Socialist to 'Agro-Imperialist' Engagement?* African and Asian Studies 9(2010): 307–333

UB on the Afro-Chinese partnership in the context of the higher education set-up. The focus is the CI and an independent degree-programme on Chinese Studies in the Faculty of Humanities. While situating Botswana in the debate, this paper pays close attention to the emerging literature on Chinese cultural polices, Chinese soft power and CIsserving as the network communication to public diplomacy.[5] The most cited work in the emerging literature on soft power and world politics is that of Joseph S. Nye.[6] Another important work is that of Kenneth King on China's aid and 'soft power' in Africa with focus on education and training.[7] Scholars (and journalists), such as Falk Hartig, have devoted much of their time between 2013 and 2014 giving a series of lectures talks/lectures, and publishing material on the globalization of Chinese soft power, CIs as innovative tools of China's cultural diplomacy, and CIs and the network communication approach to public diplomacy. Hartig, and Terry Flew and Hartig, argue that during the process of the rise of China, the People's Republic of China used its cultural institutions abroad to engage and communicate with international stakeholders in its cultural diplomacy. With a focus on CIs, Hartig further argues that such educational centres are causing foreigners to serve China's image. CIs have been mostly viewed through a soft-power angle, as "public or cultural diplomacy or as a nation branding campaign."[8] These debates will be analyzed in order

---

5. Falk Hartig, *Confucius Institutes as innovative tools of China's diplomacy*, in *Chinese Politics and International Relations*, ed. Nicola Horsburgh et al. (New York: Routledge, 2014), 121–144. See also Falk Hartig, *Making Foreigners to serve China's image: How China engages international stakeholders in its cultural diplomacy – the examples of Confucius Institutes and Panda Diplomacy*, (paper presented at Imagining Globality: China's Global Projects in Culture conference, China Institute University of Alberta, Edmonton, 2013); Falk Hartig, *Confucius Institutes and the Rise of China – How the People's Republic of China uses its cultural institutions abroad to communicate with the world*, round table participation at WIKA-Kolloquium, Instituts for Auslandsbeziehungen, Stuttgart, 2013; Terry Flew and Falk Hartig, *Confucius and the Network Communication Approach to Public Diplomacy*, The IAFOR Journal of Asian Studies 1(1)(2014): 27–44

6. Joseph S. Nye, *Soft Power. The Means to success in World Politics* (New York: Public Affairs, 2004)

7. Kenneth King, *China's Aid & Soft Power in Africa: The Case for Education & Training*, (Woodbridge: James Currey, 2013)

8. Peter Kragelund, *Chinese soft power and higher education in Africa: the Confucius Institute at the University of Zambiai*, (paper presented at the Responsible

to understand the role and significance of CIs in Botswana. In addition, the paper will study yet another related structure, a Bachelor of Arts (BA) degree programme, introduced and funded by the University of Botswana, for the purposes of comparison.

In the debate on Chinese soft power, Peter Kragelund reflects on how the China-Zambia collaboration in higher education differs from the traditional partnerships – the African higher education institutions' collaboration with Western institutions. For a very long time, soft power was the Western "strategy" to communicate their languages and culture to Africa and the rest of the world through their state-funded agencies. Obvious examples are the Alliance Française, Göete Institute and the British Council. Kragelund's focus is on the CI at the University of Zambia, across the border, north of Botswana.[9] Kragelund draws from Nye that the concept of soft power enables us to "analyze how a nation may obtain what it wants and or how it shapes what other nations do through attraction and cooperation rather than through brute force."[10] Soft power is also defined as the "second face of power", where we are required to think in terms of cooperation via agenda-setting and attraction rather than command via inducement and coercion. Attraction, and hence soft power in this sense, derives from the extent to which a country can make its culture, political values and foreign policies attractive to other countries. In the soft-power discourse, we look beyond coercion and material power to describing the ability to achieve desired outcomes.[11] We are warned that soft power is not static but changes frequently in line with the sources of soft power, i.e. culture, political values, and foreign policies including commerce and government policies.[12]

According to Kragelund, "most forcefully, a former president, Hu Jintao, used it for the first time in 2006 to describe the international

Development in a Polycentric World: Inequality Citizenship and the Middle Classes, 14th EADI General Conference, 23–26 June 2014), 2-21; Rui Yang, *Soft Power and Higher Education: an Examination of China's Confucius Institutes*, Globalisation, Society and Education, 8 (2)(2010): 235–245 : Falk Hartig, *Confucius Institutes and the Rise of China*, Journal of Chinese Political Science, 17(2012): 53–76

9. Kragelund, *Chinese soft power*
10. Ibid., 3–21
11. See D. W. Kearn, *The hard truths about soft power*, Journal of Political Power, no. 4 (1), 65-85.
12. Kragelund, *Chinese soft power*, 5

influence of China."[13] Hu Jintao made an appeal to "enhance culture as part of the soft power in the country."[14] Kragelund further argues that this position goes hand-in-hand with the "cultural going-out strategy" that seeks to promote Chinese culture abroad through cultural exchange and dialogue in order for China to be able to portray itself in developing world countries rather than rely on a Western portrayal of its culture and values.[15] This paper follows this trend in studying Chinese educational support to Africa and the response of African higher education institutions to this new form of educational (and cultural) partnership. The paper reflects further on this analysis of South-South educational collaboration using the CI situated at UB (CIUB) as a case study in analyzing external support and academic partnerships relating to the debate on soft power and power relations. The paper analyzes the impact of the Chinese Studies programme within the university, to shed light on how the China-Botswana collaboration in higher education acts in transforming the national university landscape. This paper will dissect related various issues and further reflect on the concept of soft power and cultural diplomacy to come to a greater understanding, within the context of higher education in Botswana, of the Africa-China and China-Botswana relations, including South-South university collaboration.

China-Botswana Relationship

Botswana and the People's Republic of China established diplomatic relations on January 6, 1975.[16] Since then Botswana and China have cooperated in several areas of socio-economic development and several of the Botswana officials are increasingly getting opportunities

---

13 Ibid, 5

14. This paper is drawing this quotation from Kragelund, 2014: 5, Hu Jintao cited in T. Fallon, *Chinese Fever and Cool Heads: Confucius Institutes and China's National Identities*, China Media Research, no. 10 (1), 2014: 38

15 Kragelund, *Chinese soft power*, 5, where he draws some of the ideas from Fallon, *"Chinese Fever and Cool Heads"*

16. See M. Bolaane, *China's Relations with Botswana: A Historical Perspective* in *Afro China: Past, Present and Future*, ed. Kwesi Kwaa Prah (Cape Town: The Centre for Advanced Studies of African Society Book Series, 2007). See also L Xuanxing, Chinese Ambassador to Botswana, *Memories and blessings of China-Botswana relations: A review on 35 years of diplomatic relations between China and Botswana*, Mmegi Online, April 14, 2016, accessed April 14, 2016.

to interact with the Chinese. However, their understanding of one another remains limited and language is a great barrier. Most recently newspapers in Botswana ran headlines such as, "Botswana needs to tread carefully when it comes to China", with some alleging that the Chinese embassy in Gaborone "closes shop...", suggesting a diplomatic tension between the Botswana government and the People's Republic of China.[17] Cooperation has been further cemented since the November 2006 Third Ministerial Conference of the Forum on Africa-China Cooperation (FOCAC), attended by Botswana and forty-seven African countries in China. Apart from FOCAC, China is engaging Africa through setting up Centres of African Studies in various universities of repute to study and understand Africa's physical geography and its people. These think tanks like the Center of African Studies of Nanjing University (established in 1964) have engaged in many fields of African Studies, agriculture, rural development, and natural resources' assessments in Africa. The Centres create a platform for better communications and scholarly exchange among researchers in the field of African studies, to which Africans are invited with funding extended to air travel, accommodation, meals and field trips in China.[18] Botswana, like some of the southern African countries, has participated in some of these forums, benefiting from an exchange of ideas.

Botswana's relations with China are said to be steered by a common position demonstrated through China's "Five Principles", guided by the "Eight Principles", for providing foreign aid.[19] This means Chinese aid to Botswana is provided on a principle of "no political strings attached" and these principles comprise the following: "sincere friendship"; "mutual respect and trust"; "equality, mutual benefit"; and

17. See headlines, Sunday Standard, Gaborone, 21–27 February 2016.
18. International Conference on Africa Agriculture, Rural development and Sino-African Cooperation, Nanjing, China, 21–28 September 2014.
19. T. Kalusopa, Chinese investments in Botswana, in Baah, A. Y and Jauch, H (eds) Chinese investments in Africa: A labour perspective (Accra and Windhoek: Africa Labour Research Network),2009, 124-159 & L. Maunganidze and I. Malila, Emerging Complexities and Ambiguities of Chinese Aid: The Case of Southern Africa, 2015 (unpublished), 94-95. See also an official statement from the Chinese Embassy, China Aid 'Brightness Action' Campaign in Botswana, Daily News, Gaborone, 25 June, 2015
19. Kragelund, Chinese soft power, 5

"peaceful co-existence."[20] Politically, both republics have related well and have established strong political ties, despite the recent tensions in diplomatic relations regarding Botswana's position on China and the South China Sea Islands.[21] In this respect, the Republic of Botswana strictly respects and adheres to the policy of One China and further recognizes Taiwan as being part of China, to which the Chinese officials in Gaborone often refer. Thus, these strong political ties have been expressed through several ways, for instance, the respective state leaders and high-ranking political officials have made exchange visits of common interest to both countries. Botswana presidents, Seretse Khama, Ketumile Masire and Festus Mogae, have paid visits to China. Ministers of communications; science and technology; justice; defense and security; and youth, sport and culture also made visits to China. On the other hand, Chinese leaders also visited Botswana, notably the Chinese vice-premier, Huang Ju, in November 2005, and Wu Guanzheng, member of the Standing Committee of the Political Bureau of the Communist Party of China (CPC) in September 2006.[22] The Chinese government has provided aid to Botswana on several platforms. However, much of the focus has been more on the establishment and improvement of infrastructure in Botswana – aid focused more on a holistic approach that embraces "...political high-level exchanges, cooperation in agriculture, health, aid, education, science, cultural and sports".[23] China's official representative in Gaborone often emphasizes that China strongly supports Botswana's nation-building efforts. For this reason, Botswana has been given

---

20. *An Overview of the Relations between China and Botswana,* Embassy of the People's Republic of China in Botswana, February 1, 2008, http://bw.china-embassy.org/eng/sbgx/t404979.htm; Chinese envoy tips Batswana entrepreneurs, 16 February 2009, http://bw.china-embassy.org/eng/jmw1/t535823.htm

21. A wide coverage on this issue appeared in Sunday Standard, February 2016. The hostile climate between Chinese business people and the Botswana public was captured earlier in the media, see for example Mmegi, January 27, 2009 and November 13, 2009; Botswana Gazette, February 15, 2012.

22. *An Overview of the Relations between China and Botswana,* accessed April 12, 2014.

23. See China's African Policy, in C. Alden and M. Davies, *A Profile of the Operations of Chinese Multinationals in Africa,* South African Journal of International Affairs, vol. 13 (1), 2006.

significant amounts of financial assistance that has largely included grants and preferential loans.[24] Chinese financial assistance to Botswana has mostly benefited building projects such as low-cost housing, land surveying, planning, road-network construction, health facilities and human-resources development. The government of China has also committed itself to upholding the government of Botswana's efforts to develop its infrastructure base through continued provision of concessionary loans (development assistance) as part of the *Beijing Action Plan* (2007–2009). Through the *Beijing Action Plan* (2013-2015) China has supported Botswana, carrying out "Brightness Action Campaign", providing surgical treatment to cataract patients, to enhance the health status of the local communities. In 2015 Botswana government received Chinese experts for cataract operations.

The relationship between China and Botswana is expected to grow and benefit both countries. Chinese investment in Botswana is also anticipated to increase, especially since the Chinese government has pledged to keep on offering sustenance to Chinese entrepreneurs looking for investment prospects in Botswana.[25] A series of policies devised by the Chinese government has been instrumental in promoting the undertaking of Foreign Direct Investment (FDI) in Botswana by the already-established Chinese enterprises, including medium and long-term commercial loans or soft loans from commercial banks. In order to explore other new areas of the mutually-beneficial relationship that exists between the two countries, China is set to make agreements with Botswana aimed at promoting strategies that will advance Botswana's economic diversification efforts.[26]

China has also talked about its commitment in supporting Botswana in the areas of cooperation in education and human resource development, providing statistics on the number of Chinese government scholarships given to the Botswana students to pursue post-graduate studies (master's and doctoral degree programmes) in China. These scholarships have been running since 1984, with the

---

24. *An Overview of the Relations between China and Botswana.*
25. Ibid.
26. See for example "An Overview of the Relations between China and Botswana"; Chinese envoy tips Batswana entrepreneurs, February 16, 2009, accessed August 12, 2012, http://bw.china-embassy.org/eng/jmw1/t535823.htm.

number increasing from 2007 onwards. Students are covered in respect of tuition fees, a living allowance and medical services. In addition, China provides opportunities for Botswana citizens through short-term training, which lasts from one week to a year, covering areas of information, agriculture, business and commerce, industry, sport, and military.[27] The Chinese government has over the years provided scholarships every year to Batswana students. In 2007 for instance, twenty-one scholarships were granted to Botswana. China has also been assisting Botswana in the health sector and over the years, Chinese medical teams have increased work in Botswana. A memorandum of agreement was signed on January 21, 2008, to increase the Chinese medical teams working in Botswana. China even donated (in the same year) computer equipment worth an undisclosed million dollars to the health sector.[28]

Botswana and China have also made concerted efforts towards the development of socio-cultural exchanges and cooperation. In 1991, for instance, China and Botswana signed a Framework Agreement relating to cultural exchange (e.g. handicraft exhibitions, music concerts), which is renewable every two years. This exchange with Botswana has given the Botswana cultural groups in music, dance and artists from the Thapong Visual Art Centre an opportunity to showcase their talent in China. The "Chinese Culture Focus" was in Botswana in November 2011 as part of promoting bilateral educational and cultural exchanges. The China-Botswana educational and cultural exchange was extended to the establishment of the CIUB to promote courses in Chinese language (Mandarin) and cultural study among Botswana students.

China, an Actor in Soft Power to Achieve Foreign-Policy Aims in Africa

China is not the only actor applying soft power to achieve its foreign policy aims in Africa. As observed by Kragelund, the West has a long history of using language and cultural encounters as a soft-power tool in the continent on Africa. Good examples are the widespread use of French and English as languages and their cultures, promoted through institutions like the Alliance Française and the British Council since the independence of African countries.[29] In Botswana, like in Zambia,

---

27. Ibid.
28. Ibid.
29. Kragelund, *Chinese soft power.*

the Alliance Française and the British Council, which are linked to their respective embassies, are agencies through which language and culture are being promoted. Both the Alliance Française and the British Council are located in Gaborone, but not within university premises as is the CIUB. English remains the official language of Botswana and French is offered by the Department of French within UB, and services have been extended to private schools and the Southern African Development Community (SADC) headquarters in Gaborone. Currently French is also offered to the public on a part-time basis for evening classes. The Alliance Française has over the years supported the French Department by sending UB students to spend time in France for cultural exposure and for the purpose of developing communicative skills to further their knowledge of the French language in Botswana. This set-up is supported by the Ministry of Skills and Development, viewed as being in line with the nation's overall soft-power strategies. According to a professor of French at UB, the Alliance Française was established with an objective of teaching French language and culture. He argues that "this is French soft power in a sense because they are doing all this in Botswana and everywhere in the world including China."[30] He observes that they also promote Botswana culture within Botswana by inviting young artists and writers to showcase their talent through the Alliance Française, and the French government has been supporting activities including exhibitions, art painting and sculpture-making to give young artists access to new ideas and the market. In addition, as in the case of the CIUB, they support Botswana citizens in visiting France on short training courses, but might not do so to the same extent as the Chinese government does.

The Chinese version of this soft-power tool at UB is the CI, which promotes the Chinese language, culture, civilization and philosophy. According to a former UB deputy vice-chancellor (Academic Affairs), it is expected that in the 2020s China will become the world's largest economy and this trajectory has already become apparent in the international political economy. By welcoming a CI, UB was responding to this new world order, seeking to play a role in promoting

---

30. Prof. N. Kitenge, Head of Department, French Department, UB, April 14, 2016.

relations between Botswana and China.[31] UB has to date signed numerous agreements for collaboration with partnerships in Europe and North American institutions, and through such collaboration they have received external support in the form of academic partnerships. However, in the most recent years, UB has also looked towards the East for academic partnership in the promotion of its *Research Strategy*, which has been aligned to the *National Development Plan* 10 and 11, with a strategic goal of "intensifying research performance" and "increasing international collaboration research."[32]

As noted in the introduction, China's significance in world affairs is growing dramatically, and therefore is a significant factor in the economies and politics of Africa, especially since the establishment FOCAC and the major meeting of African heads of state in Beijing in 2006. Seifude in Adem argues that China is defining its patterns of influence, including soft-power initiatives.[33] It is within this context that relations between Botswana and China in the area of higher education are analyzed, because educational aid from China has become attractive to Botswana. Against this background, UB, a significant national institution, is strongly committing to the university-university collaboration. This is in an attempt to address its policy strategy to become an intellectual centre in Africa and the world, for the study of what Frank Youngman describes as "a reciprocal need."[34] In order to address its policy in internationalization, "enhancing opportunities for UB students and staff to experience and study other countries and cultures", UB's strategy is to advance China's understanding of Africa, and Africa's understanding of China. Therefore, the institution is promoting the study of China at UB and the study of Africa in China through a partnership with universities in China that share this aspiration.

31. Frank Youngman, University of Botswana Confucius Institute Strategic Planning Workshop, September 20, 2010, University of Botswana, Gaborone; 2010 & *Discussion Paper, Strengthening Africa-China Relations: A Perspective from Botswana*, (Stellenbosch: Centre for Chinese Studies), 2013: 12

32. University of Botswana Research Strategy, approved by Senate, February 20, 2008: 1–12

33. Adem, *The Paradox of China's Policy in Africa*

34. Youngman, Strategic Planning Workshop.

University-University Partnership: Confucius Institute University of Botswana and Chinese Studies Progamme

In 2008, UB entered into a partnership with Shanghai Normal University (SHNU), and in conjunction with SHNU, established the CI, providing part-time language courses and cultural activities. In addition, a programme of student and staff exchanges and joint research was developed with academic institutions in China, including the Chongqing Technical and Business University.[35] The CIUB is an integral part of the Faculty of Humanities. However, it is run in conjunction with SNHU and receives funding from the headquarters of CIs globally, the Hanban. The CIUB is part of a worldwide network which started in 2004 and by December 2009 there were 282 institutes in eight countries – a Chinese government foreign-policy initiative to develop Chinese as an international language and to promote better understanding of China worldwide. This was a unique approach for inter-cultural cooperation based on a model of university partnership, with joint Chinese and host university directors for each institute. Each December, the global network of CIs is convened in Beijing by Hanban and while there is a standard model for a CI, each CI is expected to respond to local circumstances. Generally, the CI at UB is primarily an outreach unit of the host university, providing community service related to the Chinese language and culture through activities such as non-credit language classes for young adults and adults, training language teachers, cultural events, exhibitions, public education, performances, etc.

On March 28 and 29, 2011, an international conference on "understanding Africa-China relations" was held in Nairobi. The theme of the conference was Towards a New Africa-China Partnership: A Forum for African scholars, think tanks and researchers. This conference was organized by African research institutions and think-tanks working on Africa-China relations including the Council for the Development of Social Science Research in Africa (CODESRIA). One of the observations was that China had come up with an agenda for dealing with Africa, and the question was, "Does Africa have an agenda?" CIs in Africa could be viewed as part of China's agenda to understand Africa; hence the introduction of academic studies' departments within African universities to assist

---

35. Memorandum of Understanding was signed with Chongqing Technical and Business University in 2010.

Africa in developing a framework for its agenda, and the aim to produce young people who would understand various aspects of China.

Many host universities have academic departments that offer degrees in Chinese studies or Asian studies and undertake interdisciplinary research in these areas. These departments are separate from the CI but they can benefit from resources and the expertise that the Confucius Institute has in Chinese language teaching – thus an additional activity of a CI is to contribute to the teaching of the Chinese language in academic programmes. To complement the SHNU and UB partnership in establishing the CI in 2012, the university introduced BA Chinese Studies on main campus, a regular degree programme at the university, meeting in all respects the normal standards and expectations of UB and funded through the recurrent budget, and developing its academic expertise in all areas of Chinese studies (including the growing field of Sino-Africa relations).[36] The development of the degree programme is viewed as an organizational arrangement that would extend cooperation with SHNU to receive and host students from UB for level three of their studies. This would be spent in China for the purposes of advancing their Chinese language and study of culture. While in Shanghai, students would get an opportunity to interact with the members of Chinese society, at the university and outside of it. The development at UB was in line with the university's policy on internationalization that was approved in 2006 with a new strategic direction, containing an explicit commitment to giving priority to academic links with four major countries in Asia: China, India, Japan and Korea (Internationalization Policy, 2006). Having identified China as a key priority area for UB's international strategic engagement, the university introduced the multidisciplinary Africa-China research team to be strategically positioned in the evolving plans for the institutionalization of Africa-China scholars, while opening important opportunities for the strengthening of UB's Chinese Studies Programme.

The programme was viewed as a response to two key objectives contained in UB's strategic plan and policy of internationalization (UB

---

36. See University of Botswana Faculty of Humanities Proposal for establishing Bachelor of Arts Degree Programme in Chinese Studies, August 2010. Further discussion in Youngman, *Discussion Paper, Strengthening Africa-China Relations: A Perspective from Botswana*, 12-13

Strategy of Excellence, 2008). Given the increasingly important presence of China in Africa, the needs assessment (consultations) indicated that both the Botswana government (foreign affairs, trade and industry, police, immigration and customs, and business e.g. construction) were keen to have staff who could communicate in Chinese and who would understand the Chinese culture with which they would be dealing.[37] This is evidenced by the numerous job advertisements placed by Chinese construction companies seeking interpreters to translate Chinese into English for the workers: to "interpret some documents written in Chinese to help facilitate smooth transaction and timely running of projects. Act as a go-between negotiator for contractual and relations agreements. Knowledge of the Chinese language: good command of both oral and written language and familiarity with Chinese culture are a requirement."[38]

According to a South African academic, the CI helps to enhance Africa-China relations. The co-director of the CI at the University of Johannesburg argues that "the CIs are meant to make people understand evolving China and for the Chinese to understand Africa."[39] He said the institutes are meant to make people understand the philosophy of Confucius, comparing it with *ubuntu* in the context of southern Africa, which is an ethical concept. The aim of the CI is to promote the Chinese language and culture to achieve peace and mutual understanding in the world.[40] China's soft power has become attractive to citizens of the world, including Botswana, as is demonstrated by a case study in the paper. The introduction of CIs in Africa is based on the popular figure, teacher and philosopher Confucius. His principles have been used to brand Chinese educational tools abroad. The concepts of equality and opportunity for all through education are applied internally to keep the Chinese society together.

---

37. The author was a member of the founding committee of the Chinese Studies programme and in the process accumulated knowledge on the UB policy documents and the needs assessment that was carried out prior to the establishment of the BA degree programme.
38. Mmegi, June 20, 2012
39. D. Monyae quoted in, *Confucius Institutes enhance Africa-China Ties: S. African Academic*, Xinhua, 23 February, 2016. www.xinhuanet.com/English/2016.
40. See Hartig, *Confucius Institutes and the Rise of China*; Flew and Hartig, *Confucius and the Network Communication Approach*

The CIs offer global brand recognition and are closely associated with teaching and culture.[41] At FOCAC, China showcased its new "strategic partnership" with African countries and it is being reported that the event was decorated with selection images of Africa and banners proclaiming "Friendship, Peace, Cooperation and Development." Alden, Large and Soares de Oliveira have argued that the forum amounted to "a public declaration of China's arrival in Africa, and sought to impress this upon the African guests…"[42] One observes a similar scenario at the CIUB events, where activities are carried out with a unique public declaration of "China's arrival" in Botswana. This point will be elaborated on later in the paper.

Despite the longstanding bonds of friendship between China and Botswana, language barriers and other dynamics between the two countries frequently threatened to compromise Botswana-China relations.[43] However, the People's Republic of China, through the Embassy of China in Gaborone (and the Chinese Language Council International), together with UB worked rigorously towards a common understanding of the promotion of good relations between Botswana and China through establishing a CIUB.[44] The main focus is specifically to highlight the relevant aspects of the Chinese language and culture. While a number of Chinese nationals come to Botswana as diplomats, entrepreneurs, technicians, doctors, health workers, construction workers and small scale traders, there has been a gradual increase in the arrival of language instructors at the CIUB. The CIUB continues to spread the unique feature of China's engagement with Botswana within the higher education system. The actors within this educational cultural agency comprise a director from China and a number of young Chinese instructors paid by Hanban. Based on the partnership with UB, in addition to the manpower at CIUB are the co-

41. D. Starr, *Chinese Language Education in Europe: The Confucius Institutes*, European Journal of Education, 44 (1), (2009): 65–82; Michael Barr, *Nation Branding as Nation Building: China's image campaign*, (East Asia, Springer, 2011): 1–14

42. See Chris Alden, Dan Large and Ricardo Soares de Oliveira, *China Returns to Africa: Anatomy of an Expansive Engagement*, Working Paper 51/2008, Real Instituto Elcano; and L. O'Brien, *Africa-China Rhetoric: lessons from the World Economic Forum*, CCS Commentary, Centre for Chinese Studies, Stellenbosch, March 2, 2015

43. See for example Mmegi Online, January 17 2009 November 13 2009.

44. Youngman, Strategic Planning Workshop.

director, an administration officer, and a secretary – all paid by UB. According to the CIUB director paid by UB, there was an agreement with Hanban to bring Chinese teachers to the UB main campus and "currently the CI Headquarters is running CIUB like it is the case in other countries but in future Botswana will take over the running and management of the Institute."[45] According to the director, the idea of two directors (one from China, and the other from Botswana)is to cement the university-university partnership, so that the Botswana director would be in an advantageous position of understanding his/her local environment, understanding and appreciating the culture, national language, society, history, and how things work in Botswana; while the Chinese director would be fluent in Mandarin, and would understand Chinese society and culture, and how the Chinese do things. "In essence, someone who understands China and its system will be in a position to carry out the mandate set out by Hanban to achieve CI objectives in the educational landscape of Botswana."[46] His view is that the role of co-directors is important in facilitating the deep understanding of China-Botswana collaborators, and the role of the UB director would be extended to attending to signing for access of CIUB funds through the UB Finance, chairing of meetings, supervision of staff, immigration issues and accommodation when the language instructors arrived in Gaborone. The co-director of the CI at the University of Johannesburg observes that "CIs also give Chinese academics access to African universities and understating of African cultures."[47]

Through an activity of university-university collaboration called the "+20+20 Cooperative Plan" between SHNU and UN, several invitations have been extended to UB staff and graduate students from different faculties to access universities in China. Some have stayed at the SHNU for an academic term (e.g. September to December) and have also had an opportunity to serve as local supervisors for the Chinese graduate students who are visiting Botswana for field work. Some of the academics have attended training programmes on "Chinese market and Sino-Africa relations and Chinese culture." The training included lectures on various topics on China, including the

---

45. P.T. Mgadla interviewed, CIUB, April 6, 2016.
46. Ibid.
47. Monyae quoted in, *Confucius Institutes enhance Africa-China Ties: S. African Academic*, Xinhua, 23 February, 2016

urban history of Shanghai and Confucius classics: poetry and history. Through this arrangement visitors are taken out for various excursions to appreciate China's culture, infrastructure and industrial development, in the process gaining an understanding of and "valuing" China as a "partner with value."[48]

To embrace this partnership, UB has also provided a whole block, which is strategically located along the road and is easily accessed by visitors from outside the university, near the UB administration block, protection services, and Faculty of Humanities. In front of the building is the striking billboard with the Hanban headquarters logo and easily identifiable by Chinese red lamps and a gazebo/pavilion on a green lawn with Chinese characters. According to the instructors at CIUB, they are offering twelve levels in the study of Mandarin, starting with level one, which is "Chinese for beginners", "intermediate" and the twelfth level is advanced, with the aim of producing graduates who can speak and identify Chinese characters.[49]

Since its establishment, the CIUB has conducted a series of educational and cultural activities at UB, including outreach activities in the rural and remote areas of Botswana – a cultural tour to remote schools of Botswana, covering the junior secondary schools in Mabule (Southern District), Sojwe (Kweneng District), Kudumatse (Central District), Maitengwe (Central district), and Mapoka, (North East District). "In all these schools rudimentary Chinese language as well performances of aspects of the Chinese culture were introduced," affirmed one of the co-directors of CIUB.[50]

The teaching of Chinese in Botswana has taken place in private and elite schools in Gaborone (the capital city), such as Maruapula, Westwood, Rainbow and the language instructors are linked to the CIUB. This arrangement was made with the respective schools as a follow-up to a request for the CIUB to assist with the teaching of Chinese as one of the foreign languages together with French, etc.

---

48. The author of this paper was among the seventeen participants from the University of Botswana. See letter of invitation from Shanghai Normal University (International Exchange Division) addressed to the UB Office of International Education and Partnerships, November 22, 2013.

49. Two instructors agreed to take part in an interview with the author at University of Botswana, January 20 and 21, 2016. However, since 2015, the author has been trying to interview the CIUB Chinese Director but has not been successful.

50. Mgadla document on *CIUB Achievements*, April 4, 2016

There are also talks with the Ministry of Education, especially with those officials at a director's level, for the CIUB to teach Chinese as one optional language in public schools. According to Mgadla, South Africa adopted a policy in 2015, introducing Chinese from primary school together with other languages such as French, Portuguese, Zulu and Xhosa. The CIUB is also in cooperation with the Chinese Embassy in Gaborone to teach selected government officials the Chinese language and culture at the expense of the Chinese Embassy.

The Chinese language instructors are full time, while some are called volunteers. The full-time instructors are those with a master's degree or working in Botswana for a period of three or more years. The volunteers from SHNU teach for one to two years; some have a master's degree, while others are about to acquire the degree like the full-time instructors paid by Hanban. The CIUB, through the university management structures, signed a Memorandum of Understanding (MoU) in 2016 to introduce the Chinese language and culture at the new state-funded Botswana International University of Science and Technology (BIUST). The MoU also stipulates that the CIUB should assist in facilitating in the recruitment of six Chinese teachers (two instructors and four volunteers) to teach the Chinese language and culture. The teachers have since started teaching the Chinese language to BIUST students. The CIUB is talking about introducing its activities to the UB Francistown campus and the Okavango Research Institute (Main campus). These numerous activities will attract an increasing number of Chinese language instructors in the country, indirectly creating employment opportunities for young Chinese people in Botswana. The introduction of a multi-media facility educational system has been viewed within the Faculty of Humanities as a positive response to the UB *Teaching and Learning Policy* (2008), which notes that "the world is being dramatically reshaped by scientific and technological innovations, regional and global interdependence, cross-cultural encounters and changes in economic, political and social dynamics."[51] Therefore the multi-media facility is contributing to teaching development.

It is worth noting that in the course of this year (2016), the CIUB held celebrations for having been selected "Confucius Institute of the Year" by the Confucius Headquarters in Beijing. In his presentation at

---

51. *Teaching and Learning Policy*, University of Botswana, 2008

the CIUB celebration day, Mgadla stated that there are currently 500 CIs in the world, with over forty-eight in Africa. Amongst the CIs in Africa are those in Botswana, Ghana, Ethiopia, Nigeria, Tanzania, Egypt, Senegal, Zimbabwe, Zambia, and the South African universities (Stellenbosch University, University of KwaZulu Natal and University of Johannesburg). Mgadla further noted that in December 2015, twenty of these world CIs were awarded "Confucius Institute of the Year" and the CIUB was among the twenty. Out of the total number of those in Africa, only three qualified to be awarded "Confucius Institute of the Year." In addition, the Dean of the Faculty of Humanities where the CIUB is hosted received the award at the Global Conference held in Shanghai, China, on behalf of UB. Mgadla noted these as achievements of the CIUB. Among the achievements noted were the CIUB-organized Chinese Bridge Competitions where the Chinese language proficiency test was undertaken by both the CIUB and UB students. According to the Director at CIUB, the best student from UB was sent to China to compete with others from all over the world. "Altogether there were 133 contestants from ninety-seven countries who gathered in Hunan Province, China. The UB student, Ms Mogolo Ramalebang,[52] performed very well and ended up among the best and top ten in the world and second in Africa."[53]

Perceptions among Students and Staff: China-Botswana Relations

The students who participated in the study were between twenty-two and thirty-eight years in age; with some of the students participating in the Chinese studies programme (BA). Some had been in China for eleven months. Some had been to China twice, some for three months and others for a year.

An analysis of students' perceptions shows that China is attractive to Botswana, as noted by one of the undergraduate students: "It's cool to greet one another in Chinese *Nihau* along the UB corridors." The students also observed that when there "are Chinese dignitaries on campus engaging the audience further on Africa-China relations,

---

52. Ramalebang has recently completed her graduate studies in China. She obtained a BA degree in Chinese Studies (2015), and some advanced Mandarin level qualifications from the CIUB. She is currently working for a company in Palapye (Central district, Botswana).

53. P.T. Mgadla interviewed, CIUB, April 4, 2016

during the question and answer time, it is impressive to see the students of CIUB (various ages and genders) confidently communicating in this foreign language [Mandarin]." The responses from UB students and staff are based on their analysis of the activities of the educational programmes associated with the rising of China. There was an attempt to conceptualize whether, in the context of Botswana, the initiatives are based on mutual benefit or on unequal power relations. The students said their responses to the interview questions were influenced by what they experienced at UB, but they also shared their experiences during their stay in China. In their responses, both students and staff noted soft-power tools and some inclined towards Haugen's arguments that this was cultural diplomacy and a brand campaign, where there was cooperation through agenda setting and attraction rather than command through coercion. On the other hand, while an academic at UB acknowledges that China and Botswana relations go beyond trade agreements and diplomatic meetings, and were gradually being nurtured through the CIUB and the Chinese Studies programme, he is also of the view that it is mainly through the CI, run from Hanban, that China is making foreigners serve their image (cultural imperialism). He further observes that China is globalizing its language and culture through the CI because its cultural diplomacy is serving as a network communication strategy, "eventually these initiatives help China achieve what they want in their strategy of engagement...why would they be funding fifty students to go to China...remember when these students complete (their studies) and come back to Botswana, they will be going into Foreign Affairs, some will be permanent secretaries (in different ministries), in a way China is finding its way into the central government system."[54] In his understanding of China-Botswana relations, "this is done through collaboration rather than force; it is done through some sort of dialogue and understanding." Manatsha's view is in line with that of Nye (2004) and Haugen (2013) that it is through spreading the teaching of its language and culture that China will be able to portray a better image in a developing country such as Botswana, because they are not aggressive in the manner in which they deal with some of these countries but rather apply an effective engagement, which is working.[55]

---

54 B T Manatsha, Department of History, UB, April 11, 2016
55. B T Manatsha, April 11, 2016.See Nye, *Soft Power. The Means to success in World Politics* & H. Haugen, *China's recruitment of African university students;*

Some of the students cited examples of well-packed, elaborate and colourful CIUB cultural events, viewing them as "cultural going-out" strategies, in which China was seeking to promote Chinese culture abroad through these activities. Cultural exchange activities through poetry, music, dance, and the martial arts, which are open to the public, become a form of dialogue at the UB Student Centre, in order for China to portray its image in Botswana. Scholarship programmes are closely linked to soft-power theory with a position that students with pleasant, first-hand experiences of life abroad will admire the host country's political system and, in turn, push politics at home in the direction desired by the country they studied. The majority of those who have studied various courses through the BA Chinese Studies Programme, as well as part-time classes at the CIUB, agree that Chinese culture and language are attractive to many young people, especially in Gaborone, and may function as soft power, making the recipients' nation do what China wants it to do.[56]

According to the students in the Chinese Studies Programme and the CIUB, there is an advantage in being taught by Chinese native speakers as this helps the student to understand and practice the Chinese language and culture better. This is because they are able to listen to news broadcasts, watch films and videos, listen to songs and watch aspects of the Chinese culture all shown in the Chinese and English languages. Next door, the CIUB was hugely over-subscribed and they were receiving requests from businesses for special programmes. The programme, which has been running now for five years at UB independently of the CIUB, aims to produce graduates who will be able to communicate not only in Chinese, but will also be at home in the Chinese cultural environment. Advanced modern Chinese language-use in communication will require students to have higher language proficiency to communicate fluently and appropriately in both oral and written forms, and to express ideas precisely —as a preparation for participating in real-life situations. The aim is to develop students to acquire language skills of listening, speaking, reading and writing. The programme follows a common and successful pattern for language-based degrees, in use both at UB and elsewhere. When comparing the two programmes, the students viewed the BA

---

policy efficacy and unintended outcomes, Globalisation, Societies and Education, no 11 (3): 315-334
56. B.T. Manatsha, Department of History, UB, April 10, 2016

Chinese Studies as an inter-disciplinary programme that aims to provide a high level of language proficiency in Mandarin and to develop knowledge and understanding of Chinese culture, society, economic and politics, as well as China's relations with Africa and the world. The students noted the aims and objectives of the programme were impressive and they were confident it was a programme that could produce employable graduates with inter-cultural fluency and communication skills. Some students argued that language and culture as a strategic approach was an effective soft-power strategy because it was evident through the increasing number of the CIs that they were influencing other people in the world, and Mandarin had since become attractive and was emerging as one of the global languages in the context of international business.

A good example is that of the University of California Abroad Program and Opportunities Abroad Program offering study abroad programs at universities in Beijing, Shanghai, Taiwan, Hong Kong and Singapore, which give the students an opportunity to strengthen their Mandarin language skill and to take non-language courses on various aspects of Chinese topics.[57] State-of-the-art buildings are being opened – and are set in the heart of main campuses with dynamic spaces that are a visible testament to how much a university complements teaching and learning in the understanding of Chinese language and culture. UB is one good example where space for offices, classrooms, a conference room and language labs has been allocated for the CI not far from the administration building. Centres such as the CIUB are being supported with information technology to support classroom activities including music, poetry and Kungfu performances. Elaborate events are hosted several times in an academic year to sensitize the public on the objectives of the Chinese language programme. The students are also given a mini project to go out into Gaborone and neighbouring villages during the UB short vacation to collect life stories from the Chinese business community. This enables us to differentiate this group from other segments of Chinese presence in Botswana, such as expatriate workers, Chinese multinational enterprises, and people working at the embassy. There is an absence of data on perceptions of young people

---

57. University of Botswana Faculty of Humanities Proposal for establishing Bachelor of Arts Degree Programme in Chinese Studies, August 2010, http://chinsestdies.ucsd/edu/

in Botswana, in particular the students who have had an opportunity to pursue a programme in Chinese studies.

The students who had an opportunity to visit China shared their impression of the country: "China is big; some people are nice and some are not." Some said the visit to China changed their impressions, because they found China attractive, and interacted more with expatriates. They found the Chinese to be good people but some were rude towards blacks. Some students had opportunities to visit sports recreation centres, and places of interest including shopping and night clubs, and they formed opinions based on their understanding of China as young people from Africa. When they were asked why they would choose to study in China, they said they saw value in increasing their knowledge of China. They were interested in the language, learning it better (increasing proficiency skills), feeling the cultural impact of the Chinese, seeing the place, seeing new places including parks and museums, game rooms, restaurants and night clubs "to expose myself to new environments." Some said, "To improve cultural knowledge and learn how Chinese people speak and write the Chinese language." Some students opted to do Chinese Studies, in order to get an opportunity to travel to China for career development and they were hoping to get a job in the United Nations. Some students talked at length about the importance of appreciating China as a rising global power and having better understanding of the language, "to be fluent in Chinese and have understanding of their culture." They argued that China is very big and is a developing country, from which other developing countries could learn. One student said, "My experience in China helped me learn to be independent." The students also commented on the content of the SHNU programme of study (educational model), comparing it with the UB BA programmes.

Their view was that teaching at SHNU is intense: "They mean business there; there is no minute wasted; they are a lot of things to learn in a day compared to what they learn at UB; for instance, a day was enough to cover one lesson or a chapter, while we take more than two weeks to cover a chapter in the department of Chinese Studies, UB." One of the female students said, "Reading a book will take only a week to complete it, but at the UB, it will be three months; SHNU committed twenty hours for teaching-learning but in Botswana only six hours per week, limited time to study language." According to the students at SHNU, the learning was divided into listening, oral, reading and writing (Chinese characters) but things were different at UB. Their view was that the programme was well organized, divided into the Chinese language categories, material was broad and organized and teaching, e.g. tests and quizzes, are issued well in time. Teaching hours were long to accommodate theory and practice. They catered for extracurricular activities. Students received support – the staff committed their time to helping students. Language was given more attention; teachers were patient towards "slow learners". Students were positive about the teaching-learning process where they were able to practice what they had learnt from class. Some students saw educational program mesas being of value and relevant to their career development – such as pursuing a degree in international relations. Students also appreciated the internet which they say is "fast, convenient, reliable, everywhere, you can even buy some goods on internet and [they] could be delivered at your door step. They have great quality movies." But while noting that the TV programs were educational, they were mostly about China, promoting their culture. To most students who were interviewed, China's level of technology was an indication that it has become a global power and the environment gave one opportunities in career development.

Students also shared what they encountered as culture shock. They said the Chinese were not concerned with hygiene when serving customers especially in local businesses including restaurants, but they noted their efficiency compared to the nature of service in Botswana. They made reference to the cultural habit of spitting everywhere, for example on pavements. Some students were irritated by some questions such as "where is Botswana, in South Africa?" and asking if their hair-extensions (braids) were natural, and "why are we black…is it your first time to wear shoes…is your hair real or fake…do you have wild animals in your back yard?" The students observed that some Chinese had never been outside China, so had limited knowledge about the rest of the world, for instance seeing black females as prostitutes. "I think they are not used to fat people or our black hair. They wanted to touch our skins, our hair," said one student. They observed that race could be an issue in some sections of the population in China, where some Chinese see African blacks as beggars and looked down on them. "Some did not even want to be associated with Africans, but treated Afro-Americans differently." One of the female students who spent a whole year in Shanghai, confessed that at times she had camouflage, pretending to be an Afro-America, faking her accent, to fit in. The students' view is that some Chinese seem to idolize fair-complexion (white) people, treating them well – as superior; and that black men could be harshly treated although sometimes they caught the eyes of young Chinese women. Some would be blunt and say they didn't like black people, sometimes expressing themselves in public transport where they did not want to sit next to black people.

Conclusion

Qualifications offered by higher education institutions in Africa, which have entered into partnership with Chinese academic institutions and supported by their governments to establish CIs or to establish independent BA Chinese studies programmes in their respective institutions, are increasingly sought after. This is because for example, British and European businesses have identified a major need for graduates with Chinese language skills and an understanding of Chinese society and culture, media journalism, politics and economics. These programmes allow citizens of other countries to develop the linguistic skills and cultural awareness needed to engage with China, either as a competitor or partner, in parallel with a range of business skills. In order to be in a strategic position of engaging with the People's Republic of China, some of the academic institutions are keen to produce a crop of graduates who have developed a good working knowledge and proficiency in spoken Mandarin; familiarity with written Mandarin; and practical knowledge of the culture, society, business institutions and practices of contemporary China and the wider Chinese speaking communities. Although China came into the picture very late, it is strategically engaging Africa through expanding its own culture and language. Institutions such as UB (and now BIUST) are evoking their policy strategies to embrace China's soft power within the higher education environment. On the other hand, the increasing activities of CIs in urban and rural Botswana are an indication Hanban is sending a powerful message that China has arrived.

Bibliography

Adem, Seifudein. "The Paradox of China's Policy in Africa," *African and Asian Studies* 9 (2010): 334–355.

Alden Chris, and M. Davies. "A Profile of the Operations of Chinese Multinationals in Africa", *South African Journal of International Affairs*, vol. 13 (1), 2006.

Alden Chris, Dan Large and Ricardo Soares de Oliveira. "China Returns to Africa: Anatomy of an Expansive Engagement," *Working Paper 51/2008.*

Barr, Michael. "Nation Branding as Nation Building: China's image campaign," (East Asia, Springer, 2011): 1–14.

Bolaane, Maitseo. "China's Relations with Botswana: A Historical Perspective" in *Afro China: Past, Present and Future,* ed. Kwesi Kwaa Prah (Cape Town: The Centre for Advanced Studies of African Society Book Series, 2007).

Brautigam, Deborah. *Chinese Aid and African Development: Exporting Green Revolution* (London: Macmillan Press Ltd, 2008).

Brautigam, Deborah. "'Flying Geese' or 'Hidden Dragon'? Chinese Business and African Industrial Development." Draft Chapter, prepared for *Politics of Contemporary Africa-China Relations,* 2007.

Confucius Institutes enhance Africa-China Ties: S. African Academic, Xinhua, 23 February, 2016. Xinhuanet.com/English/2016.

Elcano Real Instituto; and L. O'Brien. "Africa-China Rhetoric: lessons from the World Economic Forum," CCS Commentary, Centre for Chinese Studies, Stellenbosch, March 2, 2015.

Fallon, T. "Chinese Fever and Cool Heads: Confucius Institutes and China's National Identities" China Media Research, no. 10 (1), 2014: 38.

Flew, Terry and Falk Hartig. "Confucius and the Network Communication Approach to Public Diplomacy," *The IAFOR Journal of Asian Studies* 1(1) (2014): 27–44.

Hairong Yan. "Chinese Farms in Zambia: From Socialist to 'Agro-Imperialist' Engagement?", *African and Asian Studies* 9(2010): 307–333.

Hanisch, Sarah. "At the Margins of the Economy? Chinese Migrants in Lesotho's Wholesale and Retail Sector," *Africa Spectrum* 3(2013): 85 – 97.

Hartig, Falk. "Confucius Institutes as innovative tools of China's diplomacy,"in *Chinese Politics and International Relations,* ed. Nicola Horsburgh et al. (New York: Routledge, 2014), 121–144.

Hartig, Falk. "Making Foreigners to serve China's image: How China engages international stakeholders in its cultural diplomacy – the examples of Confucius Institutes and Panda Diplomacy" (paper presented at Imagining Globality: China's Global Projects in Culture conference, China Institute University of Alberta, Edmonton, 2013;

Hartig, Falk. "Confucius Institutes and the Rise of China – How the People's Republic of China uses its cultural institutions abroad to communicate with the world," Roundtable participation at WIKA-Kolloquium, Instituts for Auslandsbeziehungen, Stuttgart, 2013.

Hartig, Falk. "Confucius Institutes and the Rise of China," *Journal of Chinese Political Science*, 17(2012): 53–76.

Kalusopa, T. "Chinese investments in Botswana", in Baah, A.Y and Jauch, H (eds) *Chinese investments in Africa: A labour perspective* (Accra and Windhoek: Africa Labour Research Network), 2009, 124-159.

Kearn, D. W. "The hard truths about soft power", *Journal of Political Power*, no. 4 (1), 65-85.

Kernen, Antoine. "Small and Medium-sized Chinese Business in Mali and Senegal," *African and Asian Studies* 9(2010): 252–268.

King, Kenneth. *China's Aid & Soft Power in Africa: The Case for Education & Training*, (Woodbridge: James Currey, 2013).

Kragelund, Peter. "Chinese soft power and higher education in Africa: the Confucius Institute at the University of Zambia" (paper presented at the Responsible Development in a Polycentric World: Inequality Citizenship and the Middle Classes, 14th EADI General Conference, 23–26 June 2014), 2-21.

Lee, ChingKwan. "Raw Encounters: Chinese Managers, African Workers and Politics of Casualization in Africa's Chinese Enclaves," *The China Quarterly* (2009): 647–667.

Maswana, Jean-Claude. "A Center-Periphery Perspectives on Africa-China's Emerging Economic Links," *African and Asian Studies* 8 (2009): 67–88.

Maunganidze, L. and I. Malila. "Emerging Complexities and Ambiguities of Chinese Aid: The Case of Southern Africa", 2015 (unpublished), 94-95.

Mgadla, P.T. Report on "CIUB Achievements", April 4, 2016.

Monyae quoted in Confucius Institutes enhance Africa-China Ties: S. African Academic, Xinhua, 23 February, 2016.

Nye, *Soft Power. The Means to success in World Politics* & H. Haugen, "China's recruitment of African university students; policy efficacy and unintended outcomes", *Globalisation, Societies and Education*, no 11 (3): 315-334.

Official statement from the Chinese Embassy, 'China Aid "Brightness Action" Campaign in Botswana', *Daily News*, Gaborone, 25 June, 2015.

Sautman, Barry and Yan Hairong. "Friends and Interests: China's Distinctive Links with Africa," *African Studies Review* 50 (3), (2007): 75–114.

Starr, D. "Chinese Language Education in Europe: The Confucius Institutes," *European Journal of Education*, 44 (1), (2009): 65–82; Michael Barr, "Nation Branding as Nation Building: China's image campaign," (East Asia, Springer, 2011): 1–14.

Starr, D. "Chinese Language Education in Europe: The Confucius Institutes," *European Journal of Education*, 44 (1), (2009): 65–82.

University of Botswana, *Teaching and Learning Policy*, University of Botswana, 2008.

University of Botswana Faculty of Humanities Proposal for establishing Bachelor of Arts Degree Programme in Chinese Studies, August 2010, http://chinsestdies.ucsd/edu/.

Xuanxing, L. Chinese Ambassador to Botswana. "Memories and blessings of China-Botswana relations: A review on 35 years of diplomatic relations between China and Botswana", *MmegiOnline*, April 14, 2016, accessed April 14, 2016.

Yang, Rui. "Soft Power and Higher Education: an Examination of China's Confucius Institutes," *Globalisation, Society and Education*, 8 (2)(2010): 235–245 :

YoonJung Park and Tu T. Huynh, "Introduction: Chinese in Africa," *African and Asian Studies*, 9 (2010): 207–212.

Youngman, Frank. University of Botswana Confucius Institute Strategic Planning Workshop, September 20, 2010, University of Botswana, Gaborone; 2010

Youngman, Frank. *Discussion Paper, Strengthening Africa-China Relations: A Perspective from Botswana*, (Stellenbosch: Centre for Chinese Studies), 2013: 12.

Chapter Ten. Of Myths, Stereotypes and Misconceptions – Chinese and Africans: The Case of Botswana

═══════════════════❖═══════════════════

Part Mgadla and *Oarabile Makgabana-Dintwa*

Introduction

Definition of terms

According to the Longman Dictionary of Contemporary English, "a myth is an idea or story that many people believe, but which is not true" or it is "a story without an author that is passed along and is usually intended to teach a lesson, or something that is untrue."[1] A stereotype is defined by the same source as a fixed idea or image of what a particular type of person or thing is like. A further explanation is that a stereotype tends "to decide, usually unfairly, that certain people have particular qualities or abilities because they belong to a particular race, sex, or social class."[2] A misconception is "a misunderstanding, or an inaccurate perception of something; a mistaken thought, idea, or notion."[3] It refers to an idea that is wrong or untrue but which people believe because they do not understand it properly. It is a misunderstanding due to incorrect interpretations. This

---

1. *Longman Dictionary of Contemporary English* (Essex: Longman group Ltd, 1995), 939.
2. Ibid., 1409.
3. Ibid., 906.

paper has used these terms interchangeably because they have almost similar definitions.

Myths, stereotypes and misconceptions of peoples and societies about other peoples and societies that are different from their own have been in existence since time immemorial. These myths and stereotypes tend to be negative and sometimes exaggerated, portraying negative attitudes towards other peoples or races that are different from their own. Even during the era of slave trade, misconceptions existed; for example, there was a belief that Black Africans were stronger and worked harder than other people and that they adjusted to climatic conditions and changes better than those of, say, the Indian stock.[4] During the colonial era the Europeans who colonized much of Africa came with attitudes of superiority which caused them to regard Africans as sub human beings.[5] These attitudes were not limited to a particular ethnic group but there were also "intra" stereotypes, myths and beliefs among peoples of the same ethnic, and phenotypic group. For example, White Americans from the east and north perceived their White Southern counterparts as "green horns", because they were regarded as backward and not progressive.[6] So did the Black Americans in those areas.

English people have always held to myths, attitudes, and or perceptions regarding their neighbours, the Irish; they perceive them as inferior and have attitudes of superiority towards them. Africans in different regions of the continent also have different stereotypes or myths about one another. Southern Africans believe that that Africans in countries north of their own region are susceptible to corruption

---

4. For details on the slaves and slave trade see Philip D. Curtin, *The Atlantic Slave Trade: A Census* (Madison: University of Wisconsin Press, 1969); Edward A. Alpers, *Ivory and Slaves: Patterns of International Trade in East Central Africa to the 19th Century* (Madison: Berkely, 1969); also see Elizabeth Isichei, *History of West Africa* (London and Basingstoke: Macmillan,1977), 6. Here Isichei explains why the Europeans preferred Africans to native Indians of North America or white indentured servants.

5. G. Z. Kapenzi, *The clash of cultures; Christian missionaries and the Shona of Rhodesia* (Washington DC; United Press of America, 1977), 2.

6. Generally, Southerners were regarded as people who resisted change and progress. They resisted the emancipation of the slave trade while the north encouraged emancipation.

and are unstable in their system of governance.[7] There are myths to the effect that West African foods have nutrients that make them stronger and taller than Africans in the Southern African region, thus making them better athletes.[8]

The people of Nguni descent were (and are) believed to love beef to the extent that they are noted to have the potential of eating a cow while walking.[9] Still, even within individual countries these myths and stereotypes exist especially in relation to peoples of the same country but from different regions. There exists for example a myth or stereotype in Botswana that there can never be a good wife who comes from the southern part of Botswana.[10] Those from the south also believe that men from the north do not treat their wives well. These myths and misconceptions about people other than their own are pervasive in many societies of the world, yet their origins are not known.

African contact with the Chinese

Despite having a long history of early contact with the East African coast,[11] the Chinese have not had a close association with the African people and vice-versa. This can be explained in part by the advent of European colonialism which had enveloped most of the African continent. It was not until the late 1960s and early 70s that the African nationalist movements, which sought military and logistical support necessary to topple intransigent European regimes resistant to majority rule, that Africans had close contact with the Chinese.

That said, the end of colonialism ushered in a new era of independence in which Africans became free to associate with nations

---

7. In an interview, the informant was adamant that since independence in Southern Africa, apart from Lesotho, there has never been a coup d'état and that generally the countries in Southern Africa tend to have stable systems of governance. The informant was adamant that the same cannot be said about central and some countries of West Africa.

8. Ibid.

9. Interview with C.J Makgala, University of Botswana, April 2015.

10. General assumption in Botswana.

11. See S.P. Grenville. The East African Coast: Select Documents from the First to the Nineteenth Century. (Oxford: Clarendon Press: 1962) In some of these documents Grenville discusses some of the early contacts between Africans in the Coast and people from the East mostly Indians and some Chinese.

of their choice. New African governments began to form diplomatic and bilateral relations with China. It was then that the Africans had close contact with the Chinese, but this was probably limited to official diplomatic levels. Stemming from these bilateral ties, African governments engaged in development projects with the Chinese such as building roads, bridges, railways like Tanzania-Zambia Railway Authority (TAZARA) and stadia. During this period, the ordinary African people had close contact with the Chinese – even then at a distance because they worked with them in these projects. It was here that Africans and Chinese formulated myths, misconceptions and stereotypes about each other.

Chinese contact with Africans

Mention has already been made about the long history of Chinese contact with the East African coast. Even then the contact was limited to intermittent trade so that a small number of Chinese traders interacted with Kiswahili traders on the coast.[12] Because of the intervention of European powers the trade could not be sustained for a very long time. It was these scores of traders that probably had contact with, and knew Africans closely. The majority of Chinese people in the mainland knew very little about Africans as they had little to no opportunity to have close contact with Africans. Their perceptions of Africa and Africans were probably no different from those of the Westerners who had all sorts of varied perceptions about Africa. The "Tarzan" perception was certainly ingrained in the minds of many societies that had had little contact with Africa, the Chinese being no exception. According to the "Tarzan" perception, it was believed Africans lived with animals on trees like monkeys and chimpanzees and were barbaric.

These perceptions would later be dispelled as myths, misconceptions and stereotypes with the increase in contact between the Chinese and Africans especially, as already has been stated, after the majority of African countries attained self-determination. Botswana, which attained independence in the mid-1960s, established relations with China starting way back in 1974. Like other new and developing countries, the Batswana government engaged Chinese companies in some of its developmental projects. Many of the Chinese present in Botswana today arrived in that manner and a few came as

12. Ibid.

traders. Before then, many of the Chinese knew very little about Botswana, least of all where it is located geographically in Africa. Up to the present, many Chinese, as do other countries outside the African continent, locate Botswana in relation to South Africa which known to most. For instance, it is sometimes mistaken for either being in, or being part of South Africa. Other times, it is mistaken for being part of Zimbabwe. A few of the Chinese interviewed for this paper testified to this.[13]

Alongside bilateral relations and developmental projects that saw the Chinese coming to Botswana were also Chinese traders. These Chinese, who made contact with the people of Botswana, can genuinely claim to know Batswana as they have worked with and have been in close contact with them at community level. The rest of the Chinese back in China continue to know little about Africa, just as the Batswana people who have never been in China, or have not been in close contact with the Chinese, know very little about China. In these sorts of situations, myths, stereotypes and misconceptions about other societies are inevitable.

Findings
Some Common Batswana Myths, Stereotypes and Misconceptions about the Chinese

Myths, misconceptions and stereotypes about other societies are a hindrance to the mutual understanding of societies other than one's own. They create unnecessary barriers in the furtherance of cooperation and joint ventures. They portray negative attitudes towards other societies. However, they need to be studied with the aim of analyzing them because more often than not, they are nothing more than myths, misconceptions and or stereotypes. The following are some myths, misconceptions or stereotypes by Batswana about the Chinese.

All Chinese look the same[14]

This is a common myth held by Batswana and probably by other Africans about the Chinese. Obviously, this myth or stereotype cannot

---

13. Interview with Wei Xin, Chinese language volunteer instructor, CIUB, April 2014 and Tan Ronghua, Chinese Language Instructor, CIUB, May 2015.
14. General assumptions among Africans.

be true as the Chinese, just like other people, are not the same. They are as different as people are in any society. One needs to work with them closely or visit their country to appreciate that they are different people; after all there is no country with people who look exactly the same.

The Chinese eat everything[15]

It is a common belief among Batswana that the Chinese eat everything. Those who are familiar with Chinese food know that Chinese food is not only delicious but also very healthy. To say that Chinese eat everything is indeed a myth. Different Chinese people like and dislike different kinds of their own foods. Some Batswana believe that Chinese people eat dogs and therefore if they can eat dogs then they can eat anything out there. While some people in different parts of China prefer dog meat, not every Chinese person likes or even eats dog meat. The same holds true for some regions of Botswana, where some Batswana eat mopane worms while others do not. Therefore, this remains a myth about the Chinese people.

Chinese never want to interact with local communities

Batswana interviewed for this paper indicated that what they found peculiar about the Chinese was that they had a tendency of keeping to themselves and did not easily interact with the local communities.[16]They noted further that the Chinese did not mix with Batswana communities in events such as weddings, funerals, sports and general local social life. Batswana indicated that even those with shops are not open and welcoming like Indian traders and the English whom we have had for many years in the country.[17]Asked if they ever invite Chinese to their events, it was clear that most events in Batswana communities are not per invitation but open and therefore they expect people to just come, which is different in some parts of the world. The Chinese interviewed for this paper indicated that they were not as unsociable as they were made out to be. They explained that as foreigners they needed to be cautious especially at big events to which they were not invited and where they would know no one. Once

---

15. General assumptions.
16. Interview with M. Gaetwesepe, CIUB, April 2014).
17. Interview with L. Kgaswane, ex-student of CIUB and L. Mmopi, ex-student of CIUB), March 2014.

invited, they would attend all social events without any difficulties as they were keen to learn Setswana culture.[18] Their social upbringing, especially women, was such that it did not allow them to impose themselves without knowing anybody or without invitation; hence their cautious approach to interaction. Clearly when the Chinese know you well and know that places are safe and secure they would easily interact.[19] It is, however, partly true that they do not easily interact because they want to be assured of safety and security first. It is also partly a myth because they interact easily once all their fears have been put to rest.

Chinese are always in a group
This is a stereotype that is closely related to the preceding one. In a situation where a group of people share the same language, culture and tradition, it is not easy to separate the group especially if it is in a foreign country. Similarly, if you took a group of Batswana to China or to any foreign country for that matter, they would most likely stick together because they share the same language, culture and tradition. One needs only to go to China where one would see the Chinese being as natural as anyone elsewhere in the world who would see them as individuals and in groups depending on their circumstances. Being in a group in a foreign situation could also be viewed as a safety measure as one is less likely to be exposed to danger than one would be as an individual. Batswana feel the Chinese are not interested in learning their language, culture and ways of doing things.[20] These are people's perceptions of the Chinese that are not generally true, as they have met only a few Chinese people.

Chinese have a bad attitude towards locals wanting to speak Chinese language
Locals believe the Chinese in Botswana want to know the local language, yet they do not want to teach locals Chinese. Interviews with locals for this paper indicated that the Chinese do not respond in Chinese to locals who attempt to communicate with them in their own language.[21]When they do respond, they do so in English rather than in

---

18. Interview with Tan Ronghua, April 2014.
19. Interview with Du Jin and Tan Ronghua, CIUB, April 2014.
20. Interview with M. Nthobatsang, Humanities, March 2015.
21. Interview with F. Raokgwathile, T. Mosweu former CIUB students, March 2014.

the Chinese language. This makes some locals suspicious of them. Batswana who have learnt Chinese at the Confucius Institute at the University of Botswana are eager to show what they have learnt but have had a disappointing rapport from the Chinese community. While that may be so, not all Chinese are hostile to Batswana who attempt to communicate with them in their own language. A few do respond and even try to correct them where necessary. According to the interviewees, most of the Chinese in and around Gaborone and some major villages in the country tend to be hostile to the point of arrogance. On finding out why this was so from some of the more open-minded Chinese, they state that the possible reason was that some of the Chinese were being made fun of when locals try to speak in Chinese because they say things that are not in any way close to their language. This language is based on intonation; hence the Chinese's feeling that the locals often do not pronounce the words properly. The words are pronounced in such way that it seems as if the locals are mocking the Chinese. It remains a myth, misconception and or stereotype that Chinese people in Botswana are arrogant and self-centred as is proclaimed.

All Chinese men smoke

Most Chinese men have a tendency to smoke a lot. No society is perfect of course and a comparison with Batswana men indicates that there are areas in which Batswana men do things that are viewed as out of the ordinary too e.g. drinking of alcohol. According to Batswana, who have had experiences with the Chinese men here, it looks as if they all smoke and they often smoke in public places without consideration of non-smokers in their midst.[22]The few people who have had close encounters with the Chinese indicated that some even smoke in elevators and on planes, and this has fuelled this negative stereotype about them. This remains a myth because not all Chinese men smoke.

Chinese spit a lot

Batswana and probably some Africans and other nations alike think that the Chinese like spitting a lot. Every society has habits; sometimes these are likeable and at other times they are not so palatable to outsiders. It is, however, an exaggeration to assert that all Chinese spit.

---

22. Interview with B. Mokopakgosi, May 2014 – personal experience.

On the contrary, there are some Chinese who abhor spitting. During the 2008 Olympics held in China, the Chinese government warned and discouraged its citizens from the spitting habit noting that it was not so palatable to both some of its citizens and outsiders. It cannot be held true that Chinese spit a lot from having met a few in Botswana.

Chinese do everything fast
Some of the Batswana believe that the Chinese like to do everything fast and that this ethic compromises standards and quality. Such Batswana describe Chinese merchandize as cheap and of low quality because it was made in a hurry to satisfy demands quickly and that this compromises quality.[23]The stereotype goes further to assert that Chinese goods are generally cheap because of their low quality. What most people do not realize is the fact that China has a big population, the majority of which is from either the working or peasant class. To satisfy the needs of such a huge population, including international demands, the Chinese cannot afford to be slow in the production of their goods and services. It has to be clarified that China produces both good quality and affordable goods. Thus, good quality and expensive goods are available, just as are cheap and affordable good are. The stereotype goes even further to assert that Chinese projects in Botswana are often faulty, built at a very fast pace, and at a pace viewed as compromising standards. The Chinese companies are even alleged to work late at night. If this myth has any substance in it, then the irony of it all is that Chinese cities have magnificently well-constructed, durable buildings and their work ethic is not compromised at any time, be it at home or abroad. The myth about the Chinese work ethic being too fast and that this results in compromised goods is not true.

All Chinese goods are fake
Again, this is a myth. Some Batswana who have been to China assert that the Chinese are very good imitators, especially with regard to business-related goods to the extent that it is hard to distinguish between a genuine and fake product especially if one is a foreigner.[24] Goods with famous or popular labels and brands are highly likely to be fake. According to Batswana interviewed, it is hard sometimes to

---

23. Interview with anonymous teacher in Mahupu Junior Secondary School, Kweneng West, February 2015.
24. Part Mgadla, personal experience while in China, 2011.

recognize whether an Adidas T-shirt or tracksuit is genuine or not because the imitation is so well done.[25] While there may be some truth in this assertion, it is true that for years China has produced high-quality goods for the European market and other parts of the world.

Some Chinese Myths, Misconceptions and Stereotypes about Africans (Batswana)

Africa is a poor continent with poor people

Most Chinese and Westerners who have not been to, or associated with Africans, view Africa as a poor continent whose people live in abject poverty. While this stereotype is not completely without foundation, Africa is well endowed with varied resources and even though some of its inhabitants may be poor, it also has a substantial number of people who are well-off or self-sufficient. The Western media has generally portrayed Africans in a negative light, which has regrettably found its way in most parts of the world, and the "Tarzan myth" has unfortunately been ingrained in many minds of those who have not had close contact with Africans. Africa should be viewed as a continent with a lot of potential and its people are as poor or as rich as any other.

Africa is very hot and dry

It is true that Africa is largely a hot continent. It is also true that some countries on the continent are drier than others such as Botswana or those countries closer to the desert. This perception should be cautiously viewed as some parts of Africa can be extremely cold, sometimes experiencing snow in winter, especially those countries in the south and northern part of the continent. So, it is not quite accurate that Africa always has hot and dry weather. By the same token, Africa should not be viewed as a continent that is always dry as there are counties that have a high rainfall, resulting in lush vegetation suitable for the growth of commercial crops – some of which are exported to countries outside the continent.

All Africans look the same

Chinese who have not made contact or worked closely with Africans think Africans look similar, in the same manner that some Africans

---

25. Interview with B. Mokopakgosi, L. Mmopi, L. Kgaswane; November 2014 and Part Mgadla's personal experience, 2010–2011.

think about the Chinese. It is not always possible for the Chinese to distinguish between the Africans of a particular region and those of a different country for that matter. For example, Chinese who have not been long on the continent find it difficult to differentiate between a Motswana and a Zulu.[26] The same applies to some Africans who have not made contact with the Chinese and who find it difficult to distinguish between the Chinese people and say, Japanese or Korean people. Clearly therefore Africans do not look the same just as much as the Chinese do not look the same.

African skin is black like soot and can rub off
It is not a myth that most Africans are dark skinned, but it is a myth that African skin is like soot and rubs off. Some Chinese throughout their lives have not seen black Africans at close range, having seen them only on television, and in newspapers and magazines. Some Batswana who have been to China during summer and winter camps have told stories through the CIUB about some Chinese having rubbed their skins to ascertain whether the skin would peel off.[27] Exposure to environments other than one's own helps to understand other people much better.

Africans are dirty
Through interviewing a few Chinese people for this paper, it was found that the Chinese, at least those who are here in Botswana, are impressed with African cleanliness. They are impressed by the general habitat of the Africans. Their houses are clean and their rest rooms are even cleaner than some of those found in China.[28]African people like to be clean because in some parts of the continent it is very hot. Where there is heat, there is perspiration and washing several times a day is way of cooling off and is not done to wash off dirt. It is, however, an exaggeration by the Chinese that Africans wash three times a day because they are dirty. Africans are no dirtier than any other race. Generally, Africans wash twice a day but it is not uncommon in the rural areas for some to wash once a day just like the Chinese. This is but one of those racist stereotypes according to which blacks are viewed as dirty.

---

26. Interview with Dong Jianping, May 2015.
27. Interview with L. Kgaswane, L. Sealetsa and L. Molefe, March 2015.
28. Interview with Tan Ronghua, April 2014.

Chinese think that Africa is not modernized
Again, stemming from the negative reports in the media, an impression is created that Africa is backward and is way out of step with the developed world. Some Chinese people interviewed for this paper[29] indicated that they were pleasantly surprised upon coming to Botswana to find developments that were beyond their expectations. Some did not expect to find offices with phones let alone the internet. The surprise did not stop there. They soon found out that clean water could be drunk from the tap and that electricity was available. Yet others did not expect to see highways and modern cars and could not help comparing shopping centres with those of the Western world and those of their own countries.[30]

Batswana men like drinking alcohol
One of the observations made by the few Chinese interviewed for this study indicated that Batswana men like drinking alcohol.[31] This is a perception that could not be denied except that men in general like drinking alcohol. This is not to say women do not drink, they do but they do not do so at the same rate as men. In Botswana, some Chinese observed that men can spend the whole day and night drinking and roasting beef. It is doubtful whether this is peculiar to Botswana or that men all over the world like drinking alcohol. Until this is verified to be a "Batswana-men thing", then it remains a stereotype about our society.

Batswana men like to have more than one woman
It has been observed by the Chinese here that Batswana men like to have more one woman. It is not only an observation made by the Chinese but by citizens from other nations that have been in Botswana.[32] Foreign women interviewed for this study have indicated that some Batswana men tend to be promiscuous. An American student who studied at UB told a story of Batswana young men proposing to her and when she mentioned that she already had a

---

29. Interview with Du Jing and Wei Xin, January 2015.
30. Interview with Don Jianping, February 2015.
31. Interview with Wei Xin and Tan Ronghua, March 2015.
32. Interview with anonymous foreign student in History class 416, January 2014.

boyfriend at home, the Motswana young man replied quite simply, "No problem, you can have two boyfriends, an American one and an African one!" On being asked if he himself had a girlfriend, he replied, "Of course I do, but I want you as well." Some Chinese have wondered how they can be loved by strangers as Batswana men are fond of saying, "I love you; I want to marry you", even if they don't know the woman.[33] Other Chinese have talked about hearing of "small houses" and how these tend to get more attention than the "main houses." Again, it is difficult to ascertain whether such a feature is peculiar to Batswana men or whether it happens in other parts of the world.

Batswana men force their women to prove fertility before marriage
One of the myths that came from the interviews is that most Batswana women have children out of marriage because they have to prove fertility to their partners before marriage. This is not true; as in other societies female-headed families are common due to divergent reasons and not because of having to prove fertility. It is important for the Chinese in Botswana to learn and understand why things happen the way they do here before they come to conclusions.

Chinese believe that African men are genitally gifted
This myth is not only peculiar to the Chinese but is also known to be prevalent among Westerners and other people that are not African. How this myth was generated is anybody's guess. The myth is racist as it involves the labelling of one group of people as "gifted" in the genital area. It may well be that other groups of people are also "gifted" but that this is not so widely discussed. This is a myth that is difficult to ascertain but it can only be confirmed or negated by the well-known English expression "the proof of the pudding is in the eating."

Conclusion

Myths, stereotypes, misconceptions and observations about societies other than our own have been in existence since time immemorial. While for some myths the line of reality is very thin, the majority of them are unreal, negative and based on ignorance and a lack of sufficient knowledge about other societies. The many myths and stereotypes the Batswana have about the Chinese and vice versa are largely based on a lack of sufficient knowledge about one another.

---

33. Interview with Wei Xin and Du Jin, May 2015.

Myths and stereotypes create buffers, and they hinder mutual understanding, peace, and cooperation between peoples of different ethnic and phenotypic origin. It is important therefore to study societies other than our own in order to understand them better rather than to harbour stereotypes and myths about them. That way, some of the stereotypes may be removed. Better still, one of the best ways of removing myths and stereotypes about other societies is to study their language and culture. Once you speak the language of a people, you inevitably understand their culture and once you understand their culture you understand their society. In that way, mutual relations between peoples can easily be promoted.

Bibliography

Edward A. Alpers. 1969. *Ivory and Slaves: Patterns of International Trade in East Central Africa to the 19th Century.* Madison: Berkeley

Elizabeth Isichei. 1977. *History of West Africa.* London and Basingstoke: Macmillan

G. Z. Kapenzi. 1977. *The clash of cultures; Christian missionaries and the Shona of Rhodesia.* Washington DC; United Press of America.

Philip D. Curtin. 1969 *The Atlantic Slave Trade: A Census.* Madison: University of Wisconsin Press.

Chapter Eleven. China and Tanzania as Portrayed by Chinese and Tanzanian Media

=============== ❖ ===============

Muhidin J. Shangwe

Introduction

History has proved that the media plays an important role in shaping perceptions. In light of this, the role of the media in promoting understanding among the peoples of Africa and their Chinese counterparts earned a special mention in the Forum for China and Africa Cooperation (FOCAC) circles, with the founding of the Forum on Africa-China Media Corporation. For centuries, the dominant narrative about Africa has been dominated by the *Dark Continent* tradition, according to which Africa is home to poverty, diseases, lawlessness, savagery, cannibalism, slavery and backwardness.[1] Thanks to the Western media, these perceptions are widely shared in every part of the globe.[2]

---

1. Robert R. Bates, "Africa through Western eyes: The World's Dark Continent or Capitalism's Shining Light?" Think Africa Press, October 31, 2012, accessed January 30, 2015, http://thinkafricapress.com/culture/africa-through-western-eyes-worlds-dark-continent-or-capitalisms-shining-light.
2. I recall one among many popular Latin American TV dramas broadcasted by Tanzania's ITV several years ago. One character, angered by the actions of another, wished death on her by declaring that she wished her adversary would die "from one of those terrible diseases found in Africa".

The legacy of this tradition still haunts Africa to this day despite the continent's striking historical and cultural wealth. Deborah Kaspin and Paul Landau have argued that the representations of images of Africa in the Western media are not static, but instead are complicated, nuanced and constantly transforming.[3] Kaspin observes, however, that the hegemonic myths held in the West about Africa persevere, despite the collapse of the colonial empires that the myths supported decades earlier.[4] Thus perceptions about Africa around the world and the stereotypes attached to the continent, to a great extent, are influenced by the West's version of what Africa and Africans meant and still mean to them. Such stereotypes have survived through time, as Martha Saavedra argues, so that in the contemporary world, Africa is the repository for disease, war, famine, poverty and corruption.[5]

The general understanding of Africa beyond these tragedies is therefore limited, if an understanding exists at all.[6] The same could be said about China in the eyes of Africans, as a lack of resources and an over-dependence on the international media as the main "source" of information mean that news about China in some cases lacks an African perspective. In other words, Africans do not control the narrative but rather consume what international media, including the Chinese media, feed them about China. Given the dominance of Western media in the sphere of information and the expansive Chinese media in recent years, Africans, and to a lesser extent the Chinese, are at risk of consuming information that has been filtered by the Western media, for Western audiences and interests.

---

3. Paul S. Landau and Deborah D. Kaspin, quoted here in Saavedra, "Representations of Africa in a Hong Kong Soap Opera,"764.

4. Deborah D. Kaspin, in Saavedra, "Representations of Africa in a Hong Kong Soap Opera," 765.

5. Saavedra, "Representations of Africa in a Hong Kong Soap Opera," 765.

6. Writing on the Chinese perceptions of African civil society organizations (CSOs), Xiao Yuhua observed that "[t]he majority of Chinese public has little knowledge about the African continent, let alone African CSOs." He adds, "Some people think Africa is mysterious and has a variety of indigenous cultures, but their knowledge is mostly from books, magazines, newspapers and other mass media." See Xiao Yuhua, "Chinese perceptions of African CSO: how should African CSOs engage China?" in *Chinese and African Perspectives on China in Africa*, ed. Axel Harneit-Sievers et al. (Cape Town: Pambazuka Press, 2010), 216.

This paper seeks to investigate what China means to Tanzanians and what Africa in general means to the Chinese through the eyes of both the Chinese and Tanzanian media. This is done in the context of existing structural weaknesses in Afro-Chinese relations where, as one editorial put it sometime ago, "China has an African Policy; Africa doesn't have a China Policy, only a Beijing-controlled forum in which Mandarins figure out which country to take a sweet shot at."[7] The forum in question is FOCAC, where China is not only the initiator but also the influencer. As such the author of this paper finds it irrelevant to discuss the depiction of Tanzania in Chinese media because in policy terms, as far as China is concerned, Africa is a country! That is, despite having fifty-four states, Africa is regarded as a single entity. Conversely, the depiction of China in Tanzanian media is done on the grounds that despite historical and cultural shortcomings that throw the nationhood of the Tanzanian state into question, it still considers itself as an independent nation, and is regarded as such in international politics.

Tanzania holds a special strategic place in China's engagement with Africa. Recently, China's ambassador to Tanzania stated that his government intends to make Tanzania an industrial hub in the Eastern and Southern Africa region.[8] This goes hand in hand with reports that Beijing has already been Tanzania's biggest trading partner since 2012.[9] On the other hand, a great deal of admiration is accorded to China in Tanzania, at least as expressed by Tanzanian leaders. Visiting Peking (now Beijing) in 1974, the first president of Tanzania, Mwalimu Julius K. Nyerere, expressed his admiration for the Chinese way of development. In his speech, he approvingly stated that there were two things which convinced him that socialism can be built in Africa and that this is not a Utopian vision. The first, he stated, was the fact that capitalism is ultimately incompatible with the real independence of African states. To quote his own words, "[t]he second thing which

---

7. Taylor, "China's oil diplomacy in Africa," 953.
8. Veneranda Sumila, "China eyes ATCL, port and railway projects," *The Citizen*, April 25, 2015, accessed April 30, http://www.thecitizen.co.tz/News/national/China-eyes-ATCL---10bn-port-project/-/1840392/2696976/-/4bye05z/-/index.html.
9. Adam Ihucha, "China: Tanzania's biggest development partner," *The East African*, January 25, 2014, accessed April 30, 2015, http://www.theeastafrican.co.ke/news/China--Tanzania-biggest-development-partner-/-/2558/2160314/-/wmunsez/-/index.html.

encourages me is China … China is providing an encouragement and an inspiration for younger and smaller nations which seek to build socialist societies."[10] Meanwhile, the incumbent president, Jakaya M. Kikwete, has gone on record claiming that he did not think the Chinese have a better friend on the continent than Tanzania.[11] It is on these grounds that the relations between the two countries are the focus of this paper. The aim is to find a general trend and the direction of the media reporting on the topic in question.

China's construed image of Africa and the rise of Chinese media

Philip Snow's book, *The Star Raft: Africa's Encounter with China*,[12] is a compelling work on the relations between Africa and China.[13] In the book, Snow presents three phases of the interactions between the two in a way that may help shed light on the prevailing representation of Africa in some pockets of Chinese media. We are informed that in pre-colonial times, far back in the ninth century, the dark-skinned Africans were known to the Chinese by the name *kinlun* (slaves). The name was attached to Africans who were brought by Arab slave-traders to China during the Tang Dynasty. From Kunlun, they became *shengfan* (savages) or *guinu* (devil slaves); *yeren* (wild men) or *heigui*[14] (Negroes). This was, contrary to conventional understanding, way before the *Dark Continent* narrative was invented by European missionaries and explorers. As Frank Dikotter pointed, this tendency suggests that the perception of "blacks are equal to slaves" was well established in the old Chinese mentality. According to Dikotter, the Chinese once simply

10. Bailey, "Tanzania and China,"178.
11. Interview: Jakaya Kikwete, *Financial Times*, November 6, 2007, accessed November 28, 2013, http://www.ft.com/cms/s/0/d8a07e28-72a3-11dc-b7ff-0000779fd2ac.html#axzz2lxLXE1mK.
12. Philip Snow, *The Star Raft: Africa's Encounter with China* (London: Weidenfeld and Nicolson, 1988).
13. See how Snow has contributed to this conversation in Simon Shen, "A Constructed (un)Reality on China's Re-entry into Africa: The Chinese Online Community Perception of Africa (2006–2008)," *The Journal of Modern African Studies* 47, No.3 (2009): 245–448, accessed February 5, 2015, http://www.jstor.org/stable/40538319.
14. Pleco, an English & Chinese Dictionary application popular among Chinese language learners defines *heigui* (黑鬼) as a black devil (derogatory term for a black or African person).

characterized Africa as a land of *hindun* (chaos), i.e. a primitive stage of civilization.[15] This tendency has not been helped by the Chinese word for Africa, *Feizhou* (非洲). Its meaning includes *Dark Continent*, according to popular Chinese dictionary *youdao* (有道词典). The word *fei* is particularly problematic and its many meanings include *blame, be not, mistake, wrong, error, non-, un-, incorrect, error,* etc. At face value, this carries a connotative meaning which in turn might shape Chinese society's understanding of Africa as the land of chaos, albeit subliminally.[16] Compared with the Chinese word for America, *meiguo* (美国), one could see the difference. *Mei* (美) means *beauty, beautiful, good, pretty*; thus, it could be said that it symbolizes positivity as opposed to the subliminal meaning of negativity attached to Africa. The reference to Africa as the *Dark Continent* in China brings back to this very day the painful memory of European missionaries and explorers' depiction of the continent. For the record, the *Dark Continent* narrative emphasizes all that was perceived as bad by Europeans.[17] That it still enjoys popular usage in China highlights the Chinese mentality when it comes to their understanding of Africa.

The second phase of interaction between Africans and the Chinese, according to Snow, took place during the colonial era when Chinese laborers were taken to Africa to work in Europe's various colonial enterprises. By the mid-nineteenth century, a Chinatown had emerged in Mauritius. Snow also says that the colonial experience endured by

---

15. Quoted here in Shen, "A Constructed (un)Reality on China's Re-entry into Africa," 434.
16. For most Chinese, Africa is viewed as an "off-the-map" continent. As a result, matters concerning Africa do not attract attention in ordinary Chinese conversations. For further discussion on this see Shen, "A Constructed (un)Reality on China's Re-entry into Africa," 245–448.
17. According to Vaughan, "[v]irtually all descriptions of the 'dark continent' portray its inhabitants as unattractive, heathen, and grossly uncivil. In theory, at least, the Africans' culture could be ameliorated; their physical characteristics could not. And although several aspects of African appearance – stature, facial features and hair texture, for example – displeased English eye, most striking and disturbing was the darkness of African skin. Descriptions of African people invariably stress their blackness, always disapprovingly." Quoted here from Mudimbe, *The Invention of Africa*, 130.

Chinese and Africans both at home and abroad would have sown seeds of brotherhood between the two peoples.

The third phase was characterized by the rise of Communist China in 1949. During this period and after, China presented itself as the leader of not only Africa but the entire Third World. It was then that Chairman Mao pronounced that "in making friends in the world, we should put the stress on the Third World."[18] The Chinese, we are told by Snow, saw themselves as obliged to give lessons to Africans, believing that newly independent nations were simply re-enacting the brutal feudal past of China.[19] In one case, Dikotter recalls that "the Chinese once posited themselves in a play performed in Rwanda as the saviour of an African throne from European invasion."[20] Coupled with the internationalist doctrine proposed by Chairman Mao, the Chinese once again saw themselves as superior to their "African buddies" meaning that the old image of the Africans was thus reinstated.[21] The term "African buddies" still enjoys popular usage in Chinese social circles and sometimes, mostly in social media, is synonymously used as "poor buddies" (*qiongxiongdi*).

More than two decades after the publication of Snow's book, relations between Africa and China are at their strongest in history – a new phase not captured in the book. The Maoist China is a thing of the past now and through opening up her economy, China has achieved an economic transformation never recorded in human history. This new phase has been marked by what Beijing calls *peaceful development*, a strategy that aims at, among other things, painting a positive image of the rising economic powerhouse. It is an era of "soft-power China", a concept that has been warmly embraced by Chinese leaders since it was conceived by Joseph Nye in 1990. Yu-Shan Wu has observed that during this period, Chinese leaders have realized that in the post-Cold War era, soft-power capabilities (the influence derived from non-coercive cultural appeal) are challenging the influence of the military and economic mighty, or multilateral diplomacy.[22] Wu further observes that China is seeking to win over the hearts and minds of

---

18. Wenping He, "All-Weather Friend," 25.
19. Quoted in Shen, "A Constructed (un)Reality on China's Re-entry into Africa," 434.
20. Ibid.
21. Ibid., 434–435.
22. Wu, "The Rise of China's State-led Media Dynasty in Africa," 5.

everyday people who have traditionally learned about the country through global political news circles. Commenting on the growing Chinese state-led media dynasty in Africa in relation to soft power, Wu adds, "[t]he state-led initiative is institutionalizing soft power, most recently creating its own news providers to tell the China narrative."[23] China's promotion of its soft power is understandable given the country's "not-so-attractive" past, partly due to Western media's negativity, a phenomenon still evident especially with regard to China's role in Africa. Mainly under the tutelage of the Western media, China has come in for strong criticism on the grounds that it is causing a negative impact on Africa's long-term interests by dealing with corrupt governments.[24] Thus China's expansive media aims at countering such negativity so that others may view it as a "progressive, prosperous, culturally advanced and peace-loving country."[25] Other scholars like Michael Barr, however, see more to China's embracing of soft power. He argues that soft power is essential to China and the Communist Party in particular, because it enhances its grip on power. Also, Barr argues, the very idea of soft power appeals to Chinese traditional thought, an important aspect in creating and maintaining national cohesion for the vast country. Lastly, soft power is important for China because it addresses, or can be used to address, misconceptions about the real China by foreign media as well as refuting the "China threat" theory.[26]

Barr furthermore observes that in order to expand the reach and impact of its state-run media and improve the effectiveness of mass communication as a means of state soft power, China has committed US$6.5 billion for the overseas expansion of its main media organizations. When compared with the USA, which by 2011 was spending about US$750 million annually on international broadcasting, while funding from the United Kingdom (UK)for the British Broadcasting Corporation (BBC) World Service was running at

---

23. Ibid.
24. This view is also explained by Wu, "The Rise of China's State-led Media Dynasty in Africa," 7.
25. Fook, "China's media initiatives,"545.
26. China threat theory as premised on the assumption that the rise of China is a threat to the existing international order. Understandably this theory enjoys acceptance in the West particularly in the United States of America. Barr, *Who is afraid of China*, 33–34.

less than US$400 million per annum, China's ambitious media initiative is thus put into perspective.[27]

Apart from that, we are made aware that the China Network Corporation (CNC) has established news, business and lifestyle programs broadcasted in several languages including English, French, Spanish, Portuguese, Arabic and Russian while the government-run English language channel CCTV 9 has been rebranded as CCTV News and has programs available in a hundred countries. It is also revealed that the *China Daily*, the country's leading English paper, has a weekly edition in the UK and the United States of America (USA) in the form of a publication known as the *Global Times* under the umbrella of the *People's Daily*. It was launched in 2009 with the aim to "better convey a good image of China to the world." Furthermore, China Radio International (CRI) has steadily increased short-wave frequencies from 152 in 2000 to 293 in 2009. This has been done at the time when the USA and UK have been cutting down the number of short-wave programmes with the UK announcing in 2011 that it was planning to eliminate five foreign-language services and to implement an overall phased reduction in the short-wave and medium-wave distribution of its remaining radio services. In the developing world, we are told, Xinhua is making headway by signing content deals in countries such as Zimbabwe, Mongolia, Turkey, Cuba, Venezuela and Nigeria. With a cost advantage compared to established news heavyweights such as Reuters, Associated Press (AP) and Agence France-Presse (AFP), Xinhua is steadily becoming a major source of news in Africa and much of Asia.[28]

It seems that China's aim of "conveying a good image to the world" is central in this media initiative. Speaking at the launch of the China Xinhua News Network Corporation (CNC), Xinhua President Li Congjun explained that the purpose of the television service was to "present an international vision with a China perspective."[29] Lye Liang Fook has fittingly explained the intention of such moves when he wrote:[30]

---

27. Barr, *Who is afraid of China,* 45.
28. Ibid., 46–47.
29. Fook, "China media initiatives," 554.
30. Ibid., 548.

By promoting a better understanding of China via the various media initiatives, China would like these foreign audiences to be more receptive to China or even to view China more on its own terms rather than through tinted lens. In this manner, China is laying the groundwork for others to view its culture, ideology, institutions and all that it stands for in a more "objective" light as viewed by China. Ultimately, and perhaps the most important objective of all, China would want to be able to convert its soft power resources (particularly the appeal of its culture) to realized power by effecting a change in behaviour on the part of other countries in a direction that these countries would want and which would also be in China's interest.

The promotion of Chinese soft power, apart from using the media in a public relations campaign which will include expanding the influence of Chinese media, is also being implemented through the launch of a cultural offensive and the promotion of political values and institutions.[31] In Africa, China's strategy of using the media in a public relations campaign has manifested in the form of increasing the presence of Chinese media as well as providing material and technical support to Africa's state-owned media. The former has led to, for instance, the opening of CCTV's African head office in Kenya in 2010 and the subsequent launching of the CCTV Africa program in 2012 with state-of-the-art studios in Nairobi. The latter, on the other hand, has resulted in huge financial and technical support in countries like the Democratic Republic of Congo (DRC), Gabon, Malawi, Zambia, Zimbabwe, Seychelles, Equatorial Guinea and Liberia. In countries like South Africa and Mozambique, China's involvement has taken the form of content in which China takes charge as a primary news provider. This type of support also occurs at continent-level where agreements have been reached to expand Chinese media coverage. A good example is when Xinhua launched its "China Africa News Service" to expand coverage of African and Chinese news of mutual interest in 2008. A great deal of technical support has also been given at the level of training which has been conducted on the continent.

---

31. For a detailed account on these three ways of promoting Chinese soft power see Mingjiang Li, "Soft Power in Chinese discourse."

African journalists receive training and exchange know-how with their Chinese counterparts.[32]

Africa in China's Social Media

Social media provides a special avenue for the Chinese public. China, with 600 million internet users in 2014, is the world's largest internet user and social media is one place where Chinese voices and perceptions are heard. It has been contended that in a country where full democracy and complete freedom of expression are still lacking, online communication arguably plays a particularly significant role.[33] When it comes to online topics in China, which are not frequently addressed in the public domain, the flow of information among the online community is paramount in shaping public perception.[34] In recent years, topics about Africa on social media have been on the rise, thanks to increased human interaction between Africans and Chinese. However, as we have seen earlier, Africa does not attract significant attention in Chinese social media unless there is a fundamental Chinese interest in the matter under discussion. For instance, when three Chinese nationals were arrested in November 2013 in Tanzania for possession of 706 elephant tusks, Africa's wildlife was suddenly trending. Weibo, China's equivalent of Twitter, reported that more than 11.41 million messages had been generated in an online discussion on saving elephants.[35]

In general, the representation of Africa in Chinese social media is a mixed bag but it is fair to say that, more often than not, Africa is frequently mentioned in the same line as famine, diseases, poverty and violence. Examples are numerous: for instance, it still surprises social media users when a Chinese dates a black African. In one instance, a photo portraying a romantic posture of a Chinese male and black female in Shanghai Metro went viral on Chinese social networks. Comments ranged from those admitting they could not accept Chinese

---

32. For a detailed account on Chinese media engagement in Africa 2000–2011 see Wu, "The Rise of China's State-led Media Dynasty in Africa," 13–15.

33. Shen, "A Constructed (un)Reality on China's Re-entry into Africa," 425–426.

34. Ibid., 426.

35. Lianxing Li, "Poachers' shame wrongly falls on all Chinese," *China Daily Africa Weekly*, November 8, 2013, 10.

dating black Africans to those expressing very sexist feelings against Africans.[36] A study by Simon Shen reveals that:

> The level of sexual misperception becomes much more racist once the topic is raised online. In a message warning fellow Chinese women to "beware of the Africans", various internet users said: The Negroes love to go clubbing. But their desire is not limited to dancing or drinking. Those Negroes will first try to flirt with our Chinese girls, by all possible means to flirt with us. If there had been only Negroes inside the clubs or discos, raping would have happened already (Message ID 58305, 2006). To my fellow female citizens: for the sake of your personal safety and health, for the sake of not giving birth to a black baby who will be discriminated against, for the sake of your happy marriage, please don't hang out with a Negro! (Message ID 84, 2007).[37]

In another example in 2009, Lou Jing, the daughter of an African American father and Chinese mother, suffered racist abuse by internet users, popularly known as *netizens*. Lou had participated in a talent show on Dragon TV and became famous as Shanghai Black Girl. In her defense following online internet abuse, she issued a statement in which she explained that her father was not African but American, suggesting strong resentment her abusers had against black Africans and the African Diaspora. In the story that was posted on *China Smack*, a popular site that offers English-translated stories popular in Chinese social media, one contributor claimed that "once blacks make a contribution to the world, racism against them will end", adding, "in the meantime we can enjoy watching National Geographic show pictures of caveman African tribes, hungry children covered in dirt and a continent in waste."[38] Similarly, Africans have been on the receiving

---

36. Fauna, September 6, 2006, "Chinese Black Couple on Shanghai Metro," *China Smack,* September 6, 2006, accessed February 20, 2015,http://www.chinasmack.com/2009/pictures/chinese-black-couple-shanghai-metro.html.
37. Shen, "A Constructed (un)Reality on China's Re-entry into Africa," 436.
38. Comment on Fauna, "Shanghai 'Black Girl' Lou Jing Abused by Racist Netizens," *China Smack, S*eptember 1, 2009, accessed February 20, 2015, http://www.chinasmack.com/2009/stories/shanghai-black-girl-lou-jing-racist-chinese-netizens.html.

end of stigmatization following the outbreak of Ebola in 2014. One study reveals that most online users tend to think Africans are carriers of the disease, whether they reside in China or Ebola-stricken regions on the African continent.[39] One researcher observes that for Ebola, social media users ascribe risk onto an understanding of "African-ness", whether it is located on the continent of Africa, or within African bodies when they come to reside in China, echoing previous racialized responses to HIV/AIDS.[40] Generally, social media perceptions of Africa are mostly a result of ignorance and history. Even when users have good things to say about Africa it is awkwardly done and thus unsettling. During the Beijing Olympics "in August 2008, for example, many online messages expressed amazement at the African athletes, saying things with racial overtones like 'it seems that the darkest among the Negroes are the most powerful ones'".[41] This feeling that Africans are some kind of exotic beings is so apparent in social media that it suggests knowledge about Africa and Africans is lacking for *netizens* and the Chinese society as a whole.

Africa in China's State-Owned Media

In an era of a soft-power China, it seems that the country's state-owned media has been handed a special assignment by the government. The task at hand is countering "bad press" about China which features in the Western media with considerable regularity. It is a move closely related to the country's ambitious soft-power project. Wu has argued that China's state-owned media is increasing its influence in the world as an instrument of its grander soft-power engagement.[42] In 2012, an opinion piece in the *China Daily*, the government's English mouthpiece, stated that to make the rest of the world aware of China's role in Africa, the Chinese mass media have to break the monopoly of their Western competitors in Africa and spread the facts, as well as views, of the Chinese government and think tanks

---

39. Emilio Dirkov, and Qiuyu Jiang, "From the dragon's perspective: an initial report on China's response to the unfolding Ebola epidemic," *Somatosphere*, October 29, 2014, accessed February 10, 2015, http://somatosphere.net/2014/10/from-the-dragons-perspective.html.

40. Emilio Dirkov, and Qiuyu Jiang, "From the dragon's perspective."

41. Shen, "A Constructed (un)Reality on China's Re-entry into Africa," 436.

42. Wu, "The Rise of China's State-led Media Dynasty in Africa," ii.

across the world.[43] Later on in 2012, it was reported in the same newspaper that China will invest more in mainstream media organizations, especially those targeting overseas readers in the following ten years to better present a true picture of China to the world.[44] Thus the Chinese government is using media for diplomacy, bringing a new, competitive element to influence states.[45]

China's eagerness to present the "true picture of China to the world" is having potential consequences bordering on misrepresentation and distortion. In 2003, for instance, China came under fierce criticism over its mishandling of the outbreak of the severe acute respiratory syndrome (SARS) virus. The response of near-silence from the government was criticized as irresponsible, yet it was a way of avoiding "losing face" for the leadership. Traditionally, in Chinese culture losing face, or *mianzi*, is synonymous with a loss of reputation.[46] The concept is closely associated with public appearances and image and is a significant motivator in Chinese social psychology[47]. Therefore, open and public criticism– for the world to see – maximizes the potential to lose face.[48] How does the fear of losing face impact on Afro-Chinese relations in the context of media reporting? China's desire to change the narrative about itself and Africa is enticing for Africa, where the legacy of "bad press" reached a whole new level when *The Economist* labelled Africa as the "Hopeless Continent" in 2000. However, as it was argued in an *Aljazeera* article sometime ago, the desire to change the narrative about Africa has led some to claim that Chinese media emphasizes positive, feel-good stories about the

43. Yanting, quoted in Wu, "The Rise of China's State-led Media Dynasty in Africa," 5.
44. Bo Qiu, "Investment in media to present true picture of China," *China Daily*, January 4, 2011, accessed March 20, 2016, http://www.chinadaily.com.cn/bizchina/2011-01/04/content_11791913.htm.
45. Black, Epstein and Tokita, quoted in Wu, "The Rise of China's State-led Media Dynasty in Africa," 7.
46. Murthy, in Wu, "The Rise of China's State-led Media Dynasty in Africa," 8.
47. Jian, in Wu, "The Rise of China's State-led Media Dynasty in Africa," 8.
48. Wu, "The Rise of China's State-led Media Dynasty in Africa," 8.

continent.[49] In the article, one observer is quoted as saying "[y]ou could argue that the western media tend to be too concerned about the bad news", adding that, "[t]he Chinese tend to be rather too concerned about the good news." This, however, has been disputed with others maintaining it is a myth and that the Chinese media reports both good and bad news about Africa.[50]

Whether that is true or not, there is a reason to believe that it serves China very well when its media goes the "paradise route" – that is, the preoccupation with the positive side of Africa as opposed to the perceived "hell route" portrayed by Western media, to use the aforementioned observer's analogy. It is in the interests of China to report good things about Africa for two good reasons. First, the strategy counters Western media attacks that China is only interested in African resources and will only bring havoc to the continent, much as what colonialism had done and continues to do in the shape of neo-colonialism. A *good Africa* image is a vindication of Beijing's insistence that their relations with Africa are based on principles of win-win cooperation and that the good image indicates China's role is making a difference. Secondly, by reporting the positives about Africa, the Chinese media creates a feel-good atmosphere amongst Africans, a rare comfort on the troubled continent.

It is on these grounds that China's state-owned media has been preoccupied with the "paradise route" when telling the African story. A quick glance at the Chinese state-owned media reveals tales of an exotic Africa, home to animal kingdoms, beautiful people and cultures, and most importantly for China's international image, a place where Chinese aid, trade, investment and Confucius Institutes are making a difference. A good example can be seen in a documentary *Glamorous Kenya* that was broadcast in 2012 on CCTV. The documentary emphasizes the uniqueness of China in portraying Africa. Its statement reads, "Compared to previous works on African countries, 'Glamorous Kenya' is all about looking inside the country through the

---

49. Colin Shek, "Chinese media expands Africa presence," *AL Jazeera*, January 24, 2013, accessed February 15, 2015, http://www.aljazeera.com/indepth/features/2013/01/2013120719298 22435.html.
50. Shek, "Chinese media expands Africa presence."

eyes of the crew that travelled there. Hence, the production is embedded with a Chinese perspective."[51]
The "Chinese perspective" theme is also seen in other media productions. In 2000 for instance, a twelve-part television drama, *Forever Africa (Yongyuan de Feizhou)*, went on air in China. The drama depicts Chinese medical missions in East Africa battling a highly infectious disease. The local people are more willing to work with Chinese doctors than a French doctor because the Chinese respect local traditions and work closely with local people—a theme repeated in a 2004 Hong Kong TV drama *The Last Breakthrough*.[52] In *Forever Africa,* the French doctor attempts to buy patient participation while anticipating a Nobel Prize, revealing his selfish, capitalist motivations.[53] In another documentary which is aired on a regular basis on CCTV, China's philanthropic nature and the Chinese people's work ethic are richly on display. It tells the story of the Tanzania-Zambia railway project which was built by the Chinese government from 1970-1975. The project has earned a household-name status in China in a way that everyone seems to know about it. As a Tanzanian studying in China, I have been compelled to mention the railway line on many occasions when I introduce myself to people, some of whom claim to have never heard of Tanzania, yet they know all about the railway line.

China in Tanzania's Media
The representation of China in Tanzania's media is, like Africa in China's media, a mixed bag. A quick glance at media coverage during recent years conveys China as a land of opportunities. This version of the story is usually carried out with reports about strong diplomatic ties between Tanzania and China. Chinese aid, its investment and trade between the two countries are common themes in the media in general but more so in state-owned media, understandably. This is a manifestation of the special diplomatic relations the two countries have forged over the years, as evidenced by President Kikwete's "best friends" remarks referred to in the introduction. As far as state-owned

---

51. "CCTV to air documentary 'Glamorous Kenya next January'," *China Central Television,* December22, 2011, accessed February 15, 2015, http://english.cntv.cn/program/cultureexpress/20111222/108321.sht ml.
52. Saavedra, "Representations of Africa in a Hong Kong Soap Opera," 767.
53. Ibid.

media is concerned, it should be mentioned that the Tanzania Broadcasting Corporation (TBC) is one of the biggest recipients on the continent of Chinese aid in the media sector.

In June 2014, it was announced that the TBC had received a $5 million high-definition outdoor-broadcasting van (OB) from China, which is equipped with a state-of-the-art high-definition slow-motion camera.[54] It makes Tanzania the second country in Africa, after Zimbabwe, to own such a facility. Zimbabwe's equipment, interestingly, was also donated by China. The TBC has also entered into an agreement to air Chinese drama in recent years, not to mention that it switches to China's CCTV for international news as well as special programmes about China. In 2013, the TBC launched the airing of two Chinese dramas that have been dubbed in Kiswahili. This was the second time this had occurred after another Chinese drama had been aired in 2012. The themes of these dramas vary but in general they depict social dynamics in modern Chinese society. As such, one does not expect "bad press" about China by the TBC. This might have influenced Tanzanians' perception of China, as the majority of people, especially those in the rural areas, depend solely on the TBC and other state-owned media news channels for information. A 2014 survey by Pew Research Center revealed that Tanzanians who had favorable views of China stood at a staggering 77 percent.[55]

The situation is almost similar with regard to private media, except for some elements of sensationalism and exaggeration that are in most cases a result of ignorance about China.[56] Here there is "bad press" in

---

54. Abduel Elinaza, "TBC to apply fresh tech for live matches coverage," *Daily News*, June 17, 2014, accessed February 2, 2015, http://archive.dailynews.co.tz/index.php/local-news/32663-tbc-to-apply-fresh-tech-for-live-matches-coverage.

55. "Pew Opinion of China," Pew Research Center, accessed February 2, 2015, http://www.pewglobal.org/database/indicator/24/.

56. There is a concern particularly on the Chinese side that part of the bad press about China could be a result of a deliberate campaign by the West. In one incident, a Chinese official working with a Chinese state company in Tanzania confided to me that they were surprised that some of the information on deals to be signed between his company and the Tanzanian government was already being reported by some private media outlets in Tanzania. He expressed his suspicion that there were "big forces" behind the leakage of such information and, although he stopped short of mentioning such forces, he insinuated that there was a

as much as there is "good press." This has been very much the case in recent years due to increased Chinese activities in Tanzania.[57] For instance, over the years in Tanzania, there has been an increase in drug crimes involving Tanzanians traveling to China. The depiction of the Chinese authorities regarding drug trafficking is one of no-nonsense and heavy handedness. The situation is the same when it comes to corruption. This has led to calls of "emulating the Chinese" when it comes to tackling drug trafficking and corruption. When Chen Tonghai, former Chairman of Sinopec, was sentenced to death for corruption charges in 2009, the news was not only broadly reported but was greeted with approval in many forums. On one website, the reaction of readers was almost unanimous – with most calling for the Tanzanian government to implement similar measures against corrupt officials.[58]

The reporting of such incidents usually emphasizes the tough actions taken by the Chinese government. As such, the fact that these

---

tug-of-war between China and the West on the investment front. On the concern of a deliberate campaign to smear China, it should be remembered that the West's narrative about Afro-Chinese relations is characterized by the depiction of China as a new colonial power only interested in African resources and Africa as a "weak victim of Chinese colonialism." See, Baffour Ankomah, in Franks and Ribet, "Africa-China media relations," 133. Also, the former US Secretary of State, Hillary Clinton, demonstrated this view when she warned Africa to be wary of a "creeping "new colonialism." It was believed this was a swing aimed at China. See Mathew Lee, "Hillary Clinton warns Africa of 'New Colonialism'," *The Huffington Post,* June 11, 2011, accessed April 30, 2015, http://www.huffingtonpost.com/2011/06/11/hillary-clinton-africa-new-colonialism_n_875318.html.

57. Not long ago Chinese New Year was an alien thing in Tanzania's calendar. Not anymore. The Chinese New Year is now marked with a great deal of festivity where Chinese culture is on display. The event is covered by all major news networks to the extent that it has become a familiar happening. A colleague of mine once told me, on a serious note, that only last year he did not know how to pronounce 'Confucius'. He has since acquainted himself with the term, thanks to increasing Confucius Institute's activities in Tanzania.

58. "Ahukumiwa Adhabu ya kifo kwa kupokea rushwa China," *Nifahamishe,* July 15, 2009, accessed February 27, 2015, http://www.nifahamishe.com/NewsDetails.aspx?NewsId=2516042&&Cat=2.

problems are prevalent in Chinese society is by and large not conveyed. This is a common tendency in the tabloids and social media and while this perception feeds very well into the Chinese soft-power strategy by representing a zero-tolerance from China when it comes to corruption and other social evils, at the same time it creates an image of an authoritarian China where due process of law is lacking. Commenting on the frequency of news on harsh penalties for drug trafficking and corruption in China as so regularly reported by the media in Tanzania, a university student at the University of Dar es Salaam once queried, "Do they even have due process of law? From what we read on the news it is as if people are tried and sentenced arbitrarily."[59]

In one example, a weekly tabloid *Uwazi*, published "a special report" on drug trafficking, claiming that hundreds of Tanzanians might have been hanged in China for drug trafficking.[60] The paper also claimed that the death penalty for Tanzanians in China is clandestinely carried out to the extent that even relatives of victims are left uninformed. The authenticity of such claims is debatable. In fact, the Tanzanian Embassy in Beijing, while admitting an awareness of the jailed Tanzanians in China, refuted claims of hanging, adding that those behind bars are known to the embassy and are granted permission to talk to their relatives back home over the phone.[61] Unfortunately, this version of the story usually does not attract the attention of tabloids and social media users.

Apart from that, China still conjures an image of a country that is home to counterfeit goods, illegal trade and dishonest people. Part of this has been due to unlawful activities involving Chinese nationals in Tanzania. These activities are widely reported in the media. They range from prostitution (which is illegal in Tanzania) and illegal ivory trade, to selling counterfeit products. In April 2011, for instance, a weekly tabloid, *Risasi Mchanganyiko*, ran a damning story about Chinese prostitutes in Dar es Salaam in which the editor questioned the

59. Interview with students at the University of Dar es Salaam, Dar es Salaam, Tanzania.
60. "Ripoti Maalum: Watanzania Mamia Wanyongwa China," *Uwazi*, 17 June, 2013, accessed February 10, 2015, http://www.globalpublishers.info/profiles/blogs/ripoti-maalum.
61. Millard Ayo, "Ni kweli Watanzania 50 walinyongwa China 2013? Wanaoshikiliwa je?" *Millard Ayo Blog*, January 11, 2014, accessed October 2, 2015. http://millardayo.com/tzchina/.

Tanzanian government's willingness in "getting rid of such people."[62] The story received the attention of readers and similar stories have been subjects of discussion in social-media forums. In another widely reported incident, on November 3, 2013, Tanzanians were greeted with shocking stories of the government's seizure of 706 elephant tusks at the hands of three Chinese nationals.[63] The story became a regular topic of discussion in the media. It also led to a national outrage and feelings of suspicion towards Chinese people. One article appeared in *The Citizen* where a long list of cases involving Chinese nationals in illegal ivory trade across Africa was displayed. The writer went as far as to argue that China's massive investment in infrastructure development in Africa is driven by the desire to have access to Africa's wildlife body parts![64]

Another common theme in media reporting about China in Tanzania concerns Chinese counterfeit products. Such products range from electronics to cosmetics. Cheap mobile phones made in China are simply known as *Mchina*, which otherwise translates to *Chinese person*. The popularity of this term and the poor economic conditions of most Tanzanians suggest that the majority of mobile-phone users make use of made-in-China phones. As for cosmetics and beauty products, images of people's "transformed looks" after using Chinese products are common in tabloids and social media. This is so much the case that it has become common for people to ask whether one's look is natural or *Mchina*. The most popular of these are products that allegedly increase the size of one's backside. A good example is the

---

62. "Makahaba wa Kichina warejea Bongo kwa kasi," *Risasi Mchanganyiko*, April 27, 2011, accessed February 10, 2015., http://www.globalpublishers.info/profiles/blogs/makahaba-wa-ichina?id=5398006%3ABlogPost%3A501134&page=2#comments

63. Goodluck Eliona, "Shehena pembe za ndovu yakamatwa Dar," *Mwananchi*, November 3, 2013, accessed February 24, 2015, http://www.mwananchi.co.tz/habari/Kitaifa/Shehena-pembe-za-ndovu-zakamatwa-Dar-es-Salaam/-/1597296/2058240/-/t10osh/-/index.html.

64. "Chinese and ivory poaching in the African continent," *The Citizen*, November 16, 2014, accessed May 5, 2015, http://mobile.thecitizen.co.tz/news/Chinese-and-ivory-poaching-in-the-African-continent/-/2304482/2524228/-/format/xhtml/-/sn373fz/-/index.html.

headline *Makalio Mapya ya Kichina* ("New Chinese buttocks") that appeared on the front page of a weekly tabloid *Amani*.[65] Illegal activities conducted by Chinese nationals in Tanzania are so rampant that Beijing's ambassador to Tanzania was reported in the media as having admitted that some Chinese companies engage in corruption.[66] In one instance, this report was shared in a popular online forum in which one contributor called on the Tanzanian government to carry out capital punishment on the Chinese culprits as a reprisal for "hundreds" of Tanzanians hanged in China.[67] On January 6, 2011, the government of Tanzania, through its deputy minister for trade, industry and marketing, issued a thirty-day ultimatum for illegal petty traders operating in the country's main market Kariakoo to vacate. Petty traders in Tanzania are commonly known as *Wamachinga* and stories of *Chinese Machingas* in Dar es Salaam in particular are becoming more common everyday.

The reporting of this incident in the media pointed at Chinese traders despite the fact that the deputy minister's order did not mention any specific nationals. However, the minister's earlier remarks that his government was discussing terms with the Chinese government on ways of tackling the influx of counterfeit goods might have fuelled speculations that Chinese traders were targeted. In a popular blog, *Issa Michuzi,* for instance, the majority of contributors made reference to China in a way that suggested the ultimatum was directed at Chinese traders.[68] Three months later, a tabloid covered a

---

65. "Makalio Mapya ya Kichina," *Amani,* June 7, 2012, accessed February 25, 2015,
http://www.globalpublishers.info/profiles/blog/show?id=5398006%3ABlogPost%3A1293282&commentId=5398006%3AComment%3A1293747&xg_source=activity.

66. Florence Mugarula, "Chinese bribe in Dar, admits China envoy," *The Citizen,* July 15, 2014, accessed February 25, 2015, http://www.thecitizen.co.tz/News/national/Chinese-bribe-in-Dar--admits-China-envoy/-/1840392/2384042/-/bt29rdz/-/index.html.

67. "Hii ndiyo jumla ya Watanzania waliohukumiwa kunyongwa China," *JamiiForums,* July 15, 2014, accessed February 22, 2015, http://www.jamiiforums.com/jukwaa-la-siasa/690428-balozi-wa-china-akiri-wachina-kutoa-rushwa-na-kufanya-biashara-ya-pembe-za-ndovu-tanzania.html.

68. Issa Michuzi, "Nyalandu awaondolea uvivu wamachinga wa kigeni"*Issa Michuzi Blog,* Januray 15, 2011, accessed February 20, 2915,

story of an angry crowd outside the Chinese embassy in Dar es Salaam following complaints over allegedly tightened visa application procedures. The story quoted angry visa applicants threatening to take xenophobic actions towards the Chinese on the grounds that they were restricted from entering China while their Chinese counterparts were entering Tanzania with less restriction.[69]

Conclusion: Making sense of media representations of Africa and China

China's recent media push in Africa is an encouraging development in Afro-Chinese relations. The need to ensure that Africans and Chinese take charge of the Afro-Chinese narrative instead of relying on other actors should be welcomed as a way of fostering healthy relations between the two peoples. Already steps are being taken and there is a realization that the media will have a very important role in promoting mutual understanding between Africa and China. In the African Journalist Study Tour to Beijing in 2010, for instance, it was reported that the tour allowed participants to

> [d]iscuss and better understand the role of Chinese and African media in political and economic reporting on Africa-China, as well as the role of media in shaping perceptions of China and Africa. In particular, it was found that perceptions of Africa in China, and China in Africa are driven largely by Western media coverage…, the mutual interest from both Africa and China was noted throughout the tour and provided encouragement to establish wider networks of engagement between African and Chinese journalists.[70]

Due to the fact that the Chinese media is essentially the one making inroads into Africa mainly through state-owned media, this new

---

http://issamichuzi.blogspot.com/2011/01/nyalandu-awaondolea-uvivu-wamachinga-wa.html.

69. Issa Mnally, "Vurugu mbaya ubalozi wa China," *Ijumaa*, April 5, 2011. Accessed February 26, 2015, http://www.globalpublishers.info/profiles/blogs/vurugu-ubalozi.

70. Hayles Herman, and Sanusha Naidu, "Deeping Africa-China engagement: The African Journalist Study Tour," *Pambazuka Issue* 480, May 6, 2010, accessed August 20, 2015, http://www.pambazuka.org/en/category/africa_china/64235.

development has potential repercussions. Firstly, while past and present misconceptions are still apparent, there is a risk of creating new ones by moving away from one extreme of negative representation to the other extreme of positive representation of both Africa and China. As we have seen in this paper, this is particularly evident in state-owned media where reporting is very much framed within diplomatic structures. Secondly, given the fact that African media is too dependent on foreign media as sources of news there is a risk of reporting only what they are fed by both international and Chinese media. In the context of Afro-Chinese relations, this tendency puts China in a pivotal position of shaping the new narrative that is in line with its Africa policy, sometimes at the expense of African interests.[71] Thirdly, China's global media push, seen as a move that intensifies the global war of information as signalled by the former US Secretary of State, Hillary Clinton,[72] makes Africa susceptible to external influences, be these Chinese or Western. This in turn means that such media can be used for foreign interests, including China's. Therefore, even as we try to understand the representation of China in Africa, the influence of China in affecting the narrative cannot be overlooked.

In an increasingly complex international sphere, both Africa's and China's media have a responsibility to address all sorts of misrepresentations and misconceptions while maintaining a kind of professionalism that will produce reliable information. This key responsibility comes against the backdrop of the "bad press" to which both Africa and China have been subjected by mainly the Western

---

71. The case in question here, for instance, is China's support of Zambia's state-owned media which coincided with national elections there in 1996, 2001 and 2006. Jackson Banda has pointed out that this might have potentially defused the electoral power that the opposition parties had. For more on this see Franks and Ribet, "Africa-China media relations," 131. As a vindication of how this kind of Chinese involvement can disrupt Africa's local political landscape, Michale Satta, then the leader of the opposition in Zambia and presidential candidate, became a fierce critic of China. He went on record accusing China of flooding his country "with human beings instead of investment and the government is jumping" and that, "we are becoming poorer because they are getting our wealth." For further details on this see Brautigam, *The Dragon's Gift*, 6.

72. Massey, quoted in Wu, "The Rise of China's State-led Media Dynasty in Africa," 7.

media.[73] The two are not mutually exclusive, a fact that has been acknowledged through the initiation of FOCAC in August 2012. Speaking at the launching of the forum, Cai Fuchao, minister of state administration of radio, film and television, said, "[B]y means of filing more reports on China and Africa, we hope to promote mutual understanding, and correct some of the biased opinions about us in the West."[74] This was echoed by Jean Ping, former chairman of the African Union Commission who stated, "[W]e want to give stronger efforts in having the African voices heard by the world." He added, "There're many protests and movements going on this continent, but we want to tell people what happens through our own angle and views, and have a competitive media outlet on the international stage."[75]

Clearly there is a sense of solidarity between Africa and China and the media is rightly expected to play a significant role. Although Li Anshan, a prominent Chinese scholar in Afro-Chinese relations, has suggested that the role of the media is neither devilish nor angelic,[76] yet, given the history of both Africa and China, the media's role can be both. Its role in shaping perceptions and thus affecting ways through which people interact cannot be overemphasized. For mutual understanding to happen between Africans and the Chinese, the focus must now move away from diplomatic circles to people-to-people interactions – without compromising the significance of the former. It is people-to-people diplomacy and not high-level diplomatic declarations that will eventually lead to shared values between Africans and the Chinese. This is the ideal way of addressing past and present misconceptions that have resulted in stereotypes affecting relations between the two peoples. The media is a key factor in this cause.

---

73. A report by the African Journalist Study Tour to Beijing in 2010 noted that perceptions of Africa in China, and China in Africa, are driven largely by Western media coverage. For further discussion on this see, Herman and Naidu, "Deeping Africa-China engagement."
74. "China and Africa Join Hands in Media Cooperation," China Network Television, August 23, 2012, accessed February 25, 2015, http://english.cntv.cn/program/newsupdate/20120823/105929.shtml.
75. "China and Africa Join Hands in Media Cooperation.".
76. Li Anshan, "Neither devil nor angel: The role of the media in Sino-African relations," *Pambazuka Issue* 585, May 16, 2012, accessed February 25, 2015, http://www.pambazuka.net/en/category/features/82194.

Bibliography

Bailey, M. "Tanzania and China." In *Foreign Policy of Tanzania: 1961-1981: A Reader*, edited by K. Mathews and Samuel S. Mushi, 175–178. Dar es Salaam: Tanzania Publishing House, 1981.

Barr, Michael. *Who is Afraid of China? The Challenge of Chinese Soft Power.* London: ZED Books, 2011.

Brautigam, Deborah. *The Dragon's Gift: The real story of China in Africa.* Oxford: Oxford University Press, 2009.

Franks, Suzanne and Ribet, Kate. "Africa-China media relations." *Global Media and Communication* 5, no. 1 (2009): 129-136.

Fook, Lye Liang. "China's Media Initiatives and Its International Image Building." *Journal of China Studies* 1 No. 2 (2010): 545–568, accessed January 16, 2017, http://ics.um.edu.my/images/ics/IJCSV1N2/lye.pdf.

He, Wenping. "All-Weather Friend: The Evolution of China's Africa Policy." In *Afro-Chinese Relations: Past, Present and Future,* edited by Kwesi K. Prah, 24–47. Cape Town: Centre for Advanced Studies of African Society, 2007.

Li, Mingjiang. "Soft Power in Chinese Discourse: Popularity and Prospects." In *Soft Power: China's emerging strategy in international politics,* edited by Mingjiang Li, 21–44. Maryland: Lexington Books, 2009.

Mudimbe, Vumbi Y. *The Invention of Africa.* Bloomington and Indianapolis: Indiana University Press, 1988.

Saavendra, Martha. "Representations of Africa in a Hong Kong Soap Opera: The Limits of Enlightened Humanitarianism in 'The Last Breakthrough'." *The China Quarterly,* No. 199 (2009):760–776. Accessed February 5, 2015. http://www.jstor.org/stable/27756500.

Shen, Simon. "A Constructed (un)Reality on China's Re-entry into Africa: The Chinese Online Community Perception of Africa (2006–2008)." *The Journal of Modern African Studies,* 47 (2009): 245–448. Accessed February 5, 2015, http://www.jstor.org/stable/40538319.

Taylor, Ian. "China's Oil Diplomacy in Africa." *International Affairs (Royal Institute of International Affairs 1944–)* 82, no.5 (2006): 937–959.

Wu, Yu-Shan. "The Rise of China's State-led Media Dynasty in Africa." South African Institute of International Affairs Occasional Paper No. 117, June 2012.

Xiao, Yuhua. "Chinese perceptions of African CSO: how should African CSOs engage China?" In *Chinese and African Perspectives on China in Africa*, edited by Axel Harneit-Sievers, Stephen Marks, Naidu Sanusha, 214–223. Cape Town: Pambazuka Press, 2010.

Chapter Twelve. Populism and the State in China and Africa: A Comparative Analysis (1975–2005)

═ ═ ═ ═ ═ ═ ═ ═ ═ ═ ═ ❖ ═ ═ ═ ═ ═ ═ ═ ═ ═ ═ ═

Kwesi D.L.S. Prah

The most basic thing is the unity of opposites. The transformation of quality and quantity into one another is the unity of the opposites, quality and quantity.[1]

Introduction

Afro-Chinese relations in the contemporary world have created many conversations about social, political and economic exchanges, and the futures of these relations. They have also often contributed toward highlighting popular opinion, populist theory and action; and defining *populism* as a contemporary idea and reality. This study seeks to highlight the meanings of populism within varying social contexts in Africa and China, and to show how populism as a political expression of social and economic perspective, for or against various aspects of the status quo, changed political and economic realities, over a fifty-year period of formal and informal relations.

---

1. Mao Zedong, *Mao Tse-Tung Unrehearsed*, 226

From the observations and analysis, arguments and recommendations are made based on the theoretical and physical evidence presented. These recommendations would serve as policy guidelines for future Forums on China Africa Cooperation (FOCAC) summits.

Populism: Theory and Reality

Populism is a broad concept, and as a paradigm, it finds application in so many ways that its meanings tend to be obtuse and often abstract. Generally, definitions of populism suggest that it can be understood by observing the many perspectives and roles that characterize political theories, sentiments and expressions of society. Thus, it is often argued that it is through popular culture, populist political theory and rhetoric, popular protest / action that the wealth and health of a society are judged; and this ultimately characterizes the nature of populism.

However, to avoid rigidly defining the meaning of populism, and distorting an understanding of how it is a factor in the process of change affecting Africans in China, and Chinese in Africa, it is important that it is defined as a historically rooted, ever-evolving concept and reality.

In Western contexts, the Latin phrase *argumentum ad populum*, which when translated means an "appeal to the peoples", suggests that populism serves as a philosophical and material claim to representing, or highlighting, the common interests of the majority in a given society.[2] The linguistic and philosophical roots of this idea in Western contexts commonly place the reality of populism within the contest of political ideology and organization between peoples; essentially

---

2. For a generic definition of the Latin phrase, see http://en.wikipedia.org/wiki/Argumentum_ad_populum, accessed March 6, 2014. For very general definitions of the term populism, see the online Collins Dictionary, which defines populism as "a political strategy based on a calculated appeal to the interests or prejudices of ordinary people". Accessed March 6, 2014, http://www.collinsdictionary.com/dictionary/english/populism. Also see http://www.merriam-webster.com/dictionary/populism; http://www.oxforddictionaries.com/definition/english/populist?q=po pulism#populist __10

contests between organized groups in society that seek the entrenchment of values related to particular *interests*.[3] Introducing the debate on the difficulties of defining populism as a paradigm, Margaret Canovan reminds the reader that:

> we can examine myths of past foundation and future redemption…, and the way in which such myths colour our view of popular movements happening before our eyes,… how should we regard that mythic sovereign people? We could take a robustly cynical view, treating the notion simply as a manipulative device. A less dismissive response might perhaps suggest that our familiar myths of the people as founder and redeemer of polities have rather more substance than that. If there is a kernel of truth hidden in the myths, it might be a truth about the basis of political power and political community. On that view, the hidden truth of the myth is that ordinary individual people do have the potential (however rarely exercised) to mobilise for common action. On occasion, such grass roots mobilizations generate formidable power, bringing down a regime; more rarely, they sometimes manage to make a fresh start and to lay the foundations of a lasting political community. Seen in that light, it might be the rarity, contingency and brevity of such momentous events that makes popular authority so hard to pin down, and 'the sovereign people' so mysterious and vague a notion.[4]

In the twentieth century, imperialism, commonly understood through its methods of enforcement regarding political and economic control over society (colonialism, fascism, and neo-colonialism), became a recurring theme, and gave substance to political theories defining political contests, and their global impacts. It has often been argued that these contests were theoretically based on capitalist or socialist forms of political and economic organization, and their modes of production in constant struggle.

Highlighting an example of British imperialism and its impact in Southern African contexts, B. Magubane observed that "the objective of the new state was neither the total destruction nor the transformation of traditional societies, but the incorporation of individual members as labourers with the rest available as reserve labour and to provide a market. In South Africa, the conquerors

---

3. These contestations of interests are frequently based on class, religious affiliation, ethnic association, or gender distinction.
4. Canovan, *Populism*, 241–252; 251

reconstituted the Africans as cheaper labour pools in specially designated reserves, incapable of any independent growth. The artificially preserved peasant structures became the most sinister inheritance of contemporary South Africa."[5] Therefore the use of force as the basic means to change circumstances of privilege and power became a recurring theme of populism. Observing the use of force and the idea of fascism, Palmiro Togliatti, speaking of Italy during the period 1921–1928, argued that "fascism is based on the systematic and total suppression of all forms of autonomous organization on the part of the masses", and that no other country had "...seen such a radical suppression of any possibility for the masses of creating their own autonomous organizations, under whatever form, as has Italy."[6] In fact, according to Dimitry Manuilski, "fascism is... a product of monopoly capital. It is based upon the concentration and centralization of capital and the associated development of trusts and cartels, and leads to a massive centralization of the whole apparatus of mass oppression – including the political parties, the Social Democratic apparatus, the reformist trade unions, the co-operatives, etc. Its stunted ideological forms stem from the fact that it represents the political superstructure of capitalism *in decay*."[7]

Thus in the political history of the United States (under leftist, and rightist political distinctions), certain authors argued that the term populism "was used in the United States in the 1890s to describe the People's Party, the most powerful in a series of similar movements, such as the Grangers of the 1870s and 1880s, which sought to represent the interests of small farmers, especially in the West."[8] Another narrative asserted that "*narodnichestvo*, populism, spread into Eastern Europe from Russia... with different historical background and attitude towards the problems of serfdom and of landownership, the changes in the conditions of the peasantry or at least in this class's consciousness of its own condition."[9]Others argued that populism, as a frame of reference, had older representations and usages in Western political histories, which date as far back as the Greco-Roman populist

5. Magubane, *The Political Economy of Race*, 70. For a contemporary view, also see S. Makgetlaneng's chapter titled, "The State, Politics and Democratic Consolidation in Africa", in Kondlo, *Perspectives*, 346–357.
6. See Beetham, *Marxists*, 140.
7. Ibid., 160–161.
8. Krieger, *Oxford Companion*, 679. Also, see Saloutos, *Populism*, 14–23.
9. Ionescu and Gellner, *Populism*, 99.

appeal to "civil peace" (*paxcivilis*),and Platonic hypotheses of political order.[10] Despite these differing claims to the origins of populism as a lived reality, Western social scientists such as G. Sorel, E. Laclau and F. Venturi essentially argued that populism highlighted and reflected forms of class consciousness, and served as a medium of expression in contests of power to secure political and economic interests. This explained the propensity (and *necessity* in some instances) for radical and often violent swings in local and regional disputes.[11] Ernesto Laclau, writing in 1977, summarizes this argument in the following manner: "...the emergence of populism is historically linked to a crisis of the dominant ideological discourse which is in turn part of a more general social crisis. This crisis can either be the result of a fracture in the power bloc, in which a class or class fraction needs, in order to assert its hegemony, to appeal to 'the people' against established ideology as a whole; or of a crisis in the ability of the system to neutralize the dominated sectors – that is to say a crisis of transformism."[12]

These historical perspectives remind the reader to recognize that populist expressions and agitations against "dominant ideology", and the popular movements, protests and wars that were aroused or arose from these realities, have been persistent themes in recent African and Chinese history. Populist theories and movements in Africa were influenced and affected in complex ways by physical and philosophical challenges linked to the impact of Atlantic / Arabic slavery and colonialism. Both Africa and China inherited social, political and economic constraints from either, or both these experiences; constraints that aroused populist movements, and re-affirmed the importance of populism as a dynamic and critical concept.

Populism in the Contexts of Contemporary Africa and China (1975–2005)

I defined the purpose of education as to transmit from one generation to the next the accumulated wisdom and knowledge of the society, and to prepare the young people

---

10. Norena, *Imperial Ideals*, 127–128.
11. Sorel, *Reflections*, 171–172.
12. Laclau, *Politics*, 175.

for their future membership of the society and their active participation in its maintenance or development."[13] During the first decade after the Second World War, Asia was busy with the establishment of political independence and anti-imperialism. Vietnam defeated the French in 1954; Indonesia became independent in 1945; India became independent in 1947 together with Pakistan; Sri-Lanka became independent in 1948; and Cambodia became independent in 1953. But the earliest in this line of post-colonialist experiences in Asia was Korea, in 1945. The Korean War followed in 1952 and the insurgencies in Indonesia and Malaysia occurred not too long afterwards. If Asia took the lead and set the pace for political independence, Africa, following the Manchester Pan-African Congress of 1945, was within a decade on the doorstep of colonial freedom. The Sudan obtained its independence in 1956, followed by Ghana in 1957. Soon after that, in the decade 1960–1970, two-thirds of Africa gained a form of independence from colonial rule.

The ensuing transitions – the formation of regional trading blocs such as the Economic Community of West African States (ECOWAS) or the Southern African Development Community (SADC) and continental political organizations such as the Organization of African Unity(OAU) – as a result of populist appeals to national economic independence, began breaking apart what essentially was a common interest shared amongst many Africans regarding African unity; in the face of a clearly understood concern regarding encroaching neo-colonialism.[14] The entrenched socio-political and socio-economic order (patched together by artificial states), was already configured to suit an emerging form of monopoly capitalism, championed by Western interests.[15] However, for China, these interests where cautiously re-introduced into their formal political economy, after radical movements such as the Great Leap Forward, the Cultural Revolution, and Deng Xiaoping's appeals to modernization changed popular perceptions and living conditions, and transformed the fortunes of China.

13. Lema et al. *Nyerere on Education,*124.
14. See Dani Wadada Nabudere's chapter entitled "Nkrumahism and Consciencism in the Struggle for African Emancipation in Contrast to Senghor's Negritude"in Shivji, *Chemchemi,* 38.
15. See Beetham, *Marxists,* 121–124, 309–314, 319–340.

In appraisal of the four modernizations that radically began changing the popular urban and rural landscape of China (in the decade 1980–1990), Gregory Eliyu Guldin wrote that "the intellectual climate since the 1978 Central Committee session has been the most hospitable in the history of the People's Republic despite the temporary clouds of the Spiritual Pollution campaign and the Anti-Bourgeois Liberalization campaign."[16] Furthermore, the idea of a market economy under socialist prescriptions created a consumer boom that began multiplying China's financial gains, reinforcing China's economic clout. Observing the impact of these economic reforms over a fifteen-year period (1980–1995), Conghua Li writes in 1998 that the term *xiahai* (translated *plunge into the sea*) was a popular expression used to describe "those individuals who had decided to abandon the old ways and venture into the new uncharted waters of economic reform... Those early adventurers were seen as rebels who were risking more than the security of state employment. Today, the term implies commitment to the market reforms that have transformed China. Those who are taking the plunge are seen as contributing to the new market system. However, with over 180-million people now working at non-state-owned enterprises across the country, they're no longer the exception, they're the rule."[17]

However, the aforementioned campaigns, to which Guldin alluded, were serious responses made by the Chinese Communist Party (CCP) to ensure their political authority and relevance in a tentative accommodation of what is now arguably understood to be state-capitalism. This development of populist agitation was countered by state propaganda announcing that "*bourgeois* liberalization" tended to negate socialist ideals in favour of capitalism. The "Four Cardinal Principles" were therefore evoked as an official public statement and a rebuttal to combat these developing trends. These essentially populist appeals were transmitted through its main media outlet at the time, *The People's Daily*. Thus, writing in 1984, C. C. Ching reminds the reader that

---

16. Guldin, *Anthropology*, 20. For a news report on the Spiritual Pollution Campaign, see C. Wren, "China is said to end a campaign to stop 'spiritual pollution'", *The New York Times*, January 24, 1984.

17. Li, *China: The Consumer Revolution*, 192.

in the past year our Government laid stress on raising the level of socialist ethics particularly aimed at our young generation. The measures taken are to conduct political and ideological education and to cultivate socialist moral values. Learning from the idealized model behavior of well-known persons showed good results, as illustrated by the "Learn from Lei Feng" movement. Right now we are launching a campaign on the "five stresses and four points of beauty". Decorum, manners, hygiene, discipline, and morals are stressed. The four points of beauty are (1) beautification of the mind, which means cultivating a fine ideology and moral character; (2) beautification of language; (3) beautification of behavior, which means working hard, being concerned for the other's welfare, observing discipline, and safeguarding collective interests; and (4) beautification of the environment, which includes care for personal hygiene and public sanitation. All these are for the purpose of educating the people and fostering revolutionary ideals.[18]

These perspectives represent a snapshot of the realities that defined populism in China as both the vehicle for furthering the interests of the state, as well as expressing and responding to trends in social organization and governance, laws and customs amongst the citizenry. These appeals to common interests shared between the state and the citizenry focused attention on the need for a technical and scientific modernization along scientific socialist principles. This influenced populist notions of economic self-sufficiency, social harmony, and common scientific purpose. These radical changes in contemporary China lend credibility to the observation that populism, understood as active processes of political and economic awareness, served as an important factor in the development of a Chinese "national culture", and a major influence in China's economic growth and impact between 1975 and 2005.

For Africa, post-independence nationalism and the formation of states were taking root in vastly different ways. Military manoeuvers to secure natural resources for economic gain and political power became destabilizing, and economically debilitating for many African states over the two decades 1980–1990 and 1990–2000. Economic debt and financial dependencies created bottle necks in local and regional trade, and forced many of these states across Africa to adopt / adapt policies

---

18. Ching, "Psychology," 62.

and plans that often failed and became counter-productive.[19]Alaba Ogansunwo had thus recognized that "China's policy was by no means limited to offering economic and technical assistance and improving trade relations.... China set out to develop political relations with African states and people's movements on the basis of a common solidarity against imperialism based on common experiences of imperialist exploitation. In doing this, she supported liberation movements in Africa and rendered material and propaganda help where possible."[20]

This interplay of political and economic interests between Africa and China encapsulated what essentially was a popular struggle to defend existing interests, and to attain more, political and economic freedoms from colonial / metropolitan military and economic hegemonies. Osagyefo K. Nkrumah's ideological platforms in the form of "Consciencism" and an "African Socialism", and Mwalimu J. K. Nyerere's socio-political pro-activity in the form of the *Ujamaa* indigenization project, became well-known (in both congratulatory and critical senses) articulations and representations defining populist theory under nationalist guidelines.[21] In appraisal of Mwalimu J. K. Nyerere's intellectual legacy, Issa G. Shivji contrasted the impact of the political theories and strategies shared between Osagyefo K. Nkrumah and Mwalimu J. K. Nyerere, and their attempts towards realizing Pan-African Unity:

> There is, I think, another underlying difference between the gradualist and radical approaches of Nyerere and Nkrumah, which has not been sufficiently analyzed. I will only hint at it. I think for Nkrumah, unity itself, just as liberation, was an anti-imperialist struggle, not some formal process of dissolving sovereignties. Amilcar Cabral captured the national liberation struggle as an anti-imperialist struggle well when he said, '[S]o long as imperialism is in existence, an independent African state must be a liberation movement in power, or it will not be independent.' The notion of an independent African state being a 'national liberation movement in power', I suggest, gives us the core of the ideology and politics of Pan-Africanism as a vision of not only unity but liberation. African

---

19. See Nabudere, *Imperialism– Volume I*; Nabudere, *Imperialism– Volume II;* Shivji, *Accumulation.*
20. Ogunsanwo, *China's Policy*, 262–263.
21. See Kwesi D. L.S Prah, "Tanzania-China Relations."

liberation is not complete with the independence of single entities called countries. 'Territorial nationalism' is not African nationalism. African nationalism can only be Pan-Africanism or else, as Mwalimu characterized it, it is 'the equivalent of tribalism within the context of our separate nation states'. Pan-Africanism gave birth to nationalism, not the other way round. This is a powerful argument implied in Mwalimu's ideas on African unity.[22]

The simplicity of this logic leads one to conclude that a convergence of common interests is needed, and still needs to gain traction amongst Africans at many levels of social, political and economic organization. Radical and meaningful ideas and activities bringing about constructive change in the African world historically found meaning, and still find meaning within Pan-Africanist contexts.[23] Therefore, for most African states today, the historical displacement and political / cultural / economic disempowerment of peoples require a practical, reparatory and re-distributive purpose in the aims and objectives of populist theories, intellectual trends, institutional transformations, and grassroots initiatives. In this way, populism as a paradigm must serve constructive ends.

Conclusion and Recommendations

Ingrained in every culture is a system of thought, an ideology underpinning the relations between human beings and nature. African cultures... establish specific relations between women and nature. Whatever the objective of this – exploitation of women's labour, of women's scientific knowledge and technological know-how – and its impact on women (whether they suffer from it or they use it to acquire a higher status, more power, more control over the material and spiritual wealth of their community), a debate should be embarked on.[24]

It is from within these political, economic, and cultural contexts that we can understand the degrees of popular sentiment, and the populist theories with which it is associated. The severity of current financial crises multiplies as the monopoly of capital finds increasing opposition. It is in these times that self-reflection and action are determined by the overall awareness, health, education, and freedom of choice to *create, restore,* and *sustain* ecology for as many people as

22. Shivji, *Pan-Africanism in Mwalimu Nyerere's thought.*
23. See Chinweizu's chapter titled "Pan-Africanism – Rethinking key issues," inBankie, et al., *Sustaining,* 62–95.
24. Imam et al., *Engendering African Social Sciences,* 254.

possible. Populism recently, in both Africa and China, has taken very critical approaches to the "dominant ideology", often at times to the detriment of the majority class groups concerned. The questions raised are whether populist rhetoric and political party sloganeering can address genuine crises, or serve as tools in power struggles to monopolize the distribution of resources and wealth. Therefore, at all levels of the political economic domain, serious focus on fine-tuning the idea and methods of corporate social responsibility, promoting public policy centered on developing social welfare and the elevation of indigenous knowledge systems, and re-centering monetary policy around economic exchange systems that encourage restorative based-creativity and production become key policy guidelines.

To conclude this study, it is useful to highlight how economic disposition can be a factor in altering political perception and opinion. As an example, by interrogating data about Chinese citizens either residing in South Africa, or Africans residing in China, the following derived statistics help an understanding of popular opinion about living standards, social stability, and economic opportunity. According to census data from 2011 in South Africa:

Table 1: Population born outside South Africa (China) – Census 2011

Country of birth	Number	Percentage
China	15071	0.69
Total born outside SA	2173409	

Table 2: Official employment status for those born outside South Africa (China) of working-age population (15–64 years) – Census 2011

Employment status	Number	Percentage
Employed	10472	74.93
Unemployed	395	2.83
Discouraged work-seeker	104	0.75
Other not economically active	3004	21.5
Total	13977	

*Data filtered and tabled by Anisha Panchia, STATS SA 2014

In Table 1, we note that a little over 15000 people formally registered themselves as having been born in China. Furthermore, from this total, approximately 10500 people were formally employed, which meant that well over 70 percent of the group found employment under various terms and conditions (see Table 2). Furthermore, according to work done by the Migrating for work Research Consortium (MiWORC), statistics show that peoples of Asian origin have the highest employment rate of all other groups in the Southern African Development Community (SADC) region, and the lowest unemployment rate in comparison.[25] Why is this so? Frank Youngman observed that in Botswana, Chinese immigrants "are predominantly self-employed business-people in the retail trade and employees of Chinese companies in the construction sector. Whilst the construction workers are concentrated on specific sites, the retailers can be found in small shops throughout the country, including in rural areas. Chinese people are a visible presence in a society of 2 million Batswana but there is little analysis of the interaction between the two communities."[26]Aware of the growing need for a greater awareness of these socio-economic status quos, and to gauge political sentiments and attitudes, he then concluded that "national attitudes are shaped by the national political discourse, in which politicians seek political advantage from raising the 'Chinese problem'. So far, there appears to have been no empirical research on the nature of everyday interactions between Batswana and the Chinese living and working in Botswana."[27]

In contrast, Adams Bodomo observed that between 400 000 to 500 000 Africans resided in China either as traders, students and professionals, and tourists.[28] Their employment in the Chinese formal economy is also not as well documented, or successful for various social and political reasons.[29] He observed that many African migrants in China had problems with law enforcement, and reported instances of discrimination and abuse.[30] This was because ultimately, "it is not possible to be a legitimate African Chinese (except in the case of Hong

---

25. See a summary of Deborah Budlender's work in African Centre for Migration & Society, *MiWORC Fact Sheet*.
26. Youngman, "Strengthening Africa-China Relations,"9.
27. Ibid., 10.
28. Bodomo, *Africans in China*, 12–13.
29. See Prah K.D.L, et al., *Africa-China Relations*.
30. Bodomo, *Africans in China*, 233.

Kong and Macau) with a Chinese passport and citizenship rights."[31] Serious challenges therefore face the development and survival of migrant groups in both Africa and China, and a better understanding of populist political and economic trends is necessary.

These studies also reveal that the greater impact of political and economic interaction is felt at micro-economic levels, in which the spaces for commodity exchanges are big, cheap, and people-to-people relations are more physical. Ultimately, these trends and figures highlight the need for more incentives to develop these legal and economic spaces. Better analysis of populist political trends, better understanding of popular agitation, and a re-aligning of ideological perspective make the idea and reality of populism a theoretical and practical tool for gauging change.

Recommendations:

- **Fine-tuning the idea and method of corporate social responsibility** – Realising this objective requires increasing the percentage income related to social responsibility, and creating better platforms for investment in community-based projects, and small, medium and micro-sized enterprises (SMME's).[32] As opposed to relying on populist appeals for "corporate greening" and "charity/aid", corporate social responsibility must utilize social welfare-based investment plans, as the primary basis for growth in new social, economic and political environments.

- **Promoting public policy centred on developing social welfare and the legal and economic empowerment of indigenous knowledge systems** – According to a policy brief written in 2010, Dimpho Motsamai and Siphamandla Zondi argued, "The New Partnership for Africa's Development (NEPAD) does provide a framework for social policy interventions in Africa…. These social aspects of NEPAD are generally neglected in discussions about NEPAD as a socio-economic programme for Africa because NEPAD officials, being primarily economists, have been more successful in selling its economic messages than its social initiatives. The social dimensions of NEPAD are not as explicit as the

---

31. Ibid., 233.
32. Please refer to work done by the Thabo Mbeki Foundation and the Thabo Mbeki African Leadership Institute.

economic and political facets outlined in the Action Plans." It is the thrust of this argument and policy guideline that will determine the success of empowerment initiatives.[33] Furthermore, Fatou Sow makes a very important point and argument when she states that "development policies have not always been sensitive to the place and role of women in the allocation and control of resources in production, consumption and distribution. The marginalization of women represents a very significant loss for the economy, for they constitute a considerable workforce. Sexual differentiations are especially pronounced when it comes to means of access to land and other natural resources, to equipment and materials (seeds, fertilizers, etc.), to credit and so on."[34] These issues are thus paramount when gauging, understanding, and encouraging public participation.

-   **Steering monetary policy toward economic exchange systems that encourage restorative based-creativity and production** – Issa G. Shivji noted that "there have been attempts to provide alternative frameworks, plans, and programmes such as the *Lagos Plan of Action (1980)*, *The African Alternative Framework to Structural Adjustment Programme for Socio-economic Recovery and Transformation (1989)*, *and the African Charter for Popular Participation and Development (1990)*. These alternative frameworks have underlined the need for a holistic approach to Africa's development; called for a continental program of regional integration and collective self-reliance; called upon African states not to surrender their developmental role and sovereignty in policy-making; and have attempted to develop a vision of a human-centred and people-driven development for the future of the continent."[35]As policy guidelines, these various agreements serve as important reference points for transformative agendas in the African political economy.

Bibliography

African Centre for Migration & Society.*MiWORC Fact Sheet No.1. Labour migration by numbers: South Africa's foreign and domestic migration data.* University of the Witwatersrand, Johannesburg, 2013.

---

33. Motsamai and Zondi, *Social Dimensions*, 1.
34. Imam et al., *Engendering African Social Sciences*, 52.
35. Shivji, *Accumulation*, 15.

Anthony, R. Sven Grimm and Yejoo Kim. "South Africa's Relations with China and Taiwan: Economic Realism and the 'One-China' Doctrine." Policy Briefing, Center for Chinese Studies, Stellenbosch, South Africa: November 2013.

Babawale, T., A. Alao, and T. Onwumah, eds. *Pan-Africanism, and the Integration of Continental Africa and Diaspora Africa (Volume 2)*. Lagos: Center for Black and African Arts and Civilization (CBAAC), 2011.

Bankie, F. Bankie and Viola C. Zimunya, eds. *Sustaining the New Wave of Pan-Africanism*. Windhoek: NYCN / Nigerian High Commission, 2011.

Beetham, David.*Marxists in the Face of Fascism*. Manchester: Manchester University Press, 1983.

Bodomo, Adams, *Africans in China; A Socio-Cultural Study and its Implications for Africa-China Relations*. Amherst, New York: Cambria Press, 2013.

Canovan, Margaret. "Populism for political theorists?" *Journal of Political Ideologies,9*, 3 (October 2008): 241–252.

Ching, C. C. "Psychology and the Four Modernizations in China." *International Journal of Psychology*, Vol. 19, Issue 1-4 (1980): 57–63.

Dent, Christopher. M, ed. *China and Africa Development Relations*. New York: Routledge, 2011.

Guldin, Gregory Eliyu, editor. *Anthropology in China*. New York: M. E. Sharpe Inc, 1990.

Imam Ayesha, Amina Mama and Fatou Sow, eds. *Engendering African Social Sciences*. Dakar, Senegal: CODESRIA Book Series, 1997.

Ionescu, G. and E. Gellner, eds. *Populism: Its Meanings and National Characteristics*. London: Weidenfeld and Nicolson, 1969.

Kondlo, Kwandiwe, ed. *Perspectives on Thought Leadership for Africa's Renewal*. Pretoria, South Africa: Africa Institute of South Africa, 2013, 346–357.

Krieger, Joel, editor-in-chief. *The Oxford Companion to Politics of the World*. Oxford: Oxford University Press, 2001.

Laclau, Ernesto. *Politics and Ideology in Marxist Theory*. London: NLB, 1977.

Lema Eleshi., Marjorie Mbilinyi andRakesh Rajani,eds. *Nyerere on Education / Nyerere kuhusu Elimu*.Dar es Salaam, Tanzania: Haki Elimu, E & D Ltd., The Mwalimu Nyerere Foundation, 2004.

Li, Conghua. *China: The Consumer Revolution*. New York: John Wiley and Sons, 1998.

Xing, Li andAbdulkadir O. Farah, eds, *Africa-China Relations in an Era of Great Transformations*. Farnham, UK: Ashgate, 2013.

Magubane, Bernard, M. *The Political Economy of Race and Class in South Africa*. New York and London: Monthly Review Press, 1979.

Mao Zedong, edited by S. Schram. *Mao Tse-Tung Unrehearsed (Talks and Letters: 1956-71)*. Middlesex, England: Pelican Books, 1974.

Motsamai, Dimpho and Siphamandla Zondi. "The Social Dimensions of the New Partnership for Africa's Development." *Policy Brief* No. 33, Africa Institute of South Africa, June 2010.

Nabudere, Dani Wadada. *Imperialism in East Africa– Volume I: Imperialism and Exploitation*. London: Zed Press, 1981.

Nabudere, Dani Wadada. *Imperialism in East Africa– Volume II: Imperialism and Integration*. London: Zed Press, 1982.

Norena, Carlos F. *Imperial Ideals in the Roman West: Representation, Circulation, Power*. Cambridge: Cambridge University Press, 2011.

Ogunsanwo, Alaba. *China's Policy in Africa 1958-1971*. London: Cambridge University Press, 1974.

Prah, Kwesi D. L. S. *Tanzania-China Relations in Historical Perspective: The Political and Economic Impact of Relations (1968-1985)*. Trenton, New Jersey: Africa World Press, 2016.

Prah, Kwesi. D. L. S., A. Nkenkana. and A. Asong A., eds. "Africa-China Relations: Rethinking the Afro-Chinese Partnership for Africa's Development within Socio-cultural Contexts and Experiences." Paper presented at the Africa Institute of South Africa / Human Research Science Council Conference; African Solutions to African Problems, May 2014.

Prah, Kwesi Kwaa, ed. *Afro-Chinese Relations; Past, Present and Future*. Cape Town: Center for Advanced Studies of African Society, 2007.

Saloutos, Theodore, ed. *Populism; Reaction or Reform*. New York: Holt, Rinehart and Winston, 1968.

Shivji, Issa G. *Pan-Africanism in Mwalimu Nyerere's thought*. Mimeograph, 2009, http://www.twnside.org.sg/title2/resurgence/2009/227/world1.htm

Shivji, Issa G. *Accumulation in an African Periphery*. Dar es Salaam: Mkukina Nyota Publishers, 2010.

Shivji, Issa. G. eds. *Chemchemi: Fountain of Ideas*. Issue No. 4, ISSN 1821-7036, April 2011.

Sorel, G. *Reflections on Violence*. New York, US: Collier Books, New York.

Stadnichenko, Aleksei.*Monetary Crises of Capitalism: Origin, Development.* Moscow: Progress Publishers, 1975.

Youngman, Frank. "Strengthening Africa-China Relations: A perspective from Botswana." Discussion paper. Centre for Chinese studies, University of Stellenbosch, Cape Town, 2013.

CONCLUSION

========= ❖ =========

In the chapters that make up this book, important arguments are made about the nature, plans and implications of relations and partnerships between African States and China, within local and international spaces. The arguments advanced highlight the absence of concrete theoretical frameworks, policies with little or no strategic value, and ineffective or non-existent strategic analyses with necessary Pan-Africanist perspectives. They highlight tendencies to view these relations and partnerships superficially which, more often than not, knowingly avoided serious interrogation of issues that would have constructive appeal to various Africanist development plans. Despite the fashionable 'Africa-China' discourse, in which all commentators are experts and have a claim to speaking on behalf of all Africans, most if not all of the analyses indicate a lack of ideological and methodological gravitas.

Therefore, ideologically, when trying to locate the premises for progressive Africa-China relations, one needs to formulate or strengthen a set of African International Relations positions (AIR). But what does this necessarily entail, and under what ideological and political motivation? Interpreting and answering this question rests upon the understanding that the ingredients for China's success are due largely to its general homogeneity, in cultural (language and science), political (ideology and state formation) and economic ('state-controlled, free-market capitalism') terms. In contrast Africa, with its multitude of states and differing national interests, struggles to align its political and economic strategies toward the unity of African peoples and their developmental agendas. Quintessentially, this is Africa's advantage: its social, political and thus economic heterogeneity as some have argued. Thus, as most of the authors have pointed out, the outcomes and impacts garnered from the many Africa-China partnerships are typically lop-sided, often in favour of Chinese economic and political interests. Also, collectively, Africa possesses the youngest and fastest growing population in the world, and thus is home to levels of creativity and innovation that is, and will prove invaluable to Africa's future, and the world.

Therefore, with a more nuanced analysis of interests, it appears that there is a binding theme that plays a very important role in positioning African peoples and their AIR, and the Chinese as catalysts of change. This theme, grounded in the notion of 'unity', or as Chinese foreign policy dictates, 'a harmonious world', is more than just idealistic or altruistic posturing. The most successful tool in galvanizing the productive and strategic-planning capacities of African peoples over the past century and a half has been the vision of Pan-African unity. It is only under this pre-condition that *any* meaningful economic development agenda can take root in African spaces.

For China, at a time when its soft diplomacy in Africa is being heavily scrutinized, its ability to understand the strategic interests and deficits of the various African States in fierce competition is crucial. It must realize that it is only through a shared vision of political and economic unity that it would gain any substantial benefit and advantage. In practical terms, this means shifting emphasis away from dealing with African States bilaterally. The current neo-colonial political and economic architecture in Africa does not bode well for any development agenda.

This means that any realistic developmental agenda proposed through state-political groupings such as BRICS will have to address these non-productive and unconstructive elements of political and economic organization. Although BRICS, and its corresponding banking platform (the New Development Bank), has an opportunity to facilitate the formulation and construction of long-lasting mechanisms, such mechanisms would have to seriously tackle the reform and eventual overhaul of the international financial system, and related trade agreements. Meaningful alliances would mean that African States must cooperate on strengthening intra-African parliamentary processes, which at present, is under the aegis of the poorly financed African Union (AU). By focusing on these sources of political power (women, the youth, labourers, artisans and farmers), one is then able to focus on harnessing the different skill sets and production capacities within African society, and focus efforts on supporting the necessary regional development plans (energy-producing networks, transportation networks and related services, manufacturing zones, high tech production etc.).

For development banks, such as the African Development Bank and the new BRICS Development Bank, to chart new paths and open up new opportunities, they have to defy their operational mandate: which is to primarily accrue profits from lending money, and the investments they make. Redistributing value by making bonds available to labour unions, collectives and consortiums directly related to development initiatives on the ground becomes crucial to the realization of the agendas set by the AU, and also secures the interests of Chinese investments in Africa. The new BRICS Development Bank would also have to invest heavily in indigenous and localized capacities to insure new business initiatives. By doing this, one encourages the youth within society to take initiative in how they start businesses, on their terms. Lastly, to counter-balance the pressure put on the new BRICS Development Bank by the World Bank and IMF regarding profitability, campaigning for the downgrading or erasure of national debt is imperative. The Euro-American financial oligarchies draining African economies have to account for their colonial legacy, and their business interests need to be brought into line.

Thus, to begin formulating a holistic and relevant strategic plan or blue print on future Africa-China relations, building skill capacities, industrializing certain sectors of the various economic spaces further within the African world, and fostering mutual respect amongst ethnicities and cultural groupings is essential (people-to-people and grass-roots level relations). The ideological rallying point for all these challenges must be Pan-Africanism. The nature of the nation-state in Africa, which in essence are very colonial in their structure and function as many have argued, begun their economic under-development by primarily focusing on facilitating the extraction of resources from Africa. African unity is a possibility, only through focused and coordinated African agency.

NOTES ON CONTRIBUTORS

=============◆===============

Siphamandla Zondi is professor, Department of Political Science, University of Pretoria, Pretoria, South Africa. He was Director of the Institute for Global Dialogue, a Unisa-associated foreign policy think tank based in Pretoria.

Lloyd G. Adu Amoah is acting Director, Centre for Asian Studies and Lecturer, Department of Political Science, University of Ghana. He is also, an Assistant Professor at Ashesi University College (Berekuso, Ghana).

Paul Zilungisele Tembe is a researcher, Thabo Mbeki African Leadership Institute, University of South Africa. Currently, he teaches "China's Political Relations" at Stellenbosch University.

Samuel O. Oloruntoba is senior lecturer, Thabo Mbeki African Leadership Institute, University of South Africa, Pretoria, South Africa. His research focuses on the Political Economy of Development with Africa as his core area.

Heather Chingono is senior lecturer, Department of Political and Administrative Studies, University of Zimbabwe, Harare, Zimbabwe. Her current research interests include; Africa-China Relations; African Politics; African Developmental Models; International Security; Terrorism.

Ng'wanza Kamata is senior lecturer, Department of Political Science, University of Dar es Salaam, Dar es Salaam, Tanzania. Kamata is lecturing, researching and writing on agrarian issues. He is currently involved in writing a biography of Mwalimu Julius Nyerere.

Antoine Roger Lokongo was based at Peking University, Centre for African Studies, Department of International Relations. He worked as a political journalist before going into academia. He has published many articles on the Sino-DRC Congo contracts.

Ogundiran Soumonni, is senior lecturer in Innovation Studies at the Wits Business School in Johannesburg, South Africa. His primary research interest lies in the area of innovation for sustainability from both a policy and a firm-level perspective.

Maitseo Bolaane is associate professor, Faculty of Humanities at the University of Botswana. She teaches various courses in the Department of History (mainly East & Central Africa) and with teaching responsibilities extended to Chinese Studies. She is also Director of the Centre for San Studies at the University of Botswana.

Part Themba Mgadla is professor and Director, Confucius Institute, University of Botswana. He has taught pre-colonial and colonial history of Botswana and has wide research experience.

Oarabile Makgabana-Dintwa is a lecturer in the Department of History, Univeristy of Botswana.

Muhidin Juma Shangwe is a lecturer at the Department of Political Science and Public Administration, University of Dar es Salaam. He specializes in International Relations focussing on Afro-Chinese relations.

Kwesi D.L.S. Prah lectures in World and Pan-African History at East China Normal University, Shanghai. He is a research associate with the Institute for Global Dialogue, University of South Africa, and PanGoal Institute, Beijing. His research interests revolve around critical approaches to the science of history, African and Asian Modern History, and African Philosophy.

Vusi Gumede is professor at the University of South Africa and Director of the Thabo Mbeki African Leadership Institute. Previously, he was Associate Professor at the University of Johannesburg and he lectured at the University of Witwatersrand's School of Government. Before that, he worked for the South African government in various capacities for approximately ten years.

INDEX

═══════════════════❖═══════════════════

D

E

F

G

H